THE
GUINNESS
BOOK OF

CURIOUS

W|O|R|D|S

Leslie Dunkling

GUINNESS PUBLISHING

Editor: Beatrice Frei
Design and Layout: John Rivers

The Work Copyright © Leslie Dunkling, 1994

The right of Leslie Dunkling to be identified as the Author of this
Work has been asserted in accordance with the Copyright, Design and
Patents Act 1988.

This Publication Copyright © Guinness Publishing Ltd., 1994
33 London Road, Enfield, Middlesex.

'GUINNESS' is a registered trade mark of Guinness Publishing Ltd.

Typeset in Joanna by Ace Filmsetting Ltd., Frome, Somerset.
Printed and bound in Great Britain by The Bath Press, Bath

A catalogue record for this book is available from the British Library.

ISBN 0–85112–743–6

TO THE READER

All these things heer collected, are not mine,
But divers grapes make but one sort of wine;
So I, from many learned authors took
The various matters printed in this book.
What's not mine own by me shall not be father'd,
The most part I in fifty years have gather'd,
Some things are very good, pick out the best,
Good wits compiled them, and I wrote the rest.
If thou dost buy it, it will quit thy cost,
Read it, and all thy labour is not lost.

John Taylor *Miscellanies* (1652)

CONTENTS

PREFACE

───────O───────

I was often asked, when I told friends that I was working on this book, what I meant by *curious* words. 'Well,' I heard myself saying, 'most words are curious in one way or another if you take a close look at them.' 'For instance . . .?' came the invariable demand, and I was usually able to cite a word that had occurred in the conversation a moment earlier. One had probably been used which had made me silently ask myself — 'Now where does that come from; why do we say that?' — and make a mental note to check it in the dictionary.

This process, very familiar to me, occurred as I typed the word **preface** at the head of this page. I began to wonder about the *face* part of the word. We all know that *pre-* means 'before' in words like preamble, precede, precondition, precursor, predestination, so a preface must be something that is 'before the face'. But that doesn't seem right, and a glance in the nearest etymological dictionary makes it clear that the face part of the word is misleading. 'Preface' comes from an early French form of Latin *præfatio*, a 'saying beforehand'. A more accurate form in English of the Latin word would therefore have been *prefation*, the *-fation* deriving ultimately from the Latin verb *fari, fatus* 'speak, say'. That same Latin verb leads to other English words: when we talk about what fate has in store for us, for example, we mean 'what has been "spoken" by the gods'.

The articles in this book all began when a word like preface aroused my own curiosity and sent me to the reference books. Countless scholars past and present have recorded the results of their researches in dictionaries and discursive works. They have made it a relatively easy task, for those who have the inclination and opportunity to consult them, to get at linguistic facts. Those writers have, in a sense, provided a script: my own role, therefore, has not been one of scholarship, merely of interpretation and presentation, inspired by a wish to communicate a long-standing love-affair with words and to arouse if possible a linguistic curiosity in others.

Oliver Wendell Holmes says in *The Autocrat of the Breakfast Table*: 'When I feel inclined to read poetry I take down my Dictionary. The poetry of words is quite as beautiful as that of sentences.' I understand what he means, but for my part I have preferred whenever possible to find my curious words in the works of poets and writers, and only then turn to the dictionaries. My ideal has been to discover an imaginative use of a word — with perhaps a comment on it — by a good writer, before supporting it with dictionary-style information, since linguistic facts can at best construct only the skeleton of a word. This is tacitly acknowledged by the editors of *The Oxford English Dictionary*, the greatest dictionary ever produced for any language, in their liberal use of literary quotations. Writers and poets breathe life into words and give them personalities.

On the rare occasion when my curious word has come first and has then required literary support, various concordances have once again made the task an easy one. The problem in such cases can be having to discipline oneself not to read on at length from the point indicated by the concordance. There is a constant temptation to put aside the task in hand and wallow in literary pleasure.

With preface, for example, one is led to Shakepeare's single use of the word, in *Henry VI Part One*. The earl of Suffolk has been telling the king about the charms of Margaret of Anjou, to the point where the king is eager to marry her. 'So am I driven by the breath of her renown,' says the king, 'either to suffer shipwreck or arrive / Where I may have fruition of her love.' 'Tush, my good lord!' replies Suffolk. 'This superficial tale / Is but a preface of her worthy praise.'

This comes in the final scene of the play, which Suffolk ends by declaring that: 'Margaret shall now be Queen, and rule the King; / But I will rule both her, the King, and realm.' This is a tempting invitation to read Shakespeare's continuation of the story in *Henry VI Part Two* to discover how Suffolk's ambitions are thwarted.

The Concordance to Byron's *Don Juan*, by Hagelman and Barnes, consulted on the preface question, leads a researcher to Canto V, Verse 106. Byron's only use of the word in the poem occurs when Gulbeyaz has just bought Juan as a slave:

And deem'd herself extremely
  condescending
When, being made her property at
  last,
Without more preface, in her blue
  eyes blending
Passion and power, a glance on him
  she cast,
And merely saying, 'Christian, canst
  thou love?'
Conceived that phrase was quite
  enough to move.

What happens when Juan declines to oblige the sultana, and his reasons for doing so, are then explained with typical Byronic wit. It is almost impossible not to read on, as the poem exercises its usual magic.

This preface, I see, has accidentally become an example of what follows in the book itself — namely, some two hundred word articles which combine linguistic facts with literary anecdotes. Since I believe strongly that variety is important, I have mixed in a number of literary quotations about words which seem to require no extra comment from me. I have also added some word teasers in Trivial Pursuit style, plus some examples of pairs of words which are linked etymologically in a curious way. There is also a kind of 'Shakespearean Word Alphabet' which demonstrates in itself Shakespeare's linguistic sensitivity.

The Comic Alphabet entries which introduce each section of the alphabet are fairly traditional. They occasionally take liberties with pronunciation ('G for police' = 'chief of police'; 'H for himself' = 'each for himself') but should not cause too many problems of interpretation. American readers should note that Z is to be pronounced in the British way, as *zed*. Anyone with a special interest in this subject should consult *Comic Alphabets*, by Eric Partridge, where many variants are given, as well as alphabets in other forms.

Putting this book together has given me a great deal of pleasure. I hope you enjoy it, and that I have managed to include at least some of the words that have in the past aroused your own curiosity.

Leslie Dunkling

INTRODUCTION

Derrick Van Bummel, the schoolmaster, a dapper learned little man, who was not to be daunted by the most gigantic word in the dictionary.

Washington Irving Rip Van Winkle

Shakespeare at one point compares people to words. When Henry IV says that he is unhappy about his son's unsuitable associates, Warwick tells him:

The Prince but studies his
    companions
Like a strange tongue, wherein, to
    gain the language,
'Tis needful that the most immodest
    word
Be look'd upon and learnt; which
    once attain'd,
Your Highness knows, comes to no
    further use
But to be known and hated. So, like
    gross terms,
The Prince will, in the perfectness of
    time,
Cast off his followers.

It is the fat and unprincipled Sir John Falstaff, of course, who is metaphorically alluded to as a 'gross term'. Warwick's prediction about him is ultimately proved correct, since Prince Hal does indeed cast him off when he becomes king.

Shakespeare's comparison of people with words is equally interesting when stated in reverse. In many respects words are like people. They may be familiar friends in whose company we feel quite relaxed and whom we tend to take for granted. If they have been known since early childhood, we may only meet them when we return home, but we never forget them. Other words are not so much friends as social acquaintances or working colleagues with whom we have necessary and regular contacts. There are still more words that we have met only on a few occasions. With these, as sometimes with occasional formal visitors, we may be on our guard, not quite sure how to deal with them.

Because words mirror the people who use them, the metaphor can be extended considerably. As we are judged by the company we keep, so others judge us by the words we use. Like people, those words can be described in terms of their educational, social and professional level and by the functions they perform. Many can be associated with a particular region of the English-speaking world, as well as with a certain age-group. Where the last two classifications are concerned, Ruth Rendell describes one type in terms of the other when she writes, in Talking to Strange Men: 'Mungo thought what a funny thing it was that his father and he didn't seem to speak the same language. It was rather as if, while both speaking English, they had learned it in parts of the world separated by thousands of miles, in countries where the customs and traditions were totally disparate.'

Ruth Rendell comments on a verbal generation gap: many would also argue that there is a sexual linguistic gap, that to some extent men and women of a similar age speak different versions of a language. Sheridan makes Loveless say, in A Trip to Scarborough:

Will you then make no difference,
    Amanda,
Between the language of our sex and
    yours?
There is a modesty restrains your
    tongues,
Which makes you speak by halves
    when you command;
But roving flattery gives a loose to
    ours,
Which makes us still speak double
    what we think.

No sensible man ever engages, unprepared, in a fencing match of words with a woman.

Wilkie Collins The Woman in White

Shakespeare's comment on women's language comes in *Cymbeline*. Guiderius tells Arviragus: 'Prithee have done, / And do not play in wench-like words with that / Which is so serious.' The words Guiderius has in mind are poetical references which compare Imogen to flowers. These differences between male and female word usage are not always easy to spot, but sometimes become apparent when a married couple are of different nationalities. A foreign husband whose English has mostly been learnt by listening to his wife will sometimes use words which sound inappropriate. The words themselves may be correct; what is wrong is that they are 'wench-like', not suited to a male speaker.

'You'd be a pretty child if you kept yourself clean.' I looked down in sudden shame for the girl's word 'pretty'.

William Golding Free Fall

There are also words which many speakers believe to be unsuitable for mixed company. Swear words belong to this group, and are traditionally avoided by both men and women when members of the opposite sex are present. 'The first time I said fuck in her presence,' writes Philip Roth in *Portnoy's Complaint*, 'such a look of agony passed over The Pilgrim's face, you would have thought I had just branded the four letters on her flesh. Why, she asked so plaintively once we were alone, why had I to be so "unattractive"? What possible pleasure had it given me to be so "ill-mannered"?' Another man, hearing such language used, may be embarrassed on the woman's behalf. Joseph Heller, in *Good as Gold*, has: ' "Sid, you're fucking me over again!" Gold shouted. Victor, who did not like bad language ever in front of women, reddened further.' Other taboo words between the sexes have varied at different times — see, for example, the article on LIMB, page 106.

'Some of these Irish chaps are damned rogues. I beg your pardon, Mrs O'Grady, for saying damn before a lady;' and he made a low bow to Mrs Egan, who was obliged to leave the room to hide her laughter.

Samuel Lover Handy Andy

Words, then, like people, can differ sexually, socially, educationally, regionally and by age-group. This book pursues the analogy of words as people in yet another way. Words are thought of as having individual personalities and life stories. They are seen as members of extended families, with parents, grandparents, uncles, aunts, cousins and perhaps children who need to be introduced. Most of the words dealt with are still very much alive, still adapting themselves to changing circumstances. Some are no longer with us, but are commemorated in records of the past.

The words that each of us 'knows' in one way or another — the meanings we ascribe to them, the manner in which we pronounce and spell them — form the equivalent of our human social and professional circles. We all have personal vocabularies or idiolects (Greek 'own words'). As the etymology of the word suggests, each person's idiolect is unique. The words we use and the way we use them constitute a kind of linguistic finger-print — a term which comes to mind partly because idiolectal evidence is now increasingly used for forensic purposes. Whereas fingerprints, however, remain unnoticed in normal circumstances, we often become at least partly aware of a person's idiolect. We probably react in some way to a speaker's social and regional accent. We may notice the use of words and expressions which a speaker uses with particular frequency. Some speakers may even use words of their own invention. Len Deighton writes, in Close-up, of a young actress: 'Suzy is verbal about things she doesn't like ("blah things" in Suzy's language). Politics are blah and so are "pigs" and cabbage and weekend parties where they dress for dinner.'

The Deighton comment indicates, incidentally, the typical way in which imaginative writers individualise their characters by their idiolectal quirks. One thinks of Armado, say, in Love's Labour's Lost, a man of 'fire-new words, fashion's own knight'. There are more famous examples, such as Sheridan's Mrs Malaprop. Samuel Lover, in Handy Andy, gives a lengthy description of a character's odd linguistic habit: 'Whenever O'Grady was in a bad humour, he had a strange fashion of catching at some word that either he himself, or those with whom he spoke, had uttered, and after often repeating it, or rather mumbling it over in his mouth, as if he were chewing it, off he started into a canter of ridiculous rhymes to the aforesaid word, and sometimes one of these rhymes would suggest a new idea, or some strange association which had the oddest effect possible.'

O'Grady is in one of his tantarums, as his wife calls them, when a nurse gives him some pills. Lover writes: 'O'Grady made a face at the pill-box, and repeated the word "pills" several times, with an expression of extreme disgust. "Pills – pills – kills – wills – ay – make your wills – make them – take them – shake them."'

Idiolectal recognition can also work in reverse — we are likely to form an image in our minds of a person who is said to talk frequently about 'champers', say, or uses the expression 'old boy'.

She had to be on her guard against saying 'pardon' and 'jolly decent' and other innocent phrases which she had always employed, for if they slipped out, they were instantly derided.

Frederic Raphael The Limits of Love

It could be argued that we constantly make use of other people: we certainly make use of words. They enable us to communicate both subjective feelings and objective thoughts, either in speech or by writing. Often feelings and thoughts are intermingled, but sometimes we attempt to remove all traces of subjectivity — as in a piece of scientific, technical or academic writing. By contrast, we may be overwhelmingly concerned with making someone aware of our emotional state. There is a kind of law which governs these different uses of language. Words become progressively less important in *themselves* as we move from written objectivity to spoken subjectivity.

Anything he saw was by way of distressing conjecture, and proceeded more from the Marchesa's tone than from her words.

J.I.M. Stewart A Use of Riches

This apparent devaluation of word-meaning in emotional or attitudinal speech occurs because of the various other channels of communication that are available to speakers. Although we think of words as conveying specific meanings, in a spoken context the supposed meaning of a word can easily be modified or reversed. Deliberate use of a particular tone of voice can immediately make it clear that we mean the opposite of what we are saying. Joyce Cary makes the point in The Horse's Mouth: '"I believe you, old son," said Bert, meaning that he didn't.'

The 'walk in' was uttered with closed teeth, and expressed the sentiment, 'Go to the deuce.'

Emily Brontë *Wuthering Heights*

A human voice can superimpose on to the words it utters an extraordinary range of information about the speaker's attitude to what is being said. That information can remain even when the words themselves convey no sense. 'Upon my knees, what doth your speech import?' says Desdemona to Othello. 'I understand a fury in your words, / But not your words.' In more normal circumstances, the words and the information conveyed by the tone in which they are spoken are understood simultaneously. Visual or tactile information may also be part of the multi-channel communication.

'As a family, we just don't communicate, do we?'
The term 'communicate' amused Mrs Babcock. It was such a cliché, on the lips of every intense TV talk-show guest in the country. 'Yes, I am aware that we don't — communicate,' she replied. 'But you have to understand that that's one of my few remaining pleasures.'

Lisa Alther *Kinflicks*

The written or printed word remains a humble linguistic unit with a dictionary meaning; in speech it becomes part of a multi-layered sandwich. When we listen to emotional speech we are, as it were, experiencing the blended taste of those layers. In more academic terms, we are responding not just to semantic content but to paralinguistic and prosodic features.

Those who happen to be dealing with unemotional ideas need not worry about what is lost when their words are written rather than spoken. Writers of

fiction have more of a problem. If they are reporting an emotional conversation they must enable a reader to 'hear' how the words were said. They must also inform the reader of any other communicative acts, things that were 'said' visually or by touch. Some of the words they use to do this may directly 'translate' a gesture. The etymology of 'innuendo', for example, has to do with nodding. 'Supercilious' refers to the lifting of the eyebrows.

The writer's literary skill dictates how unobtrusively and accurately this vital information is given. An article later in this book (see SAID, page 166) deals with so-called 'said-substitutes'. These give an indication of the different ways in which words can be spoken. Often the formula used by a novelist is 'said' itself followed by an adverb. The latter can also provide an indication of what, in Desdemona's phrase, was in the words.

In terms of frantic endearment she uttered his name over and over again.

Iris Murdoch *The Bell*

An extreme example of subjective, attitudinal information conveyed by the way a word is said rather than by the meaning of the word itself comes in the use by lovers of each other's name. R.F. Delderfield, in *Theirs Was the Kingdom*, has: 'She pulled him down on her, kissing his cheeks and eyes and mouth, and murmuring his name over and over again. No more than that, just "Giles . . . Giles . . . Giles . . ." so that she invested it with a sort of glory and he heard it as music more enthralling than anything Herrick or Marvell had written on the subject of love.'

In such instances the name itself obviously conveys no message — the person addressed knows who he is. Everything is in the tone of voice and the actions that accompany speech. Normal words temporarily become superfluous, though only to the people concerned. Delderfield's character may have preferred the repetition of his name to the verses of Herrick or Marvell, but the rest of us are glad that Herrick penned such lines as:

Whenas in silks my Julia goes,
Then, then, methinks, how sweetly
    flows
The liquefaction of her clothes!
Next, when I cast mine eyes and see
That brave vibration each way free,
O how that glittering taketh me!

We are also grateful that Marvell relied on rather more than the murmured name of his coy mistress, reminding her of time's passing in such lines as:

But at my back I always hear
Time's wingèd chariot hurrying near;
And yonder all before us lie
Deserts of vast eternity.

The empassioned repetition of a lover's name forms part of what was first dubbed the 'little language' by Jonathan Swift. In *Wives and Daughters* Elizabeth Gaskell refers to translating the 'little sentences in "little language"' of letters sent by a French wife to her English husband. H.G. Wells, in *A Story of the Days to Come*, has: 'Their silence ended; and Denton, speaking in a little language of broken English that was, they fancied, their private possession — though lovers have used such little languages since the world began — told her how they too would leap into the air one morning out of all the obstacles and difficulties about them . . .'

Little seems to be an appropriate description for this special 'language', since it tends to be spoken in a little voice. 'On their wedding night', writes Lois Battle in *War Brides*, 'she longed to talk to him in an intimate way, with whispers, pet words, private bedroom jokes, to reveal all the passion she'd been

---

He conversed in a low tone that could not be overheard — for the language of love is never loud; but where is the female ear so dull that it cannot catch the softest whisper of the lover?

Washington Irving The Spectre Bridegroom

---

forced to hide.' Swift may also have had in mind the language of 'little people', since lovers sometimes resort to baby-talk. Sinclair Lewis reports on such usage in *Elmer Gantry*, where the hero is at one stage told by his lover: 'Oh, issums such cwoss old bear! Issums bad old bear! So cwoss with Lulukins!' Elmer himself, despite the fact that he has been told admiringly, 'You're so terribly educated — you know such long words,' writes a note which runs: 'Dearest ittle honey-kins bunnykins, oo is such a darlings.'

This kind of thing is all very well between adult lovers, if it remains private, but is not recommended for real babies or young children. It does the latter no good to hear their imperfect attempts at pronunciation reinforced by adult speakers. As it happens, once they have a basic vocabulary, children usually respond intelligently to words they do not already know. An exchange between a mother and child in *Kingfishers Catch Fire*, by Rumer Godden, runs: '"We shall be poor and frugal. We shall toil." "What is toil?" asked Teresa. "Work very very hard," said Sophie.'

Miss Godden perhaps supposes that Teresa will have guessed the meaning of 'frugal', if she did not already know it, because of its juxtaposition with 'poor'. With 'toil' she has no contextual help. She therefore asks to be introduced to the verbal stranger who has appeared on the scene. A similar exchange occurs in John Updike's *Should Wizard Hit Mommy*, where a father is telling his young daughter a story. 'Go through the dark woods, under the apple trees, into the swamp, over the crick—' 'What's a crick?' 'A little river.' Later the father says: 'Eventually they got used to the way he was and did not mind it at all.' 'What's evenshiladee?' 'In a little while.'

———————○———————

I see her voice, a jagged shape of scarlet and bronze, shatter into the air till it hangs there under the sky, a deed of conquest and terror.

William Golding *Free Fall*

———————○———————

Updike's respelling of 'eventually' is a reminder of the visual nature of the written word, and of the devices sometimes used by writers to exploit that fact. Written dialogue often attempts to be as close an imitation as is possible of what was supposedly said spontaneously. As part of the imitation process, novelists often change the conventional spellings of words to indicate sub-standard or dialectal pronunciation. In Sinclair Lewis's *Elmer Gantry*, 'Lez go out and start a scrap. You're a lil squirt, Jim,' indicates drunken pronunciation. In the same novel, 'Strolling through the shaaaaady lanes,' captures the way a word is sung. Spellings like 'dunno' have become almost standard to indicate the laziness of relaxed speech.

Sometimes spelling changes become visual jokes. In *Barnaby Rudge*, for instance, Dickens uses spelling variation to describe the increasing speed of a turning wheel: 'Whirr-r-r-r-r. The grindstone was soon in motion . . . Whirr-r-r-r-r-r-r.' Elsewhere in the

———————○———————

People who for any reason wanted to get on the soft side of him called him The Christian — a phrase whose delicate flattery was music to his ears, and whose capital T was such an enchanting and vivid object to him that he could see it when it fell out of a person's mouth even in the dark.

Mark Twain *Was It Heaven? Or Hell?*

———————○———————

novel Dickens plays with capital letters: '"IF", said John Willet . . . uttering the monosyllable in capitals.' P.G. Wodehouse, in *A Slice of Life*, has a similar joke: '"Sir Jasper Finch-Farowmere?" said Wildred. "ffinch-ffarowmere," corrected the visitor, his sensitive ear detecting the capital letters.'

———————○———————

I rough out my thoughts in talk as an artist models in clay. Spoken language is so plastic, — you can pat and coax, and spread and shave, and rub out, and fill up, and stick on so easily, when you work that soft material, that there is nothing like it for modelling. Out of it come the shapes which you turn into marble or bronze in your immortal books, if you happen to write such.

Oliver Wendell Holmes
The Autocrat of the Breakfast Table

———————○———————

An awareness of other visual possibilities, besides spelling changes, was shown by the earliest novelists. In *Tristram Shandy*, the 18th-century writer Laurence Sterne uses a squiggly line on the page at one point to show how a stick was flourished in the air; a black page reinforces a verbal account of Yorick's death. Sterne also makes intensive use of italicisation and other printing devices, often for bawdy purposes. A scene between a servant and the hero as a young child becomes: 'The chambermaid had left no ********** under the bed: — Cannot you contrive, master, quoth Susanna, lifting up the sash with one hand, as she spoke, and helping me up into the window-seat with the other, — cannot you manage, my dear, for a single time, to **** *** ** *** ******?'

Other typographical devices that have been used by imaginative writers include Lewis Carroll's change of type face in *Through the Looking-Glass*. When Alice has a conversation with what turns out to be a gnat, the passage runs: '"It sounds like a horse," thought Alice to herself. And an extremely small voice, close to her ear, said, "YOU MIGHT MAKE A JOKE ON THAT — SOMETHING ABOUT 'HORSE' AND 'HOARSE', YOU KNOW."' The French poet Louis Aragon set out the words of his poem on rain so that they trickled down the page. Many other poets have made their verses form appropriate shapes.

Once words are written down, whether as literature or non-fiction, they constitute what is almost a separate language. The range of words used, for example, is likely to be greater than in conversation, since in proper circumstances as much time as is necessary can be taken to coax words, as Oliver Wendell Holmes once expressed it, into the right shapes. What is written is frequently that which has been rewritten. The reader in turn is able to reread, to take time to pause as necessary to think about what is being said, unless the pressures of life enforce skimming rather than reading. As for the writer, even when journalistic or other deadlines place artificial limits on writing time, there are still some advantages over speech. Most people speak about seven times faster than they write. There is therefore usually time to edit a sentence mentally as words are written or typed.

———○———

Someone once said of me, and it was not entirely unjust, that I read poetry for the grammar. As I have said, I never wanted to be a writer. I loved words, but I was not a word-user, rather a word-watcher, in the way that some people are bird-watchers. I loved languages but I knew by now that I would never speak the languages that I read. I was one for whom the spoken and the written word are themselves different languages.

Iris Murdoch *A Word Child*

———○———

Writers of non-fiction do not normally need to use orthographical variants, but they frequently make use of pictures and diagrams to assist their texts. Such visual help now occurs even in books about words, such as dictionaries. The benefits are to be seen in publications such as the two-volume *Reader's Digest Great Illustrated Dictionary*, probably the best work of its kind for family use. But even when pictures as such are not used, careful attention to page layouts and the use of different typefaces can make a great difference to the communicative process between writer and reader. The visual appearance of the page, for example, may create for the writer the pleasant general effect that an attractive personal appearance creates for a speaker. In general terms it is obviously correct for the written word to be made as visually interesting as possible. Most speakers, after all, use facial and bodily gestures to illustrate what they say. Words and their meanings, as we have seen, are only one means of communication, and it is usually helpful to support them in other ways.

———○———

PANDARUS:
Here's a letter to you from yond poor girl.
TROILUS:
Let me read.
PANDARUS:
What says she there?
TROILUS:
Words, words, mere words, no matter from the heart.

William Shakespeare *Troilus and Cressida*

———○———

That having been said, words written or spoken do remain the prime instruments of human communication and are of great power and importance in themselves. It is therefore astonishing to remember that, in one sense, all the words in the English language are in their written forms merely permutated arrangements of letters drawn from a total stock of 26. When spoken they consist of similar permutations of basic sounds, or phonemes. English makes use of 45 such sounds, such as those which distinguish between 'bat', say, and 'cat', or 'bat' and 'bet', 'bat' and 'bag', as well as the so-called open juncture that allows us to know when someone is saying 'that stuff' rather than 'that's tough'. But the groups of letters or sounds, having become recognisable words, are then symbols which can influence our minds and emotions to an astonishing degree.

———————O———————

'You will discover very soon, sir, that actions speak louder than words.'

'I believe that is so,' said the Master Philologist, 'just as the Jewish mob spoke louder than He Whom they crucified. But the Word endures.'

James Branch Cabell *Jurgen*

———————O———————

It is natural for us to ask why a particular combination of letters or sounds symbolises in English one object or abstract meaning rather than another. This book often tries to answer that question in relation to individual words, but is by no means meant to be a systematic history of the English language in general. Many full-length works have already covered that ground. There are also excellent summaries to be found in such works as *The Oxford Companion to the English Language*, in articles on 'The History of English' and related topics. All historical descriptions of English deal with the development of Old English — a basically Germanic language spoken in Britain from the fifth century — from a postulated Indo-European language. Old English, sometimes known as Anglo-Saxon, gave way to Middle English midway through the 12th century. The next three centuries were marked by the adoption into English of large numbers of French and Latin words. Modern English dates from the mid-15th century, but at all times the language has continued to change and expand.

It is also natural for those who use the English language every day for social and professional purposes to be interested in English words in a general way. Those who have more than a passing interest we know as 'word-buffs'. Some study words with great seriousness, others forage among them as a hobby. Those who are philologically inclined, drawn instinctively to questions of history and etymology, are likely to relax with a cryptic crossword. Serious Scrabble-players, by contrast, sometimes take a more mathematical view of the language. They may see words in a computer-like way, as strings of letters which are especially useful or high-scoring for Scrabble purposes. Championship players have been known to memorise lists of such words without either knowing or caring what the words mean.

Between the extremes of half-hours spent with the cryptic crossword and championship Scrabble lie many other word games which can provide amusement from childhood onwards. Hangman, for example, is rather grimly named, but it has long allowed an intriguing verbal battle of wits between those who play it. Such games are often encouraged by parents and teachers, who know that anything which helps to arouse a child's interest in words is worth-while. There are even word-game families, like the one described by Sumner Locke Elliott, in *Edens Lost*: 'Their games were constant and curious. You might have to go a day without using prepositions. You might be the last fool to guess why on a journey you could take a cat but not a kitten, a blanket but not a sheet.'

The second game mentioned by Elliott is obviously more teasing when the person being questioned does not see the words spelled out. His 'preposition' example reminds us that words have job-descriptions — labels which describe their grammatical functions — and hints at another level of word-game sophistication. A 17th-century game of similar type is demonstrated in *Cynthia's Revels*, by Ben Jonson, where the characters play Nouns and Adjectives. Several players randomly choose an adjective, one chooses a noun. The players are then asked to justify the description of the noun by the adjective they chose. In the play the noun chosen is 'breeches'. 'Why *odoriferous* breeches, guardian?' 'That which contains most variety of savour and smell we say is most odoriferous; now breeches, I presume, are incident to that variety, and therefore odoriferous breeches.'

Breeches are then explained as *popular* because everyone wears them, not just courtiers. They are 'humble', because they are used to being sat upon. They are 'barbarous', 'because commonly, when you have worn your breeches sufficiently, you give them to your barber'. They are even said to be 'Pythagorical', 'by reason of their transmigration into several shapes'. After these explanations the player who chose the noun is asked to explain its etymology. 'Breeches, *quasi* bear-riches; when a gallant bears all his riches in his breeches.'

Jonson shows that a master wordsmith is able to relax with the tools of his trade and that he enjoys a pun. It is good to be able to share in his pleasure. This book is also meant, at a much humbler level, to be such a sharing. It is written by one for whom the English language creates an almost child-like excitement. Constant discoveries are made; there is a constant wish to say to others, 'Come and look at this.'

Professional word-lovers are sometimes seen by others in rather gloomy terms. They are thought of as being chained to their desks, 'buried' in their reference books. The novelist Eric Linklater was able to describe vividly and more positively the word-lover's inner vision. In *Magnus Merriman* Linklater says of his hero: 'Magnus in a vision saw the torrent of the English language flung down before him, with sunlight in its hair and the trapped strength of long centuries in its limbs, and heard alike the liquid melody of its verse and the clatter of its common little words and the sonorous fulmination of its most imperial majesty and Miltonic measure. He longed to throw himself into the stream below and battle in its strongest current and dive in the deepest pools for pearls.'

The book is an attempt to explain, justify and communicate a love of words, written by one who threw himself into the stream.

VIOLA:
They that dally nicely with words may quickly make them wanton.

CLOWN:
I would, therefore, my sister had had no name.

VIOLA:
Why, man?

CLOWN:
Why, her name's a word; and to dally with that word might make my sister wanton. But indeed words are very rascals since bonds disgrac'd them.

VIOLA:
Thy reason, man?

CLOWN:
Troth, sir, I can yield you none without words, and words are grown so false I am loath to prove reason with them.

William Shakespeare Twelfth Night

FOR
'ORSES

ABILITY

———◇———

A draught upon my neighbour was to me the same as money; for I was sufficiently convinced of his ability.

Oliver Goldsmith *The Vicar Of Wakefield*

———◇———

Ability is not today a word which immediately suggests 'money' but that was not always the case. Between the 16th and 18th centuries it was often used specifically to mean the ability to provide money. In Shakespeare's *Twelfth Night*, for example, when Antonio asks Viola to return his money, she replies: 'Being prompted by your present trouble, out of my mean and low ability I'll lend you something.'

One of the pleasantest instances of the word's use in this sense comes in the letter written by Sir Philip Sidney to his brother Robert, on 18 October 1580: 'My dear Brother, For the money you have received, assure yourself (for it is true) there is nothing I spend so pleaseth me; as that which is for you. If ever I have ability, you shall find it so: if not, yet shall not any brother living be better beloved than you, of me.'

During the same period **disability** was used to mean not having the means to provide money — being unable to meet one's liabilities, in other words. **Liability** looks as if it is associated with ability, but it has in fact a completely different origin. 'Ability' derives ultimately from Latin *habere* 'to hold', and is based on the idea of something that is 'handy, suitable for a purpose'. 'Liability' is from Latin *ligare* and has to do with 'that which can be bound (by law)'.

ABRACADABRA

———◇———

Still rings in his ear, distinct and clear, Abracadabra! that word of fear!

Richard Harris Barham *The Ingoldsby Legends*

———◇———

Abracadabra is a word known to most children, who would probably be able to explain that it is used by magicians and conjurors when casting spells. The word has no meaning in the ordinary sense, and its origin is — fittingly — unknown. Its earliest occurrence is in a second century poem by Q. Severus Sammonicus, but it is not clear whether it derives from Greek or Hebrew. The latter is more likely, and a popular explanation of the word makes it a kind of acronym, using letters of the Hebrew words *Ab, Ben, Ruach, Acadosch* 'Father, Son and Holy Spirit'. In former times its letters were set out in triangular form and worn round the neck as a charm.

The word occurs in many other European languages. In French it has been adapted to form the adjective *abracadant(e)* 'surprising, extraordinary, marvellous'.

ACME

———◇———

Thus it is, by slow steps of casual increase, that our knowledge physical, metaphysical, physiological, polemical, nautical, mathematical, enigmatical, technical, biographical, romantical, chemical, and obstetrical, with fifty other branches of it, (most

Teaser: What is curious about the word 'almost'?
(Answer page 230) **??**

of 'em ending as these do in ical), have for these two centuries or more, gradually been creeping towards that acme of their perfections, from which, if we may form a conjecture from the advances of these last seven years, we cannot possibly be far off.

Laurence Sterne Tristram Shandy

Acme is used in English to mean 'highest point'. English writers began to use the word in the 16th century, at first leaving it in its Greek form. It was not until the 18th century that it was felt to be thoroughly English. It has links with Greek *akros* 'topmost extremity' and therefore with words like **acropolis** 'elevated part of town' and **acrobat** originally 'walking on tiptoe'.

In making use of 'acme' in the passage above, Laurence Sterne comments on the many English words that end in *-ical*. This is a double suffix which forms what is called a secondary adjective. Since the 18th century, when Sterne made his comment, there has been a tendency to simplify *-ical* to *-ic* where possible. We would certainly now say **romantic** rather **romantical**, and most speakers would use **obstetric** rather than **obstetrical**. Occasionally there is a slight difference of meaning between the two forms. We would speak of **economic** science but an **economical** person, a **historic** occasion but a **historical** treatise. Both **music** and **musical** have become nouns, but the latter is still able to function as the adjective.

ADAMANT

When Eve upon the first of Men
The apple press'd with specious cant
Oh! what a thousand pities then
That Adam was not Adamant!

Thomas Hood Reflection

APPLAUSE

Epilogue:
The King's a beggar, now the play is done.
All is well ended if this suit be won,
That you express content; which we will pay
With strife to please you, day exceeding day.
Ours be your patience then, and yours our parts;
Your gentle hands lend us, and take our hearts.

William Shakespeare All's Well That Ends Well

At the end of a play, Roman actors would say to the audience *Plaudite!* 'applaud!' Our form of the Latin word is **plaudit** 'round of applause' or 'emphatic expression of approval'. **Applause** itself, needless to say, is an oblique form of **applaud**, which itself comes from the same Latin verb — *(ad)-plaudere* — that led to 'plaudit'. Another word in this group is **plausible**, originally 'deserving of applause' before coming to mean 'having an appearance of truth or worth'.

Roman audiences were not always pleased. They could drive actors off the stage by clapping in an unappreciative way and hissing. For this they had the verb *explodere*, a form of *ex-plaudere*. This has become our word **explode**, together with the noun **explosion**. The modern meanings of these words have come a long way from the original idea of 'driving from the stage', though when we talk of 'exploding a theory', in the sense of showing it to be worthless, then we are still at one with disgruntled Romans.

Young children seem to clap their hands instinctively when pleased, like dogs wagging their tails, but the action has become conventionalised. While clapping is now mainly a response to a public performance, it can be used by an

. . . the weird (when you came to think about it) human activity called 'clapping'. If you saw a grasshopper rubbing its legs together, or a seal flapping its flippers, you said 'How quaint'. But humans, who also possessed other, very highly sophisticated means of communication and expression, beat their hands together and thought it quite a reasonable thing to do. Why not a rhythmic clashing of the teeth?

Alexander Fullerton *Other Men's Wives*

ANGLO-INDIAN

We looked like what we were —
Anglo-Indians, Eurasians,
cheechees, half-castes, eight-
annas, black-whites. I've
heard all the names they call us,
but I don't think about
them unless I'm angry.

John Masters *Bhowani Junction*

individual in a private conversation. A slow, exaggerated hand-clap, deliberately making little sound, is sometimes used as ironic congratulation when something silly has been said or done. Since this is the opposite of applauding in a genuine way, we could perhaps describe that as a modern form of 'explauding'.

AQUILINE

Nabir's mother was as handsome as her sons; she had a beautiful aquiline face, fine black eyes and hair that was still raven black.

Rumer Godden *Kingfishers Catch Fire*

The passage quoted above is unusual in its use of **aquiline** 'eagle-like'. The word is from Latin *aquila* 'eagle' (**eagle** itself being an adaptation of French *aigle*, which in turn is directly from *aquila*). The point about aquiline is that almost invariably in literature — the word is seldom used in conversation — it is used to describe a nose, the distinctive type of nose that resembles an eagle's beak. Such noses have commanded attention through the centuries. Isaac Disraeli tells us in his *Curiosities of Literature*, in an essay

on 'Female Beauty and Ornaments', that in ancient Persia 'an aquiline nose was thought worthy of the crown'.

One problem faced by those who have such a nose is that it is exposed to danger. Robert Graves ruefully says, in *Goodbye to all that*, that he is 'untruthfully described as having no special peculiarity. For a start, there is my big, once aquiline nose, which I broke at Charterhouse while foolishly playing rugger with soccer players. (I broke another player's nose in the same game.) That unsteadied it, and boxing sent it askew. Finally, it was operated on by an unskilful army surgeon, and no longer serves as a vertical line of demarcation between the left and right sides of my face.'

Sometimes, startlingly clear-cut in the half light, could be glimpsed a profile of some gaunt Southern labourer, or backwoodsman; and it was the profile of a portrait seen in some gallery or in the illustration of a book of history. A nose high-bred, aquiline; a sensitive, haughty mouth; eyes deep-set, arrogant . . .

Edna Ferber *Show Boat*

Charles Dickens has at least two characters whose noses call for the aquiline description. Miss Tox, the particular friend of Mrs Chick in *Dombey and Son*, has a 'nose, stupendously aquiline'. Mrs Veneering, in *Our Mutual Friend*, is said to be 'aquiline-nosed and fingered, each of her aquiline fingers looking so very like her one aquiline nose that the brand-new jewels on them seemed necessary for distinction's sake'.

The bearer of an aquiline nose can be described with considerably less elegance as 'hook-nosed'. Jesse Hexam, a waterman who also features in *Our Mutual Friend*, is 'a hooknosed man', perhaps because he is not on the same social level as Mrs Veneering. But Dickens, as always, can add a few words to complete the portrait. With his nose 'and his bright eyes and his ruffled head, he bore a certain likeness to a roused bird of prey'.

———————○———————

A kind of sleepy Venus seem'd Dudù,
Yet very fit to 'murder sleep' in those
Who gazed upon her cheek's transcendent hue,
Her Attic forehead, and her Phidian nose.

Lord Byron Don Juan

[Phidias was a famous sculptor in ancient Greece.]

———————○———————

One would normally call such a description a **thumbnail sketch**; it would be tempting to suggest that a *thumbnose sketch* exists, were it not that 'thumbnose' implies a rude gesture. Candidates for the new category, whatever it was named, would include Washington Irving's hilarious portrayal of Ichabod Crane, in *The Legend of Sleepy Hollow*: 'His head was small, and flat at top, with huge ears, large green glassy eyes, and a long snipe nose, so that it looked like a weathercock, perched upon his spindle neck, to tell which way the wind blew.' Dickens himself, of course, would hold his own even in such company. In *Bleak House* he makes the throwaway remark, of Mr Snagsby's unnamed niece, that she has 'a sharp nose like a sharp autumn evening, inclining to be frosty towards the end'.

———————○———————

I like the saucy retroussé,
Admire the Roman, love the Greek;
But hers is none of these — it's a Beak.

Edwin Meade Robinson *A Disagreeable Feature*

[French *retroussé* 'tucked up', is used to describe a nose that is 'turned up at the tip'.]

———————○———————

Dickens, in fact, is especially strong on noses, with a variety of descriptive terms at his disposal. Anybody who has read *Nicholas Nickleby*, for instance, remembers Miss La Creevy, the portrait painter. On one occasion Nicholas meets her when she 'had got up early to put a fancy nose into a miniature of an ugly little boy, destined for his grandmother in the country, who was expected to bequeath him property if he was like the family'. 'That's the convenience of living in a thoroughfare like the Strand,' she tells Nicholas. 'When I want a nose or an eye for any particular sitter, I have only to look out of the window and wait till I get one.' 'Does it take long to get a nose, now?' Nicholas asks. '**Snubs** and **Romans** are plentiful enough, and there are **flats** of all sorts and sizes when there's a meeting at Exeter Hall; but perfect aquilines, I am sorry to say, are scarce.' 'Indeed!' says the ever-helpful Nicholas. 'If I should meet with any in my travels, I'll endeavour to sketch them for you.'

Such a conversation ought to be enough on the subject for one novel, but Nicholas is later obliged to return to it. His mother, discussing Frank Cheeryble, asks: 'What may you call his nose, now,

➤◠◄ ASSASSIN HASHISH ➤◠◄

Both adapted from an Arabic word 'hashish-eater'. The original assassins were Muslim fanatics who prepared themselves to murder their victims, usually Crusaders, by eating hashish.

my dear? What style of nose — what order of architecture, if one may say so. I am not very learned in noses. Do you call it a Roman or a **Grecian**?' 'Upon my word, mother,' Nicolas replies, 'as well as I remember, I should call it a kind of composite, or mixed nose. But I have no very strong recollection on the subject, and if it will afford you any gratification, I'll observe it more closely, and let you know.'

———————O———————

Knows he that never took a pinch,
Nosey, the pleasure thence which flows,
Knows he the titillating joys
Which my nose knows?
O Nose, I am as proud of thee
As any mountain of its snows,
I gaze on thee, and feel that pride
A Roman knows!

Alfred A. Forrester To My Nose

[The first line refers to a pinch of snuff.]

———————O———————

The most famous Dickensian nose, however, is in Hard Times. Allusions to 'the **Coriolanian** style of nose' of Mrs Sparsit, Mr Bounderby's housekeeper, are scattered throughout the novel. We are told, for instance, that Mrs Sparsit 'took her classical features downstairs again, and entered the board-room in the manner of the Roman matron going outside the city walls to treat with an invading general'. Or, 'her manner of sitting was so perfectly serene, that most observers would have been constrained to suppose her a dove, embodied, by

some freak of nature, in the earthly tabernacle of a bird of the hook-beaked order'. When she is caught out in the rain, 'rills ran down her bonnet and her Roman nose'.

When this formidable lady upsets Mr Bounderby he exclaims: 'Why don't you mind your own business, ma'am? How dare you go and poke your officious nose into my family affairs?' Dickens remarks that 'this allusion to her favourite feature overpowered Mrs Sparsit'. She is still foolish enough, however, in a later chapter to say: 'Pray, sir, do not bite my nose off.' 'Bite your nose off, ma'am!' says the ungallant Mr Bounderby. 'Your nose!'

———————O———————

He had thought, at first, that the Italian women had noses too long — from the nasal standard of American cover-girls — but presently he was convinced that these almost long noses were part of a medieval grace and long flying lines that ought to be seen not in the chopped-off smart New York styles which prosperous Italian women wear today, but in a fluency of trailing silk, soft green trimmed with silver and rare furs. He noted with comfort that Olivia Lomond's nose was one-hundredth of an inch longer than the severe Colorado norm, and he felt that if ever he should see Roxanna Eldritch's pert snub nose again he would consider it truncated and vulgar.

Sinclair Lewis World So Wide

———————O———————

A hundred years before Dickens was to amuse himself and his readers at the expense of Mrs Sparsit's nose, Laurence Sterne had published Book Three of Tristram Shandy. In it was a lengthy description of Walter Shandy's obsessive interest in Noses — a subject which Sterne was at pains to define: 'I define a nose as follows — intreating only beforehand and beseeching my readers, both male and female, of what age, complexion, and condition soever, for the love of God and their own souls, to guard against the temptations and suggestions of the devil, and suffer him by no art or wile to put any other ideas into their minds, than what I put into my definition — For by the word *Nose*, throughout all this long chapter on noses, and in every other part of my work, where the word *Nose* occurs — I declare, by the word I mean a nose, and nothing more, or less.'

This disclaimer reads oddly to mod-

-*INE WORDS*

Aquiline 'eagle-like' is one of a family of words based on Latin names for animals and birds. A useful source for specialised adjectives of this type is *Modifiers*, edited by Laurence Urdang. Some examples of -ine words are listed below, where the meaning in each case is 'of' or 'like [the animal/bird]'. Such words are sometimes used jokingly, as Oliver Wendell Holmes demonstrates in *The Autocrat of the Breakfast Table*: 'If you expect me to hold forth in a "scientific" way about my tree loves, — to talk, for instance, of the *Ulmus Americana*, and describe the ciliated edges of its samara, and all that, — you are an anserine individual.' There is also the 'learned' version of a well-known proverb:

It is permitted to the feline race
To contemplate even a regal face.

Accipitrine — hawk, falcon
Acipenserine — sturgeon
Alcelaphine — antelope
Anserine — goose
Asinine — ass
Bombycine — silkworm
Bovine — ox
Canine — dog
Capreoline — roebuck
Caprine — goat
Cardueline — goldfinch
Cathartine — buzzard, vulture
Ceratorhine — rhinoceros
Cervine — deer
Ciconine — stork
Colubrine — snake
Columbine — dove
Crotaline — rattlesnake
Cygnine — swan
Delphine — dolphin
Didelphine — opossum
Elephantine — elephant
Equine — horse
Feline — cat
Formicine — ant
Fringilline — finch

Hippocampine — seahorse
Hippotigrine — zebra
Hircine — goat
Hirundine — swallow
Icterine — oriole
Larine — gull
Leonine — lion
Leporine — hare
Limacine — slug
Lupine — wolf
Lutrine — otter
Macropodine — kangaroo
Membracine — treehopper
Mimine — mockingbird
Murine — mouse
Muscicapine — flycatcher
Musteline — weasel
Myoxine — dormouse
Ostracine — oyster
Ovine — sheep
Pantherine — panther
Parine — titmouse
Passerine — sparrow
Pavonine — peacock
Perameline — bandicoot

Percesocine — barracuda
Perdicine — partridge
Phalacrocoracine — cormorant
Piscine — fish
Pluviaeline — plover
Porcine — pig
Psittacine — parrot
Ranine — frog
Sciurine — squirrel
Scolopacine — woodcock
Serpentine — serpent
Sittine — nuthatch
Soricine — shrew
Sturnine — starling
Suilline — swine
Taurine — bull
Trochilidine — hummingbird
Turdine — thrush
Turnicine — quail
Ursine — bear
Vaccine — cow
Vituline — calf
Viverrine — civet
Vulpine — fox
Vulturine — vulture
Zibeline — sable

ern eyes, but a literary joke of the 18th century was that by **nose**, **penis** should be understood. Sterne is reminding his readers of the fact, though he pleads innocence. He remarks that his great-grandmother insisted on a large jointure from his great-grandfather on the grounds that 'you have little or no nose, sir'. To this his great-grandfather replied that it was 'a full inch longer than my father's'. Sterne then adds: 'Fair and softly, gentle reader! — where is thy fancy carrying thee? — if there is truth in man, by my great-grandfather's nose, I mean the external organ of smelling, or that part of man which stands prominent in his face.'

Sterne knew perfectly well where the fancy of his readers was taking them — exactly where he wanted it to go — but he declares: 'Heaven is witness, how the world has revenged itself upon me for leaving so many openings to equivocal strictures — and for depending so much as I have done, all along, upon the cleanliness of my reader's imagination.'

Few men of great genius have exercised their parts in writing books upon the subject of great noses: by the trotting of my lean horse, the thing is incredible! and I am quite lost in my understanding, when I am considering what a treasure of precious time and talents together has been wasted upon worse subjects — and how many millions of books in all languages, and in all possible types and bindings, have been fabricated upon points not half so much tending to the unity and peace-making of the world.

Laurence Sterne Tristram Shandy

Having established his terms of reference, Sterne is now free to explain his father's theory of noses. He is in favour of long ones, believing that a 'number of long and jolly noses, following one another in a direct line,' will raise a

family to the highest social levels. There follows a mock-learned discussion about scholars of the past who have devoted themselves to **rhinology**, the study of noses. The greatest of these, says Sterne, was Hafen Slawkenbergius.

Sterne's style is not to everyone's taste, and he is not easy to read, but his contribution to English literature is unique. Here he is on the subject of Walter Shandy's supposed love of the imaginary scholar: 'Slawkenbergius in every page of him was a rich treasure of inexhaustible knowledge to my father — he could not open him amiss; and he would often say in closing the book, that if all the arts and sciences in the world, with the books which treated of them, were lost — should the wisdom and policies of governments, he would say, through disuse, ever happen to be forgot, and all that statesmen had written or caused to be written, upon the strong or the weak sides of courts and kingdoms, should they be forgot also — and only Slawkenbergius left — there would be enough in him in all conscience, he would say, to set the world a-going again. A treasure therefore was he indeed! an institute of all that was necessary to be known of noses, and everything else — at matin, noon and vespers, was Hafen Slawkenbergius his recreation and delight.'

AVAILABLE

'Eat, drink and love; what can the rest avail us?' So said the royal sage Sardanapalus.

Lord Byron Don Juan

In the 16th century to say that something was **available** meant that it was

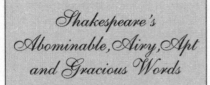

Shakespeare's Abominable, Airy, Apt and Gracious Words

CADE:
It will be proved to thy face that thou hast men about thee that usually talk of a noun and a verb, and such abominable words as no Christian ear can endure to hear.

Henry VI Part Two

PRINCE:
Three civil brawls, bred of an airy word,
By thee, old Capulet, and Montague,
Have thrice disturb'd the quiet of our streets.

Romeo and Juliet

ROSALINE:
His eye begets occasion for his wit,
For every object that the one doth catch
The other turns to a mirth-moving jest,
Which his fair tongue, conceit's expositor,
Delivers in such apt and gracious words
That aged ears play truant at his tales,
And younger hearings are quite ravished.

Love's Labour's Lost

etymologically with **value**, from Latin *valere* 'to be worth'.

In the 17th and 18th centuries **vails** (usually in that form) was the tip which a house-guest gave to a servant when he left the house where he had been staying. Such vails were very important to the servants, making up a large part of their annual income. Jonathan Swift therefore wrote, in 1729: 'I advise you of the servants . . . who expect vails, always to stand rank and file when a stranger is taking his leave.'

The custom of giving vails to servants died out to some extent by the end of the 18th century, though a visitor to Ireland in 1805 referred to 'the vale, or parting token, which the menial servants still in many houses expect'. A. Clarke, writing in 1823, refers to vails as 'that sovereign disgrace to their masters', presumably because employers paid low wages and forced servants to depend on gratuities.

AWFULLY

They had a lingo of their own. Quite common things, according to them, were 'scrumptious', or 'awfully good', or 'awfully rotten', or just 'bally awful'. Cigarettes they called 'fags'; their bicycles their 'mounts', or 'my machine' or 'my trusty steed'; the Candleford Green people they alluded to as 'the natives'. Laura was addressed by them as 'fair damsel', and their favourite ejaculation was 'What ho!' or 'What ho, she bumps!'

Flora Thompson Candleford Green

'capable of producing a desired result'. It was of **avail** 'useful'. We still avail ourselves of something when we make use of it, but these days we mostly use 'avail' negatively; we did something **to no avail**. The word 'avail' in its turn is derived from **vail** and is connected

Flora Thompson is describing in the above passage members of a typical early cycling club. They were young men who 'had a great sense of their own importance, and dressed up to their part in a uniform composed of a tight navy knickerbocker suit with red or yellow braided coat and a small navy pill-box cap embroidered with their club badge'. They would cycle out into the country-side on a Saturday afternoon, stopping at a post office when they reached their destination. 'Cycling was considered such a dangerous pastime that they telegraphed home news of their safe arrival at the farthest point in their journey. Or perhaps they sent the tele-grams to prove how far they really had travelled, for a cyclist's word as to his day's mileage then ranked with an an-gler's account of his catch.'

Miss Thompson worked in a village post office and was able to note the cyclists' slangy use of language. **Aw-fully**, as she reports, was a favourite intensifier, though this usage rather debased the word's meaning. **Awe** has the basic sense of 'fear', and **awful** once described anything which inspired fear or dread. By the 17th century the word was also used to mean 'solemnly im-pressive'. In theory something which is 'awfully good' is good enough to in-spire feelings of reverential awe; in fact it is now merely something which a speaker believes to be 'very good'. The weakened meaning of the word no doubt makes it difficult for modern students who come to Shakespearean lines such as that spoken by Richard II: 'How dare thy joints forget / To pay their awful duty to our presence?'

FOR
MUTTON

BASIATION

Love that seems to the scoffing world to go slinking into basiation's obscurity.

George Meredith *The Egoist*

It is fitting that George Meredith should refer to obscurity in the passage quoted above. He could never resist an obscure word in favour of a simple one. His **basiation** is from Latin *basiare* 'kiss' and therefore means 'kissing', but his sentence remains obscure even when basiation is translated. Theoretically, he could also have used the verb **basiate** 'to kiss'. The learned adjective, if one should ever need such a thing, which means 'to do with kissing' would be **osculatory**, from another Latin verb *osculari* 'kiss'.

Shakespeare and his contemporaries often used **buss** for 'kiss'. Ulysses uses both words in *Troilus and Cressida* when he says:

For yonder walls, that pertly front
   your town
Yond towers, whose wanton tops do
   buss the clouds,
Must kiss their own feet.

This 'buss' was earlier **bass** and is presumably also from Latin *bastiare*, or its derivative French *baiser* 'kiss'.

English perhaps now needs more than one word for 'kiss', to distinguish between the social peck, used at greeting and parting, and the more romantic 'silent petition', as Ben Jonson calls it in *The Devil is an Ass*. **Kiss** itself is a Germanic word found in a similar form in several languages. In English, where the verb originally had an o rather than an i, it has been used in interesting compounds as well as independently. In the 17th century, for example, there was a word for what was later called in slang a **sky-scraper**: had things worked out differently we might have been able to speak of the **kiss-clouds** of New York.

BASTARD

'The bastard.'
The mere word had startled him — rather as it would have if suddenly used by a bishop or contumacious curate. His mind even tried to take it literally — in its application, say to one of his own children. Jill hadn't given it any accent to stagger him. She hadn't attached it to Anrander as a covert term of indulgence or endearment. She meant it — or thought she did. But — just as a bit of vocabulary — it didn't belong to her.

J.I.M. Stewart *A Use of Riches*

Many people have wondered why children born out of wedlock should be stigmatised. Their illegitimacy was not of their choosing, nor are they mentally and physically different from other children. Shakespeare's thoughts on the subject are put into the mouth of Edmund, bastard son to Gloucester, in *King Lear*:

Why bastard? Wherefore base?
When my dimensions are as well
  compact,
My mind as generous, and my shape as
  true,
As honest madam's issue? Why brand

BARBECUE

'Barbecue and poppycock,' Fiona said. 'Isn't it a strange tongue the English have? A body wouldn't understand one half that's said.'

Alice Dwyer-Joyce *The Penny Box*

Teaser: Which common ten-letter English word begins and ends with 'b'?

(Answer page 230)

??

they us
  With base? with baseness? bastardy? base, base?
  Who, in the lusty stealth of nature, take
  More composition and fierce quality
  Than doth, within a dull, stale, tired bed,
  Go to th' creating a whole tribe of fops
  Got 'tween sleep and wake?

Edmund follows this vigorous defence of the illegitimate child with sneering comments about Edgar, his legitimate brother. 'Fine word "legitimate"!' he says in passing, and ends with the exhortation: 'Now gods, stand up for bastards.'

It is a crime to assist a woman condemned to the tittering gossip that can be worse than death by helping her avoid what is quaintly known as an 'illegitimate baby' — as though one should speak of an 'illegitimate mountain' or an 'illegitimate hurricane'.

Sinclair Lewis *Ann Vickers*

In modern English, **bastard** is only occasionally used in its technical sense of 'illegitimate child'. When it is used in that way, according to Mr Brownlow in Dickens's *Oliver Twist*, it reproaches not so much the parents or the child as the person who employs the word. That comment could apply even more, perhaps, to the frequent occasions when the word is meant as a general term of abuse. It can also be, as J.I.M. Stewart points out in the passage quoted above, a term of indulgence ('the poor bastard') or endearment ('you old bastard').

To call men love-begotten, or proclaim
Their mothers as the antipodes of Timon,
That hater of mankind, would be a shame,
A libel, or whate'er you please to rhyme on;
But people's ancestors are history's game;
And if one lady's slip could leave a crime on
All generations, I should like to know
What pedigree the best would have to show?

Lord Byron Don Juan

'Bastard' has an uncertain status in English. Some speakers use the word frequently in relaxed conversation and think of it as a mild insult. Others see it very much as a swear-word, on a par with the American phrase **son of a bitch**, to be avoided along with other taboo words. As such it can be subjected to euphemistic treatment. **Basket** is a common substitute, **baa-lamb** is another — though the latter is not in R.W. Holder's *Faber Dictionary of Euphemisms*. Holder does list, however, a wide range of terms for 'illegitimate child', including **by-blow**, **by-come**, **chance-bairn**, **chance-born**, **chance-child**, **chanceling**, **fly-blow** (influenced by by-blow and referring to eggs left by a fly on meat), **love-child**, **mishap**, **windfall**.

The original meaning of bastard refers to the supposed place of conception, which was not in the marriage bed but on a **bast** 'a pack saddle'. The pack saddle was used by muleteers as a bed when they stayed overnight in an inn, but it could equally well be used in a field. Phrases such as *fils* (*homme*) *de bast* 'pack saddle son (man)' arose in Old French. The pejorative ending -*ard*, found in other French words such as *vieillard* 'old man', *canard* 'duck' was then added to *bast* to give *bastard*, modern French *bâtard*.

Let the bantlings be sent to the hospital.

Tobias Smollett *The Adventures of Peregrine Pickle*

English formerly had a word **bantling** 'a small child, brat', often used as a synonym for bastard. This was possibly a corrupt form of German *Bänkling*, referring to a child begotten on a bench 'in the lusty stealth of nature'. Not that the begetting of a child in an unorthodox place automatically led to bastardy. If the parents subsequently married, the child would be considered lawful, though legal opinion seems to vary as to whether the marriage must have occurred before the child was born.

BEAUTEOUS

Think'st thou I saw thy beauteous eyes,
Suffused in tears, implore to stay;
And heard unmoved thy plenteous sighs,
Which said far more than words can say?

Lord Byron *To Caroline*

Byron switches into a conventional poetic register when he uses **beauteous** for **beautiful**, **plenteous** for **plentiful** in the above passage. Such words reflect a school of thought that believes that poetry requires a separate language, or the use of words that are not bandied about in ordinary conversations. Others would want poetry to use real language to talk about real subjects.

Byron could have inherited these particular words from Shakespeare. 'Black men are pearls in beauteous ladies' eyes', is quoted by Proteus as 'an old saying' in *The Two Gentlemen of Verona*. There are many other occurrences of

'beauteous' in the plays. 'Plenteous' is less frequently used by Shakespeare, but 'plenteous tears', for example, are mentioned in *Richard III*.

Tears and sighs, says Byron, said 'far more than words can say'. He is adding his testimony to those who speak about 'the soul's language' (see SOUL, page 175), the mainly wordless communication of emotion.

BED

Musical beds is the faculty sport around here.

Edward Albee *Who's Afraid of Virginia Woolf?*

Bed seems to be a simple word which is easy to define. It merely describes 'something a person sleeps on'. Yet the same word is capable of thousands of subjective interpretations. Its compound forms hint at its range of powerful associations, its brief summation of the human condition: child-bed, marriage-bed, sick-bed, death-bed.

The bedchamber, no doubt, was a chamber of very great and varied experience, as a scene of human life: the joy of bridal nights had throbbed itself away here; new mortals had first drawn earthly breath here; and here old people had died.

Nathaniel Hawthorne
The House of the Seven Gables

Subjective definitions of certain keywords can be very interesting. At a serious level they can assist the psychoanalyst in what they reveal about the definer. At the party-game level they allow a display of wit. For Tobias Smollett, for instance, in *Peregrine Pickle*, a bed ironically becomes an 'academy'. He is talking about a domineering wife and a hen-pecked husband who have retired for the night to 'that academy in which all notable wives communicate their lectures'.

At least one word in the 'bed' group qualifies as curious. **Bed-ridden** means 'confined to bed through sickness or infirmity', but the word appears to be saying that the person concerned is like a horse, 'ridden' by the bed. It is similar to **hag-ridden**, which did originally mean 'ridden by hags or witches', before it took on the sense of being 'troubled by nightmares and lack of sleep'.

Bed-rid was the earlier form of 'bedridden', the change probably being made by analogy with 'hag-ridden'. Earlier still the word in Old English was bed-rida 'bed-rider'. The sick person who could not walk, in other words, had to be carried everywhere on a bed. He was riding the bed instead of a horse.

BEHOVE

―――――○―――――

It does not behove God-fearing persons to speak with disrespect of the divinely appointed Prince of Darkness.

James Branch Cabell *Jurgen*

―――――○―――――

The verb **behove** is something of a linguistic fossil, especially in spoken English. 'If it behoves you to do something,' explains *Collins Cobuild English Dictionary*, 'it is right, necessary, or advantageous for you to do it.' In American English the correct pronunciation of the word is usually indicated by the spelling: 'It **behooved** him to tread warily . . .' writes Mary McCarthy, in *The Groves of Academe*. The word is so seldom

heard in normal conversation that many speakers would now pronounce it to rhyme with rove, grove.

'Behove' and **behoof**, its associated noun, are Germanic words. There is a very obscure connection with the verb **heave**, but it is almost impossible to unravel the changes of sense that have occurred over a thousand years. Perhaps, to use a literary cliché, it ill behoves us to try.

BELLY

―――――○―――――

Fie, fie, this belly, beauty's mint,
Blushes to see no coin stamped in't.

Thomas Randolph *A Pastoral Courtship*

―――――○―――――

Belly is now curiously avoided in polite conversation. Speakers switch to euphemisms such as **stomach** (or its babyish equivalent **tummy**), **midriff**, **breadbasket** and the like. 'Stomach' is the middle-class word, having been promoted from a Greek word which originally meant 'throat, gullet'. It was then used figuratively of the mouth of the stomach before coming to mean the stomach itself. Old English bælig, by contrast, meant a 'bag, skin-bag'. The word developed in two different ways, leading to 'belly' for the part of the body and **bellows** as a 'blowing bag'. By the 14th century 'belly' was the normal literary word, used for example in the Authorised Version of the Bible far more frequently than 'stomach'.

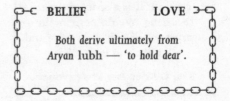

BELIEF   LOVE

Both derive ultimately from
Aryan lubh — 'to hold dear'.

Your belly is a heap of wheat, encircled with lilies.

Old Testament *Song of Solomon*

Shakespeare uses both 'belly' and 'stomach', but it would sound ludicrous to apply the latter word to Sir John Falstaff. He himself had no doubt about the word to use. In *The Merry Wives of Windsor* he speaks of Mistress Page, 'who even now gave me good eyes too, examined my parts with most judicious oeillades; sometimes the beam of her eye gilded my foot, sometimes my portly belly. O, she did so course o'er my exteriors with such a greedy intention that the appetite of her eye did seem to scorch me up like a burning-glass!'

In compounds like **belly dance**, **belly flop**, **belly laugh**, 'belly' has managed to survive more or less intact. **Belly-ache** would probably have been lost, but it has managed to take on a new meaning as a verb. We tell the doctor we have a **stomach-ache**, but accuse someone of belly-aching if he is constantly complaining in an unreasonable way.

BELONG

'I can't belong physically to two people.'
'"Belong physically"? Whom are you reading, Louise? Where do you get these phrases? People don't "belong", physically or any other way, my girl. Anyway, I don't. Love is an hour we give and take, a need we fulfil in each other, a mood, a release, a perception. It is a span of time, recurring. We do not own the instrument of that — we use and bless and love it.'

Kate O'Brien *Pray for the Wanderer*

BLEACH

Bleach is a curious word because at one time it could refer to both 'white' and 'black'. Old English had both *blæc* 'black' and *blac* 'white, shining'. They were originally perhaps the same word, meaning 'absence of colour'. That was also the first meaning of **bleak**, though by an easy transposition it came to mean 'absence of vegetation'. *Blac* led to a verb bleach meaning 'make white' by washing and exposing to sunlight. *Blæc* also led to a verb bleach, meaning 'blacken', though this is now obsolete.

GARNET:
I wish you could take the white and silver to be married in. It's the worst luck in the world, in anything but white. I knew one Bet Stubbs, of our town, that was married in red; and, as sure as eggs, the bridegroom and she had a miff before morning.

Oliver Goldsmith *The Good-Natur'd Man*

The use of **white** and **black** in English is also curious at times. We drink 'white' wine, for instance, which is always coloured in some way, if only with the lightest touch of green or yellow. Nor do 'white' people deserve that description. The former **White Sunday** became **Whit Sunday** and in Scotland changed to **Whitsunday** or **Whitsun Day**. The latter has been fixed since 1693 as 15 May, which means that in Scotland what was once a Sunday can fall on any day of the week.

The police wagon known as a **black Maria** is said to allude to an American woman who helped police handle prisoners, but the story is impossible to prove. The criminals inside such a vehicle might have been **blacketeers** at one time, if they were black market racketeers. If instead they were **blackmailers**, the allusion was to **mails** 'payments' formerly extorted from farmers on the Scottish borders as protection money. It has been suggested that payment made with black cattle accounted for the first part of the word.

───────○───────

Helena looked around the apartment. It was painted black, so as not to show the dirt, she would have presumed if Norine had been practical. But doubtless the colour was a banner or slogan of some kind, as in Putnam's shirt, though a puzzling one to Helena, since black, she had always understood, was the colour of reaction, of clerical parties and fascists.

Mary McCarthy *The Group*

───────○───────

As for **blackguards**, a word which is now rarely used, it referred ironically in the 16th century to the dirty followers of the court or an army who carried the pots and pans. Such kitchen servants soon earned a reputation for being **scoundrels**, to use another old-fashioned word. *The Oxford English Dictionary* dismisses them as 'the dregs of the community'.

BLUE

───────○───────

In ancient Hebrew, Greek and Latin, some of the colour words were clearly not as explicit as they are today. It seems very strange to us, but our word for **blue**, in an early form *blavus*, probably links with Latin *flavus* 'yellow'. The shared sense was possibly something like 'gleaming or glowing with colour, colourful'. Similarly, Greek *glaukos*, to judge by the things the word was

applied to, seems to have covered blue, grey, green and silvery. In ancient times it was simply not considered important to distinguish between fine shades of colour.

───────○───────

'Miss Kirkpatrick's eyes must always be perfection. I cannot fancy any could come up to them: soft, grave, appealing, tender; and such a heavenly colour — I often try to find something in nature to compare them to; they are not like violets — that blue in the eyes is too like physical weakness of sight; they are not like the sky — that colour has something of cruelty in it.'

'Come, don't go on trying to match her eyes as if you were a draper, and they a bit of ribbon; say at once "her eyes are lodestars" and have done with it!'

Elizabeth Gaskell *Wives and Daughters*

───────○───────

We are said to 'feel blue' when we are depressed; earlier people in such a state were visited by the **blue devils**. There may be a connection with the hangover effects of drinking cheap gin, which was also known as **blue ruin**. Those who were drunk were said to see everything through a bluish haze. When a blue ribbon was adopted as a symbol of temperance at the end of the 19th century, there may have been a wish to remind drunkards of such matters, though 'blue' was also vaguely associated with 'goodness' and 'excellence'.

───────○───────

Blue ladies there are, in Boston; but like philosophers of that colour and sex in most other latitudes, they rather desire to be thought superior than to be so.

Charles Dickens *American Notes*

───────○───────

The 'blue ladies' that Dickens refers to in *American Notes* are **bluestockings**. This derogatory name for literary or intellectual women arose in the 18th century when women gathered for intelligent conversation at private houses. The fact that one of the men who attended such meetings, Benjamin Stillingfleet, wore blue worsted stockings instead of the silk stockings which were fashionable, was enough to cause them to be known as 'blue stocking societies'.

In the same book, Dickens also refers to Hartford, 'the seat of the local legislature of Connecticut, which sage body enacted, in bygone times, the renowned code of "Blue Laws", in virtue whereof, among other enlightened provisions, any citizen who could be proved to have kissed his wife on Sunday, was punishable, I believe, with the stocks'.

These Puritanical **blue laws** are thought to have been published originally on blue paper, and were as strict as Dickens suggests. A married couple, for example, were required to live together whatever the state of their relationship. Prison rather than divorce was a couple's only option. Americans are still likely to use this 'blue law' to describe any regulation that is thought to be too strict or severe. The term may also have given rise to the use of blue to mean 'rude, immoral'.

The **Blue Peter** is the flag that is flown when a ship is about to leave harbour. The reason for the 'Peter' is unknown. The suggestion that it represents French *partir* 'go, leave' is ingenious but there is unfortunately no evidence to support the theory.

BLUSH

Love may again be likened to a disease in this — that when it is denied a vent in one part, it will certainly break out in another; what her lips, therefore, concealed, her eyes, her blushes, and many little involuntary actions betrayed.

Henry Fielding Tom Jones

Words can easily be used to conceal our thoughts, but as Fielding points out (above) we may reveal them in other ways. **Blush** is a pleasant-sounding word, and is probably connected etymologically with **blaze**. Our cheeks redden as if they are burning. It is then left to someone else to decide why they have done so, whether we are confused or ashamed. In *The School for Scandal* Sheridan creates a scene where a blush is 'construed', as he puts it. Sir Oliver Surface says, in the presence of Maria, that Charles is in love with her. He continues: 'And, with the young lady's pardon, if I construe right, that blush — '. He does not finish his sentence, but he obviously means: 'If I interpret that blush correctly, you love him too.'

Great writers constantly make comments about the ways in which people communicate without words. They report not only what is said, but what has been understood. A typical Shakespearean comment on the blush and its significance occurs in *All's Well that Ends Well*. The Countess of Rousillon says to Helena:

You love my son; invention is asham'd,
Against the proclamation of thy passion,
To say thou dost not. Therefore tell me true;
But tell me then, 'tis so; for, look, thy cheeks

Confess it, th'one to th'other; and
   thine eyes
See it so grossly shown in thy
   behaviours
That in their kind they speak it . . .

BOOK

But what strange art, what magic can dispose
The troubled mind to change its native woes?
Or lead us willing from ourselves, to see
Others more wretched, more undone than we?
This Books can do; nor this alone; they give
New views to life, and teach us how to live;
They soothe the grieved, the stubborn they
   chastise,
Fools they admonish, and confirm the wise:
Their aid they yield to all: they never shun
The man of sorrow, nor the wretch undone:
Unlike the hard, the selfish and the proud,
They fly not sullen from the suppliant crowd;
Nor tell to various people various things,
But show to subjects what they show to kings.

George Crabbe The Library (extract)

Book is from an Old English word meaning 'beech'. It is thought that the earliest runes, or letters, were scratched on beech bark. Many other terms to do with writing are derived from the materials on which words were inscribed. **Bible**, for example, is ultimately from a Greek word which referred to the inner bark of the **papyrus**, the rush which once grew abundantly in Egypt and was used to prepare a primitive **paper**. Other words of the 'Bible' family are **bibliography**, **bibliomania**, **bibliophile**, where biblio- has the more general sense of 'books'.

The library in which books are gathered is from Latin liber, which again refers to the material used for writing. In this case the reference was to the 'inner

bark of a tree', used before papyrus. Other words in this family are **libretto** and **libel**. Librairie confuses English-speakers who study French because it is a bookshop. In Old French it was a 'library', which is now denoted by bibliothèque.

A good book steals the mind from vain pretences,
From wicked cogitations and offences,
It makes us know the world's deceiving pleasures,
And set our hearts on never-ending treasures.
Men know not thieves from true men by their looks,
Nor by their outsides, no man can know books:
Both are to be suspected, all can tell,
And wise men ere they trust will try them well.

John Taylor An Arrant Thief

Books require **readers**, who are so called because they 'deliberate, consider' what is before them. The archaic *rede* 'counsel' is the same word as **read** in its former sense. From the same Old English source comes the word **riddle** 'enigma, something requiring explanation'. An 'explanation' of a book is sometimes provided by the special kind of reader who is a **reviewer** — who theoretically 'looks again' at a work. By an odd convention, a reviewer is often very different from the typical reader an author had in mind — perhaps a fellow professional working in the same field rather than someone who needs to be gently introduced to a subject.

There is a natural wish for a reviewer of this type to demonstrate his own cleverness at the expense of objectivity. The problem is by no means a new one. Sir John Harington, writing in the early 17th century, has a little poem entitled 'Against Writers That Carp At Other Men's Books':

The readers and the hearers like my
    books,
But yet some writers cannot them
    digest.
But what care I? For when I make a
    feast,
I would my guests should praise it,
    not the cooks.

Most people concerned with producing serious books hope that the works will have some kind of positive influence on their readers, though they may never know about it. It was nearly two hundred years before a young John Keats was introduced to John Chapman's translation of Homer. We have been aware ever since of the impact the book made on Keats:

Then felt I like some watcher of the
    skies
When a new planet swims into his
    ken;
Or like stout Cortez — when with
    eagle eyes

He stared at the Pacific — and all his
    men
Look'd at each other with a wild
    surmise —
Silent, upon a peak in Darien.

BOURGEOIS

—○—

'Values' was not the only emancipating discovery of Theodore's expanding and complicating mind. He was among the first of those who brought the phraseology of Communism into the rich abundant world of art-studio talk. He anticipated 'Proletart' with his 'Art of the Social Revolution'. When he drew he put revolutionary feeling (whatever that was) into his line. He imposed upon all that slow earthbound Fabian stuff the word 'bourgeois'.

Professor Broxted also became bourgeois; all science indeed was presently bourgeois; and Florentine art, and the Royal Academy, and most portraiture (except when it was 'plutocratic' and so even worse), comfort, bathrooms, punctuality, duty, were all jumbled and deflated together under the blight of that word. He learnt to use this word bourgeois with the same finality as Bernstein; it became his leading card, his Joker in discussion; it beat everything.'

H.G. Wells The Bulpington of Blup

—○—

Bourgeois was given a specific meaning by Karl Marx, who referred to the **bourgeoisie** as the capitalist ruling class that exploited the working class. In normal English usage the word indicates the middle-class concern for material possessions and social status, or the conventionally respectable and conservative behaviour associated with the middle classes. Ernest Weekley was preparing his entry on the word for his *Etymological Dictionary of Modern English* in December 1917. He remarked caustically that 'bourgeois' was 'applied by "intellectuals" to those who pay their way and look after their children'. He added that 'Russian "citizens" are very busy massacring the *bourgeoisie*'.

───────○───────

He was always saying snotty things about my suitcases, for instance. He kept saying they were too new and bourgeois. That was his favourite goddam word. He read it somewhere or heard it somewhere. Everything I had was as bourgeois as hell. Even my fountain pen was bourgeois. He borrowed it off me all the time, but it was bourgeois anyway.

J.D. Salinger *The Catcher in the Rye*

───────○───────

In French *bourgeois* originally meant inhabitant of a *bourg* 'borough', a city-dweller. In colloquial speech the word also became 'employer'. A modern French *bourgeois* is 'middle-class', with perhaps a tendency to be 'upper middle-class'.

Etymologically, 'bourgeois' is connected with borough, which began as a word meaning a fortified 'castle' or 'manor-house', then extended its meaning to a larger area. There is a link also with the *-burg* ('fortress, stronghold') of German place names such as **Hamburg** and thus with the very non-bourgeois **hamburger**.

▬▬▬▬▬▬▬▬▬▬

BRUSH

───────○───────

She learnt to flash a smile brilliant as Cedric's own. 'I make her say "brush" before she comes into a room,' he told me. 'It's a thing I got out of an old book on deportment and it fixes at once this very gay smile on one's face.'

Nancy Mitford *Love in a Cold Climate*

───────○───────

Most people would think of **cheese** rather than **brush** as the word that

achieves the effect described by Nancy Mitford, but her comment does raise the interesting topic of words which have a non-linguistic usefulness. Dickensians will immediately think of **prunes** and **prism** in this context. In *Little Dorrit* Amy makes the mistake of saying: 'I think, father, I require a little time' in the presence of Mrs General. This aristocratic widow has been engaged by Mr Dorrit to improve the minds and manners of his daughters, and she constantly demonstrates her value. On this occasion she tells Amy that 'Papa is a preferable mode of address. Father is rather vulgar, my dear. The word Papa, besides, gives a pretty form to the lips. Papa, potatoes, poultry, prunes and prism, are all very good words for the lips, especially prunes and prism.'

Flora Thompson, in *Candleford Green*, shows how 'prunes and prism' was taken into general use. She is referring to young women who remained at home with their parents when she says: 'According to them, their parents' old-fashioned ideas were their main obstacle. "Pa's so old-fashioned. You'd think he had been born in the year dot," these would say. "And Mama's not much better. She'd like us to talk prunes and prisms and be indoors by ten o'clock and never so much as look at a fellow before he had shown her a certificate of good character."'

> **BOSH**
>
> Rebecca knew in her heart that her ladyship's proposition was what is called *bosh* (in that noble Eastern language with which Wilfrid the Crusader was familiar), or fudge, in plain Saxon.
>
> **William Thackeray** *Rebecca and Rowena*

BUST

Busts and bosoms have I known
Of various shapes and sizes
From grievous disappointments
To jubilant surprises.

Anon

The anonymous poet quoted above uses **bust** and **bosom** as synonyms, referring to a woman's breasts in an old-fashioned way. The former word is popularly linked with the verb and the idea of **bursting out**, but there is no connection between the two. Italian *busto*, French *buste* referred to a sculpture of a person's head, shoulders and chest and gave us 'bust' in that sense. The ultimate origin of the word is unknown, but some scholars have linked it with **busk**, referring to a tree trunk.

Similar words to 'bosom' are found in

According to Harald, her deep-bosomed figure, as revealed by her bias-cut blouses, gave promise of sensuality.

Mary McCarthy The Group

other Germanic languages. The original meaning of the word was probably the space embraced by the two arms, the spatial sense being retained in a phrase like 'in the bosom of one's family'. 'A bosom friend' is also one who might be embraced. 'Bosom' is now rarely heard but amongst Shakespeare and his contemporaries it was in common use. It occurs in most of the Shakespeare plays, for instance.

He then put his hand in my bosom, and indignation gave me double strength, and I got loose from him by a sudden spring, and ran out of the room.

Samuel Richardson Pamela

Buxom looks almost as if it might be a blend of 'bust' and 'bosom', but it is a separate word. It is linked with **bow** and had originally the basic meaning 'easily bowed or bent'. From this it came to mean either 'obedient, submissive, obliging' or 'physically pliant, yielding to pressure'. An obliging person was usually 'good-tempered' and the word eventually took on that sense, together with a meaning of 'healthy'. In former times good health and plumpness were rather more closely associated with one another than they are today, so a 'buxom woman' was well-rounded.

FOR YOURSELF

CANNIBAL

○

No sooner had he reached the sidewalk (little cannibal that he was) than Jim Crow's head was in his mouth.

Nathaniel Hawthorne
The House of the Seven Gables

○

The child mentioned in the passage quoted above is merely eating a gingerbread man, and is therefore a **cannibal** only by humorous exaggeration. The word is a corrupt form of **Caribal**, which in turn refers to the **Carib** tribe of the **Caribbean** islands. In the native language, 'Carib' is said to mean 'brave, daring'. The Caribs were reported to Columbus as being **anthropophagi** 'maneaters', so that their name in the form 'cannibals' was subsequently used in that sense. The change from initial *Car-* to *Can-* has often been put down to the influence of Spanish *can* 'dog', but Columbus himself believed that the tribesmen were subjects of the Great **Khan** (of Tartary).

○

OTHELLO:

And of the Cannibals that each other eat,
The Anthropophagi, and men whose heads
Do grow beneath their shoulders. This to hear
Would Desdemona seriously incline.

William Shakespeare *Othello*

○

The name of **Caliban**, Shakespeare's monster in *The Tempest*, is usually explained as another variant of cannibal. Shakespeare was certainly familiar with the latter word, using it several times in his plays.

There is a racial reference of a different kind in Hawthorne's use of **Jim Crow**. This was the name of a stereotype Negro in a 19th-century song-and-dance act. Jim Crow was later used as an offensive term for any male Negro, while **Jim Crowism** described ethnic discrimination against black Americans.

CERTAIN

○

The Maypole was really an old house, a very old house, perhaps as old as it claimed to be, and perhaps older, which will sometimes happen with houses of an uncertain, as with ladies of a certain age.

Charles Dickens *Barnaby Rudge*

○

Dickens appears to be making the point that we can be certain of nothing when it comes to the meanings of words. **Certain** does seem to behave in a peculiar way when a woman is described as being of 'a certain age'. As Dickens points out, the word appears to reverse its meaning completely. What we should apparently be talking about is a woman of 'an **uncertain** age'.

Why, then, do we say a certain age? We do in fact use 'certain' in a similar way in other contexts. We might say to a child that 'we know a certain little girl who ought to be in bed'. The little girl's name is certain — known for sure — but we choose not to say who she is. This applies to the woman of a certain age. Her age is known, to her at least and perhaps to others, but by tactful common consent it is not mentioned.

Teaser: What is curious about the word 'clinker'?
(Answer page 230) **??**

Dickens may have picked up on the oddity of 'a certain age' by reading Lord Byron, who plays with the phrase in *Beppo*:

> She was not old, nor young, nor at
>   the years
> Which certain people call a *certain age*,
> Which yet the most uncertain age
>   appears.

Byron obviously enjoyed this sally and returned to the theme in *Don Juan*, Canto VI:

> And lo! a fifth appears; — and what
>   is she?
> A lady of a 'certain age', which
>   means
> Certainly aged — what her years
>   might be
> I know not, never counting past
>   their teens.

CHILLI

———○———

Ayah's tales were like the chilli juice that the drivers squirt into the eye of a wounded elephant; the smart of the juice diverts the elephant's attention from its wound.

Rumer Godden *Kingfishers Catch Fire*

———○———

Chilli, or **chile**, **chili** as it becomes in its American spellings, must be one of the most misleading words in English. The name of the seed pod and the seasoning derived from it came to us from Mexican Spanish, but chilli is ultimately an Aztec word. When it was first introduced to England it was thought to be from **Chile** the country, but there is no connection.

As it happens, the name of the South American country means 'the cold, snowy land'. The Peruvian Incas who conquered part of it gave it such a name in their own language because, for them, the country was cold compared to their homeland. Our own words **chill** and **chilly** are from a family of words that includes **cold** and **cool**, but the resemblance between Chile and chilly is coincidental.

There is a well-known scene in Thackeray's *Vanity Fair* where Becky Sharp falls into the trap of believing that 'chili', as Thackeray spells it, must be chilly. Becky is trying to ensnare Joseph Sedley, the Collector of Boggley-Wallah, into marriage, so she pretends to like all things Indian: '"Give Miss Sharp some curry, my dear," said Mr Sedley, laugh-

CAD

In the 1940s, not even the machines for destroying lives and cities were more ingeniously developed than the novelties in the American vocabulary. The ancient four-letter words pertaining to generation and digestion were brought from the garden fence to the Junior Misses' schoolroom, and in the lower reaches of etymology, there was also a treasury of new labels for the sort of male once described with relish as 'an agreeable scoundrel'. He could now be referred to not merely as a cad or a bounder, but as a heel, a drip, a punk, a lug, a jerk, a louse, a stinker, a rat, a twirp, a crumb, or a goon. There were exquisite distinctions among the precise meanings of those words, but most of them were allied to 'wolf', the contemporary term for a confirmed seducer or amateur pimp, a type well thought of at the time.

Sinclair Lewis *Cass Timberlane*

CHEMISTRY

Who can explain the whys and
wherefores of attraction between
the sexes? As I remember, the
word we used in those days to
acknowledge the inexplicability
of it all was chemistry. The
chemistry was right or the
chemistry was wrong.

Howard Jacobson Redback

ing. Rebecca had never tasted the dish
before. "Do you find it as good as
everything else from India?" said Mr
Sedley. "Oh, excellent!" cried Rebecca,
who was suffering tortures with the
cayenne pepper. "Try a chili with it,
Miss Sharp," said Joseph, really interested. "A chili," said Rebecca, gasping.
"Oh, yes!" She thought a chili was
something cool, and was served with
some. "How fresh and green they look!"
she said, and put one into her mouth. It
was hotter than the curry; flesh and
blood could bear it no longer. She laid
down her fork. "Water, for Heaven's
sake, water!" she cried.'

CIAO

Ciao, the Italian word used as both a
greeting and word of farewell, is now
listed in dictionaries because of its fairly
frequent use by English-speakers. The
word recalls the formula '**Your servant**,
sir/madam', which was similarly used
in English in times past. Ciao literally
means '(your) slave', being a dialectal
alteration in Italian of schiavo, Latin sclavus.
Slave in turn is linked with the **Slavs**,
who formerly were reduced to slavery
by conquest.

CINEMA

One of the most popular American entertainments
is kissing. Young men and young girls pull up on
the highways and kiss each other between 6.30 and
10.30 p.m. This kind of amusement is considered
perfectly decent, probably because it keeps you from
going to a cinema.

George Mikes Down With Everybody

When the cinématographe was invented in
France at the end of the 19th century it
was given a name based on Greek words
meaning 'motion' and 'writing, drawing'. The American version **motion
picture** was thus very close to the
original idea. This remained true of the
more colloquial **moving picture**, though
this was inevitably shortened. Americans were soon going to the **movies** to
see a **movie**.

In Britain people might similarly talk
of going to the **pictures** to see a **picture**.
This sounds a little like a childish treat,
and in more dignified speech they go to
the **cinema** to see a **film**. Cinema is used
both for the building where a film is
shown — a motion-picture theatre —
and for the industry concerned with
film-making.

British and American speakers of English have thus tended to go their separate
ways in this matter. The British have
ended up taking yet another word from
French and pronouncing it more or less
in the same way. Not that it happened
without a struggle. A glance into local
English directories of the early 20th
century shows that the buildings springing up on all sides were also described
at the time as **cinematograph halls,
electric empires, electric palaceums,
electric theatres, kinemas, kinematic
theatres, pictoriums, picture dromes,
picture houses, picture palaces, pic-**

ture pavilions, picture theatres, talkie theatres.

There was a good reason for kinema and kinematic, since cinema derives from Greek *kinema* 'movement', itself from *kinein* 'to move'. We retain the initial k- in learned and technical words like **kinesics** 'the study of body movements and gestures which contribute to communication', and **kinematics** 'the branch of mechanics concerned with the motion of objects'. Had the English been more inventive than the French, then, we would no doubt have had a **kinematograph** and would today be speaking of the *kinema*.

Cinema has some unexpected links with other words. Because the Latin verb *ciere* 'to set in motion' is a member of the same family as Greek *kinein*, it is fitting, from an etymological point of view, that we should be **excited**, or even **incited**, by what we see on the screen. There are other words which derive from the same source, all with an underlying idea of setting in motion. **Cite** 'call upon to appear in an ecclesiastical court', acquired a secondary meaning of 'call upon, quote by way of authority or example'. **Recite** is an obvious derivative; rather more removed is **resuscitate**, which literally means 'to stir up again'. Perhaps that, too, is something that good cinema can do for us.

CLUB

. . . the dismal and enormous Mansions of Silence which society has raised to Ennui in that Omphalos of town, Pall Mall, and which, because they knock you down with their dulness, are called Clubs . . .

William Thackeray
George de Barnwell

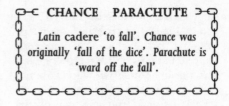

CHANCE PARACHUTE

Latin *cadere* 'to fall'. *Chance* was originally 'fall of the dice'. *Parachute* is 'ward off the fall'.

CLOSET

KING JOHN:
. . . to my closet bring
The angry lords with all expedient haste.

William Shakespeare *King John*

Shakespeare uses the word **closet** to mean either a private room, as in the above passage, or a cabinet where private papers are kept. The latter sense is seen in *Macbeth*, when a Waiting-Gentlewoman says: 'I have seen her . . . unlock her closet, take forth paper . . .' In French a *closet* was a small *clos*, from Latin *clausum* 'enclosure', ultimately from *claudere* 'to shut'. **Enclosure** itself is clearly from the same word, as is **cloister**. Used with a prefix, *claudere* usually becomes -*cludere* or -*clusus*. The word is present in words like **include**, **conclude**, **recluse**, **exclude**, **exclusive**.

'My mother's room is very commodious, is it not? Large and cheerful-looking, and the dressing closets so well disposed!'

Jane Austen *Northanger Abbey*

'Closet' was ruined in its 'private room' sense when the term **water-closet** appeared in the 19th century. This soon became **WC**, which is now rarely heard or seen. The main modern meaning of closet, especially in American English, is a cupboard, but the idea of privacy has survived both in **closeting** oneself away and in keeping one's beliefs, habits or feelings 'in the closet'. In American slang of the early 1970s a **closet queen** was a male homosexual who chose not to make a public statement about his sexual nature. 'To come out of the closet' therefore came to mean to make such a statement. The phrase was perhaps linked in people's minds with revealing the 'skeleton in the cupboard'.

COCKNEY

FOOL:

Cry to it, nuncle, as the cockney did to the eels when she put 'em i' th' paste alive; she knapp'd 'em o' th' coxcombs with a stick, and cried 'Down, wantons, down.'

William Shakespeare King Lear

Those who know their Shakespeare would not need to be told that the words quoted above are spoken by the Fool to his royal master. No other character in the plays uses **Nuncle** as a term of address, and it is only ever used to Lear. The word is a form of **uncle**, arising from a false division of 'an uncle'. More interesting, however, is the Fool's use of **cockney** in this speech. He certainly does not mean a Londoner born within the sound of Bow bells, as the word now suggests. He had in mind a 'squeamish woman'.

COMMISSIONAIRE

Craine's father would have liked this set-up. But he would have snorted if you called a porter a commissionaire.

J.I.M. Stewart A Use of Riches

Shakespeare's only other reference to cockney comes in Twelfth Night, where the Clown says: 'I am afraid this great lubber, the world, will prove a cockney.' In other words, 'I am afraid this great stupid fellow, the world, will prove to be an effeminate milksop.'

Cockney has clearly experienced many changes of sense. In the 14th century the word appears to have meant a 'cock's egg'. This was probably a derisive name for an especially small or misshapen egg which a hen occasionally produces. By the end of the century the word was also used of what was later known as a **nestle-cock**, the last-hatched bird and weakest of the brood, requiring its mother's special attention. In human terms the cockney was an over-protected 'mother's darling' who never achieved independent maturity.

Cockney was then applied by countrymen as a term of contempt for townsmen. In 1617 the Bow-bells definition first appeared, but in modern times it is not always applied too strictly. Suburban Londoners tend to think of anyone who speaks with a strong working-class London accent as a Cockney. The word is certainly now only linked with accent and social class; it carries no suggestion of contempt for lack of manliness.

EMILIA:

O murderous coxcomb! What should such a fool Do with so good a wife?

William Shakespeare Othello

Lear's fool in his speech also refers to **coxcomb**. This is another spelling of **cock's comb**, the crest on the head of a cock. Eels clearly do not have such crests, but coxcomb was commonly used in the 17th century as a jokey word for 'head'. The word could also mean a 'conceited fool'.

The *x* for *cks* in the spelling 'cox' is frequently found in names, such as

CONSCIENCE

Richard: Conscience is but a word
that cowards use,
Devis'd at first to keep the strong
in awe.
Our strong arms be our
conscience, swords our law.

William Shakespeare Richard III

Shakespeare's
Calm, Cholerick,
Comfortable Words

KING JOHN:
Behold, the French amaz'd vouchsafe a parle;
And now, instead of bullets wrapp'd in fire,
To make a shaking fever in your walls,
They shoot but calm words folded up in
smoke,
To make a faithless error in your ears.

King John

ISABELLA:
Great men may jest with saints: 'tis wit in
them;
But in the less foul profanation.
That in the captain's but a cholerick word
Which in the soldier is flat blasphemy.

Measure for Measure

QUEEN:
O full of careful business are his looks!
Uncle, for God's sake, speak comfortable
words.

Richard II

Nixon for 'Nick's son'. It is a shorthand form, rather than an attempt to disguise an embarrassing word. Even as 'cox' it seems to have embarrassed the father of Louisa May Alcott, author of Little Women. He changed the family name from **Alcox** to **Alcott** so that the offensive syllable did not need to be uttered. Another way of side-stepping the problem is seen in the pronunciation Co'burn of the name **Cockburn**. In American English **cock** itself is usually avoided — the bird becomes a **rooster**.

'Do you always smoke arter you goes to bed, old cock?' inquired Mr Weller of his landlord, when they had both retired for the night.

'Yes, I does, young bantam,' replied the cobbler.

Charles Dickens The Pickwick Papers

The bird's name is no doubt imitative of the sound it produces — onomatopoeic as the rhetoricians have it. The shape of the bird's head caused cock to be applied to the kind of tap known as a **stopcock**. By the 17th century the shape and function of this tap caused the word to be humorously used in slang for 'penis'. That sense then became widely established, affecting our perception of words like **cockpit** 'pit used for cockfights', **cocksure**, originally 'thoroughly reliable', as reliable as the cock greeting the dawn. Cocksure now means 'swagger-ingly sure of oneself' and carries a suggestion that this presumption is due to sexual prowess.

GRUMIO:
Cock's passion, silence! I hear my master.

William Shakespeare The Taming of the Shrew

Cock can mean other things besides 'male fowl' and 'penis'. In **haycock** it refers to an egg-shaped heap of hay, and may derive from a dialectal use of French *coque* 'egg'. **Cockboat** 'small ship's boat' is ultimately from **cogboat**, a separate word which has nothing to do with the bird. Shakespeare refers to such a boat in *King Lear* when Edgar says: 'Yond tall anchoring bark / Diminish'd to her cock; her cock, a buoy / Almost too small for sight.' Yet another meaning of cock occurs in oaths from the late 14th century, where the word is a euphemism for 'God'. Our ancestors were apparently to be heard exclaiming **'Cocks body! Cock's bones! Cock's heart!'** and the like. **'By Cock!'** was also a variant form of **'By God!'** Such expressions were doomed once a euphemism for cock itself became necessary.

CONCUBINE

○

'Who is she? Your concubine?'
    'Damn it, Margaret!' he exploded, 'you've got to stop using that language.'
    'It's just a word,' she said. 'Why are you so scared of words? It's a word for someone who lives with you without being married.'

Judith Rossner *Any Minute I Can Split*

○

The definition of **concubine** given above is not quite accurate. Although at one time the word could refer to either the man and woman of a couple who lived together without being married, it has for centuries been used only of the woman. In polygamous societies she is recognised by law but is inferior in status to the wife. In western societies she formerly had no legal standing, but would now be regarded as a common-law wife.

    Concubine literally means a person who 'lies together with' another, from Latin *con-cubare*. The same Latin root leads to **incubate**, literally 'to lie upon' and **incubus**, the male demon who was supposed to molest women sexually while they slept. The female equivalent of this personified nightmare was the **succubus**, from *sub-cubare* 'lie under'. *Cubare* also had a nasalised form *cumbare* which led to words like **incumbent** 'lie upon oneself, apply oneself to' and **succumb** 'sink under pressure'.

    Judith Rossner's character reacts to concubine as if the word is an obscenity, which it is not. It merely refers to a state of affairs that once caused far more social embarrassment than it does now. The word is not used, but that is presumably because of the implied inferior status. Americans involved in a live-in, unmarried relationship recently began to refer to their **posslq** (pronounced possellcue), the word being an acronym of 'person of opposite sex sharing living quarters', but an uglier neologism is hard to imagine.

○

He cut across a remark of Amelia's to the effect that marriage with the right woman so added to a man's comfort. 'I'm not married, if that's what you mean.'
    'Then who — ?'
    'My keep,' said he baldly.
    'Hah! You call a spade a spade, Mr Reddin.'

Mary Webb *Gone to Earth*

○

In the *Longman Guide to English Usage* Sidney Greenbaum and Janet Whitcut mention posslq while discussing the difficulty of introducing 'the sexual partner with whom one lives outside marriage'. They continue: 'My *lover* sounds too emotional, my *man* or my *woman* too primitive and earthy, and my *mate* far too biological. *Boyfriend* and *girlfriend* are possible, but slightly coy. My *friend* is vague. *Cohabitant* and *cohabitee* sound like legal jargon. *Concubine* would be an interesting choice, but one can scarcely imagine its becoming popular.' The Scottish term **bidie-in** is also considered and rightly rejected.

Incubus and succubus could presumably be used by humorists, and **incubine** or **succubine** suggest themselves, whichever is appropriate. But the discussion, while interesting, is surely unnecessary? If a person introduces someone else in a social context as his or her **partner**, is there any doubt about its meaning?

CONQUEST

—◯—

He felt that, if he particularly wanted to, he could make a conquest of this Sophie. The word 'conquest' had reality to him — he liked the idea of supremacy and believed, correctly, that women want to be prevailed upon.

Shirley Hazzard The Evening of the Holiday

—◯—

Conquest has been used to refer to captivating a person, as well as subjugating a people, since at least Shakespeare's time. Shirley Hazzard seems to imply in the quotation above that it is always men who do the conquering. Beaumont and Fletcher, *A King and no King* (1611), were already speaking about the reverse situation: 'Nature did her wrong, / To print continual conquest on her cheeks, / And make no man worthy for her to take.' Similarly, Lord Lytton says in *Godolphin*: 'Constance, dressed for conquest, sat alone in her dressing-room.'

Conquest is clearly related to **conquer**, the verb deriving from Latin *conquaerere*. This had the original sense 'search for', which led on to the idea of **acquiring** something by making an effort. The 'seeking' theme of *quaerere* is found in many other related words. A **quest**, for example, can be either 'the act of seeking' or 'the object that is sought'. To **enquire** means to 'seek information', to pose a **question** or **query**, while an **inquest** or an **inquisition** is a specialised kind of **enquiry**. Those who make a **request**, or write out a **requisition**, are also seeking for something in return.

Shirley Hazzard says that women want to be conquered, which she equates with 'prevailed upon'. The etymology of the word suggests rather that they wish to be sought after and won by effort.

COULD

'When a man is not loved, it is no use for him to say he could be a better fellow — could do anything — I mean, if he were sure of being loved in return.'
'Not of the least use in the world for him to say he *could* be better. Might, could, would — they are contemptible auxiliaries.'

George Eliot Middlemarch

CONTANGO

—◯—

'You won't get your stockbroker on Monday. It's Contanger Day or something with them every Monday.'
'Contanger? It sounds like a new kind of guano.'

A.A. Milne More Cricket

—◯—

Contango is a curious term used by British stock-brokers. On Contango Day a buyer of stock pays to the seller a percentage of the sum owed, the rest to be paid on the next Settlement Day, eight days later. The percentage that is paid is itself referred to as the contango. The word has been in use since the mid-19th century, and its origin, as befits a word that has to do with stocks and shares, remains a matter for speculation. It is usually said to be a corrupt form of **continuation**, which presumably would have arisen through an intermediary *continuango*.

'Contango' seems to appeal to novelists. Barbara Jefferis used *Contango Day* as the title of a novel, published in 1954. The story has nothing to do with the Stock Exchange, but concerns the birthday and suicide of an elderly woman. James Hilton had earlier published *Contango*, a complicated international story where once again the title is used as an obscure metaphor. The book was by no means as successful as *Lost Horizon*, which followed a year later, or the subsequent *Goodbye, Mr Chips*.

CURIOUS

'Curiouser and curiouser!' cried Alice (she was so much surprised, that for the moment she quite forgot how to speak good English).

Lewis Carroll *Alice's Adventures in Wonderland*

Curious is entitled to be called a curious word, having been used in English in many different shades of meaning. It derives from Latin *curiosus* 'careful', ultimately from *cura* 'care', and at first had that meaning in English. 'He should take him unto his own cure,' says a 15th-century writer, 'and be to him as curious as he would be unto his own child'. Related words from the same Latin source include **cure**, **curable**, **incurable**, **manicure**, **pedicure**, **curate**, **curator**, **sinecure** — used of a job which is **secure** 'without care' because it involves little work — **procure** 'obtain by care and effort'.

Of late years, an abundant shower of curates has fallen upon the north of England: they lie very thick on the hills; every parish has one or more of them; they are young enough to be very active, and ought to be doing a great deal of good.

Charlotte Brontë *Shirley*

By the 17th century Shakespeare was able to use 'curious' in various senses. The 'careful' meaning is there in *All's Well that Ends Well*, when the King tells Bertram: 'Frank nature, rather curious than in haste, Hath well compos'd thee.' He means that nature was particular or fastidious about what it was doing. By the reference in *Henry VI* Part Three to 'a curious bed', Shakespeare means one which has been carefully and skilfully made. In *Cymbeline* he uses the word to mean 'anxious, concerned'. Iachimo has with him 'jewels of rich and exquisite form, their values great'. He is afraid of being robbed and says, 'I am something curious to have them in safe stowage.'

> ## CRITIC
>
> This word critic is of Greek derivation, and signifies judgement. Hence I presume some persons who have not understood the original, and have seen the English translation of the primitive, have concluded that it meant judgement in the legal sense, in which it is frequently used as equivalent to condemnation.
>
> **Henry Fielding** Tom Jones

'Is there any point to which you wish to draw my attention?'

'To the curious incident of the dog in the night-time.'

'The dog did nothing in the night-time.'

'That was the curious incident,' remarked Sherlock Holmes.

Sir Arthur Conan Doyle Silver Blaze

CUCKOO WORDS

'See how out of sin comes good.' Sister Mary Fanny was given to what Mother Morag called 'cuckoo-words' or platitudes. But in this case they were true.

Rumer Godden The Dark Horse

Curiosity in the meantime had developed from its earliest sense of 'carefulness' and was coming to mean 'an over-careful interest in unimportant things'. It was on the way, in other words, to becoming a synonym of 'inquisitiveness'. Once it reached that point, curiosity could also be transferred to an object which aroused great interest. Curious could also take on its modern meanings, as when people say that they are curious — 'eager to know' — about something, or that something is curious — 'arouses interest', often because it is odd in some way. The 'caring' meanings have been left aside.

Charles Dickens was well aware that curiosity, a powerful word in itself, would make an excellent component in his title The Old Curiosity Shop. The action of the novel does indeed begin in the shop, but Little Nell and her grandfather are soon on their enforced travels. The chapter which describes the death of Little Nell is usually cited as an example of Victorian sentimentality at its worst, but it is movingly written. The funeral description has even been cited as a curiosity in its own right. C.C. Bombaugh points out, in his Oddities and Curiosities of Words and Literature, that many of the sentences are beautifully formed and stand the test of being set out as blank verse:

Along the crowded path they bore her now;
Pale as the new-fallen snow
That covered it; whose day on earth
Had been so fleeting.
Under that porch where she had sat when Heaven
In mercy brought her to that peaceful spot,
She passed again, and the old church
Received her in its quiet shade.

DAINTY

○

To describe Pat Bramble, in any record, no matter how realistic, the word 'dainty' would have to be fetched forth from the boarding-house of shabby and pensioned words. Dainty. Out of a Victorian novel. Kin to Little Nell and Miss Nickleby . . .

Sinclair Lewis *Ann Vickers*

○

Sinclair Lewis is rather unfair to **dainty** in the above passage. He is presumably thinking of the word in its 'delicately pretty' sense. Little Nell and Kate Nickleby are also angelic of character. For most people the word also suggests something good to eat, a choice morsel or delicacy. But why should Lewis think the word 'shabby', one that has been 'pensioned'? It is also surprising that he should link it in literary terms with Victorian novels. It suggests more immediately Bottom's 'O dainty duck!' in *A Midsummer Night's Dream* or perhaps Prospero's 'my dainty Ariel' in *The Tempest*.

'Dainty' has changed its meaning century by century. It was originally a noun meaning 'estimation, honour', having come into English from French. The French word in turn looked back to Latin *dignitatem* 'worthiness', found again in **dignity** and **indignant** — which originally described one's feelings at finding someone or something 'unworthy'. By the 14th century 'dainty' was an adjective meaning 'excellent, delightful', to the eye or palate. It then imitated **nice** in that it could also be used to mean 'fastidious'. Now it simply means 'small and pretty' or 'small and good to eat', and is one of those words that possesses a verbal quiddity (see page 156): it somehow suggests by its shape and sound what it means. 'Dainty' is, as it were, a dainty word.

DANDRUFF

○

Before putting away the comb in his breast pocket, he examined it minutely for signs of falling hair. Except for a few flakes of oily dandruff, there was nothing to be seen.
'Good', he said.

Patrick Boyle *Like Any Other Man*

○

Dandruff appeared as an English word in the 16th century. It is a curiosity because no one knows where it came from, though many learned suggestions have been made. It was often spelt **dandriff** in the 17th century, and sometimes became **dandro** or **dander**. There is just a slight chance that the latter form accounts for **get one's dander up** 'become ruffled or angry' — 'get in someone's hair', so to speak. Cures for dandruff were already being sought in the 17th century, though special shampoos had not yet appeared. Philemon Holland, writing in 1601, declared that 'the juice of garlic being taken in drink cleanseth the head from dandruff'. The smell of one's breath probably also cleansed the room of one's friends.

DATING

○

'You're funnier than the boys I'm used to dating,'
she said.
*   I can't stand that word 'dating'. I don't like 'formal' either when they mean evening dress.*

Richard Bissell *The Pajama Game*

○

The Romans used to begin a letter with a formula of the type *Data Romæ prid. Kal. Apr*

Teaser: What is curious about the word 'delightful'?

(Answer page 230)

??

'given at Rome on the 31st March'. *Data* was a plural past participle form of the verb *dare* 'give', and is the same word we use when we talk about collecting **data** '(given) facts'. From its constant use in specifying when and where a letter had been written, 'data' took on the meaning of '(specific) day or time'. The word passed into French in that sense, then came into English as 'date'.

Having already undergone this massive change of meaning, 'date' was ready to change still further. From the idea of 'agreeing on a date' to meet someone, a 'date' came to mean 'a social engagement between two people of the opposite sex'. Later still 'date' could be applied to either of the persons involved in that appointment, as in 'Who's your date tonight?' or 'John's my date.' It also became possible to speak of dating someone, partnering that person, perhaps on a regular basis. The useful shorthand phrase **blind date** came into being to describe a date between two people who had not previously met.

As is fairly obvious, none of the dates mentioned so far has anything to do with the fruit of the date-palm. The kind of date we eat takes its name from its shape, which the ancients likened to a 'finger', Latin *dactylus*, Greek *daktylos*. Curiously enough, this kind of date also came to be applied to persons in an expression like **soppy date**, used as an affectionate term of address.

The Oxford English Dictionary records another 'date' curiosity. The Scottish verb **daut** or **dawt** 'fondle, caress' was sometimes written as 'date'. A 16th-century Scottish writer, for instance, said that 'the father will make much of his son, and allure him; so the Lord dates and

allures us'. The origin of the word in this sense is unknown, but there is no connection (etymologically at least) between 'going out with someone on a date' and 'fondling'.

DEUTEROGAMY

'You here see that unfortunate divine, who has so long, and it would ill become me to say successfully, fought against the deuterogamy of the age.'

Oliver Goldsmith The Vicar of Wakefield

Deuterogamy is from Greek *deuteros* 'second' and *gamos* 'marriage' and therefore refers to a 'second marriage' which occurs after death or divorce. It is obviously not the same as **bigamy**, where two marriages exist at the same time. 'Bigamy' is from an ecclesiastical Latin translation of the Greek word which gives us **digamy**, 'two marriages'. Digamy has been used in the past to describe both legal and illegal second marriages, but is now a rare word. We are more familiar with **monogamy** 'one marriage', **polygamy** 'several marriages' and **misogamy** 'hatred of marriage'.

Polygamy may well be held in dread,
Not only as a sin, but as a bore:
Most wise men with one moderate woman wed,
Will scarcely find philosophy for more.

Lord Byron Don Juan

A person who is 'afraid of marriage' might be described as **gamophobic**. By contrast there is the **gamomaniac**, who suffers from a form of insanity characterised by 'strange and extravagant proposals for marriage', as *The Oxford English*

DEVIL

'Poor devils,' said Mad.
Why devils, Emma wondered.
Was it a term one used
automatically when enemies were
wounded or killed?

Daphne du Maurier Rule Britannia

Dictionary expresses it. **Hypergamy** has to do with 'marriage into a higher caste or social group'.

Other terms based on *gamos* 'marriage' are used by botanists. A **phanerogam** is a seed plant or flowering plant, though the word literally means 'visible marriage'. A **cryptogam**, literally 'hidden marriage', is a plant such as a fern, moss or fungus which does not produce flowers or seed. The marriage references relate to the manner in which the plants reproduce themselves.

DIMPLE

Men, of course, grow virtuously zealous in an instant on behalf of the lovely dame who tells them bewitchingly, she is alone and defenceless, with pitiful dimples round the dewy mouth that entreats their guardianship and mercy!

George Meredith Evan Harrington

Friedrich Kluge, in his *Etymologisches Wörterbuch*, links the German *Tümpel* 'pool' with **dimple**, saying that both derive from a word meaning a 'depression' in the ground. Professor Weekley also pointed to the English dialect words **dimble** and **dumble** 'ravine'. Ultimately 'dimple' is connected with **deep**.

'I don't think I am pretty,' thought Molly, as she turned away from the glass; 'and yet I am not sure.' She would have been sure, if, instead of inspecting herself with such solemnity, she had smiled her own sweet merry smile, and called out the gleam of her teeth, and the charm of her dimples.

Elizabeth Gaskell Wives and Daughters

The *Oxford English Dictionary* remarks in passing that a facial dimple is 'regarded as a pleasing feature'. This has certainly been true since at least the 17th century, when Milton spoke in *L'Allegro* of 'wreathéd smiles, Such as hang on Hebe's cheek, And love to live in dimple sleek'. The charm of the dimple lives on in modern times. 'Dimple', previously as a pet name for a girl, is now quite often used by British Asian families as a first name.

DISCOMMODE

'I'll tell my wife and daughter,' he said. 'We didn't know we were discommoding you so.'
Norma liked that word and she said it over under her breath.
'Discommode — I wouldn't want to discommode you, Mr Gable, but I think you should know . . .'
The man with the mustache got up from his chair and limped painfully to the counter, groaning under his breath. He brought the sugar bowl back with him and sank, with grimaces, back into his chair.
'I would have got that for you,' Norma said with concern.
'I wouldn't want to trouble you,' he explained bravely.
'It wouldn't discommode me none,' said Norma.

John Steinbeck The Wayward Bus

disable, disabuse, disadvantage, disagree, disallow, disappear, disappoint, disapprove, disarm, disarrange, disassociate, disavow — to mention only those where the main verb begins with *a*. Of these, 'disappoint' is the one which is now used figuratively. It originally meant to deprive someone of an appointment or fail to keep an appointment, either of which was likely to cause considerable frustration to the person concerned.

While English has retained the words mentioned above, the use of many others with this prefix has been, as it were, **discontinued**. To restrict the **discussion** (originally Latin *discutere* 'detach by shaking') once more to those words where the main verb begins with *a*, we have lost **disaccept**, **disaccompany**, **disacknowledge**, **disacquaint**, **disadvance**, **disadvise**, **disaffirm**, **disalarm**, **disanchor**, **disanimate**, **disapparel**, **disappreciate**, **disarray**, **disarrest**, **disassent**, **disassist**, **disattach**, **disauthorise**. Some of these do survive in a simpler form — **depreciate**, **detach**, **dissent**. For others we use a different word: **obstruct** or **hinder** for disassist, **release** for disarrest. Disarray remains as a noun but not a verb.

DISSING

◦

'I can't tell you how much I disenjoyed this evening.'

Iris Murdoch A Word Child

◦

In the passage quoted above Iris Murdoch uses the prefix dis-, which normally reverses or negates the meaning of the verb that follows, to create a word which is easily understood, though unfamiliar. English-speakers are used to the pattern created by such verbs as

'Why it is that long-stage coachmen possess such insiniwations, and is always looked up to — a-dored I may say — by ev'ry young 'ooman in ev'ry town he vurks through, I don't know. I only know that so it is. It's a reg'lation of natur — a dispensary, as your poor mother-in-law used to say.' 'A dispensation,' said Sam. 'Wery good, Samivel, a dispensation if you like it better,' returned Mr Weller; 'I call it a dispensary, and it's always writ up so at the places vere they gives you physic for nothin' in your own bottles'.

Charles Dickens The Pickwick Papers

◦

Dis- is, then, disappearing from the English language to some extent, though it has come into its own in youthful street slang. A ritual exchange of insults, known in the past as a **slanging** or **scolding match**, a **flyting** when in versified form, became a **sounding** or **playing the dozens** in black American usage. From this verbal contesting, which carries great prestige for skilful contestants, has developed **dissing** — showing **disrespect** or being **dismissive** in words and actions. To **diss** (occasionally **dis**) someone is to put him down verbally.

———————◯———————

What's that word beginning with dis? Disembodied? No, not disembodied. Distemper? No, not distemper. Disconcerted, that's the one. I was disconcerted. I should imagine that if you happened to wander by accident into the steam room of a Turkish bath on Ladies' Night, you would have emotions very similar to those I was experiencing now.

P.G. Wodehouse Much Obliged, Jeeves

———————◯———————

Some will think this rather a **dismal** linguistic development, though this particular curious word does not belong to the group under discussion. Dismal is a form of Latin *dies mali* 'evil, unlucky days', of which there were 24 in the medieval calendar, said to have been computed by Egyptian astrologers. Anyone who gives credence to such matters should be especially careful on the following days: 1, 25 January; 2, 26 February; 1, 28 March; 10, 20 April; 3, 25 May; 10, 16 June; 13, 22 July; 1, 30 August; 3, 21 September; 3, 22 October; 5, 28 November; 7, 22 December. According to the ancients, they are days on which it is best stay at home in bed.

DONATION PARDON

Latin *donare* 'to give'. Pardon is *per-donare* 'for-give'.

DUMBFOUNDED

———————◯———————

And all the people of the lulled and dumbfound town are sleeping now.

Dylan Thomas Under Milk Wood

———————◯———————

Dylan Thomas's use of **dumbfound** as an adjective in Under Milk Wood forces the reader or listener to reappraise the more familiar **dumbfounded**. In Thomas's usage, the town of Llareggub, which appears to have a suitably Welsh name but is an ananym, or back-spelling, is 'found/discovered to be dumb/silent'. It is not 'temporarily rendered speechless with astonishment'.

It is not immediately obvious why something surprising should dumbfound us. Why **found**, which normally means to 'establish' or to 'work with molten metal'? It is difficult to see a connection with either of these meanings, though there is in fact a link with the second.

What seems to have happened is that dumbfound was formed by analogy with **confound**, which has much the same meaning. The latter word is from Latin *confundere* 'to mix together, confuse'. *Fundere* itself means 'melt, pour', which leads to 'found' in the sense of pouring molten metal into a mould. Dumbfound thus contains the idea of being unable to speak because of mental confusion.

In North America **dumb** is frequently used to mean 'stupid'. A person might be described derogatively as a **dumb-ass**, **dumb-bell**, **dumb bunny**, **dumb cluck**, **dumbo**, **dumb ox**, **dum-dum**, **dummy**. These are all influenced by German *dumm* 'stupid', found also in *Dummkopf* 'blockhead'. The 'speechless' meaning is rendered in modern German by *stumm*. English **stammer**, which also has to do with difficulty of speech, is ultimately connected with it.

English dumb and German *dumm* are obviously closely related. The word which led to both is thought to have had a basic meaning of 'incomprehension'. A deaf-mute was both unable to understand what was said, and unable to make others understand by speech. In an early form of German, therefore, the same word meant both 'deaf' and 'dumb'. It could also mean lack of understanding due to mental incapacity.

In these rather more enlightened times we are aware that a deaf and dumb person is as intelligent as anyone else. The close scrutiny of language in terms of political correctness that now occurs may help English to cleanse itself of the 'stupid' associations with 'dumb'.

───────○───────

I exercise myself an hour every morning upon a dumb bell, that is placed in a corner of my room. My landlady and her daughters never come into my room to disturb me while I am ringing.

Joseph Addison Spectator No. 115

───────○───────

'Dumb-bell' is worthy of a moment's separate attention. The double-headed weight used in a gymnasium is not very bell-like. The word made more sense at a time when the bells of every village church were rung on numerous occasions. It was then applied to an apparatus like that used for swinging a church bell, though no bell was attached to it. Bell-ringers used the dumb-bell to learn their craft, while others exercised by 'ringing' the non-existent bell. The smaller dumb-bells were presumably used to exercise the wrists in preparation for hand-bell ringing.

─────────────────

DUNKLE

───────○───────

Without very deeply dunkling the truth.

Anon Lawrie T

───────○───────

The above quotation appears in *The Oxford English Dictionary* to support the definition of the Scottish verb **dunkle** 'make a dint in'. Given the name of its author, the words could perhaps serve as a modest review of this book. The resemblance between the verb and the surname Dunkling is a mere coincidence — the place-name origin of the surname is fully explained in *The Guinness Book of Names*.

FOR
BRICK

EARTH

What is earth, Sexton? — A place
to dig graves.
What is earth, Rich man? — A
place to work slaves.
What is earth, Greybeard? — A
place to grow old.
What is earth, Miser? — A place
to dig gold.
What is earth, Schoolboy? — A
place for my play.
What is earth, Maiden? — A place
to be gay.
What is earth, Seamstress? — A
place where I weep.
What is earth, Sluggard? — A
good place to sleep.
What is earth, Soldier? — A place
for a battle.
What is earth, Herdsman? — A
place to raise cattle.
What is earth, Widow? — A place
of true sorrow.
What is earth, Tradesman? — I'll
tell you tomorrow.
What is earth, Sick man? — 'Tis
nothing to me.
What is earth, Sailor? — My
home is the sea.
What is earth, Statesman? — A
place to win fame.
What is earth, Author? — I'll
write there my name.
What is earth, Monarch? — For
my realm it is given.
What is earth, Christian? — The
gateway of heaven.

Anon (quoted by Carolyn Wells *A
Whimsey Anthology*)

EFF

*'I could have dropped through the floor when he
started effing and blinding it.'*

Stan Barstow *A Kind of Loving*

Eff is listed in modern English dictionaries as a verb, but its use is highly
restricted. In an expression like 'Eff off!'
it manages to convert an offensive four-
letter word into an almost as offensive
three-letter word — not much of a gain.
Chambers English Dictionary calls 'eff' a
euphemism: some might say that it is a
euphemism in need of a euphemism.
Pee is a similar conversion of an initial
letter into a verb for supposedly euphemistic purposes, though no one would
say 'Pee off!'

The phrase used by Stan Barstow,
quoted above, is used to mean 'swearing' in a general sense. We know what
the effing refers to, but the **blinding** is
no longer obvious. It dates from the
1880s, when it was widely used in
military slang. Eric Partridge, in his
Dictionary of Historical Slang, quotes Kipling:

If you're cast for fatigue by a
sergeant unkind,
Don't grouse like a woman, nor
crack on, nor blind.

In *The Cockney*, Julian Franklyn comments
on 'the incessant swearing that flows
with the stream of cockney conversation'. He says that the Cockneys themselves do not think of it as swearing —
'it is merely a generous allowance of
lubricating oil to language'. Real swearing occurs only under special circumstances and is then 'always appropriate'.

Franklyn continues: 'Such a linguistic
firework display is not called swearing.
That is too weak a word. The term used
is blinding: "'E made me that wild I was
blinding at him for half an hour!" or,

"'Arry 'it 'is thumb with the 'ammer. Did 'e blind!".'

The allusion was to curses such as 'Blind your eyes!' which were formerly in use. The most frequent oath of this type was 'God blind me!', turned by Cockney speakers into **Gorblimey**! or **Blimey**!

Since Franklyn was writing in the early 1950s, he was obliged to be rather coy about the effing that accompanied the blinding. He nevertheless had much of interest to say about the 'first among unprintables' and its use at various social levels. Even those who used it incessantly amongst themselves considered it strictly taboo in the presence of doctors, nurses, clergymen and the like. They would also have been deeply shocked, as the Stan Barstow quotation indicates, to hear the word used by a middle-class person. With **fuck** no longer considered to be either unprintable or unsayable on stage and screen, the delicate taboo system that once governed its use is rapidly breaking down.

ELEVATOR

In England Fran had learned to say Lift for Elevator, Zed for Zee, Lábóratory for Láboratory, Schenario for Scenario, and Shi for Ski.

Sinclair Lewis Dodsworth

As is well known, what people in Britain would call a lift is what Americans and Canadians would call an **elevator**. In a friendly argument about which term was more 'correct', an Englishman was heard to argue that 'it must be lift, because that is the English term and the English invented the language'. 'And who invented the elevator?' came the reply.

EMPIRIC

All economical and practical wisdom is an extension or variation of the following arithmetical formula: $2 + 2 = 4$. Every philosophical proposition has the more general character of the expression $a + b = c$. We are mere operatives, empirics, and egotists, until we learn to think in letters instead of figures.

Oliver Wendell Holmes
The Autocrat of the Breakfast Table

A quack doctor in the past was sometimes called an **empiric**, from Greek empeiros 'skilled', ultimately from peira 'experiment'. This may suggest that the word was complimentary, but it was not. An empiric based his treatments on anything that was believed to work, without having any theoretical knowledge that might have helped him understand why something was effective. His methods could be summed up by the phrase 'trial and error'. This is broadly true of **empirical** studies in any field.

There is an etymological link between the **empiricist** and the **pirate**. The latter is someone who 'attempts everything'. In a sense, the quack doctor was practising a kind of piracy in the high street rather than on the high seas. Greek peira is also closely linked to Latin periri, for which see the article on Expert on p. 63.

ETCETERA

'Bless your heart, etc.'
'You be careful with your etcs,' said Cokey. 'This is a respectable house.'

Joyce Cary The Horse's Mouth

ENDURE

◯

What courage can withstand the ever-during and all-besetting terrors of a woman's tongue?

Washington Irving Rip Van Winkle

◯

Irving's **ever-during** in the passage quoted above means 'ever-enduring, ever-lasting'. The author is being playfully hyperbolic and continues his exaggeration with his **all-besetting** 'persistently harassing'. **Endure** is based on Latin durus 'hard', as are words like **durance, duration, duress, obdurate**. Had he been using modern colloquial idiom, Washington Irving might have asked: 'What can any man do when a woman decides to give him a hard time?'

EVER

◯

'Can I have a baby?' Rennie said to Daniel.
  'Do you mean right now?' said Daniel.
  'I mean ever,' said Rennie.
  'Ever,' said Daniel. 'Ever is a pretty big word.'
  'I know. Big words get you in trouble,' said Rennie. 'They told me that at school.'

Margaret Atwood Bodily Harm

◯

It is interesting to see **ever** described as a 'pretty big word' in the above quotation, but we know exactly what is meant. The word is of awesome significance if seriously used. For Edna O'Brien, in Girl with Green Eyes, it is also a 'dangerous word': '"That ring has to last you a long time," he said. "How long?" "As long as you keep your girlish laughter."

Shakespeare's Empty, Ethiop, Evil Words

ANGELO:
When I would pray and think, I think
    and pray
To several subjects. Heaven hath my empty
    words,
Whilst my invention, hearing not my
    tongue,
Anchors on Isabel.

Measure for Measure

ROSALIND:
Women's gentle brain
Could not drop forth such giant-rude
    invention,
Such Ethiop words, blacker in their effect
Than in their countenance.

As You Like It

ADRIANA:
'Tis double wrong to truant with your bed
And let her read it in thy looks at board;
Shame hath a bastard fame, well
    managed;
Ill deeds is doubled with an evil word.

The Comedy of Errors

I noticed with momentary regret that he never used dangerous words like "for ever and ever".'

For ever may be a dangerous phrase, but it is used all too easily in the language of amorous popular songs. 'I love you' is seldom felt to be a strong enough statement. 'I will **always** love you,' as Whitney Houston expresses it in one of her great successes, has become almost a minimum verbal commitment. If the 'always' is not present, a suitable replacement has to be found. **Eternally** would no doubt feature strongly in any word count based on popular lyrics, together with phrases like **till the end of time**.

For ever and a day is another synonymous phrase, suggesting that even 'for ever' is not long enough. The original phrase in this case was probably **for ever and ay**, where **ay** (or **aye**) is an archaic word for 'ever'. As for real curiosities, there is **till the cows come home**. This ought to mean 'until the evening' but the cows in this expression stay out in the fields for an indefinite period.

'For ever' occurs so frequently as a collocation that it has long been written, especially in the USA, as **forever**. 'After ten forevers Dr Reynolds returned' writes Harper Lee, in *To Kill a Mockingbird*. The author is recapturing a young child's sense of time, which can stretch a few minutes into what seems like an eternity. Perhaps it is a similar distortion which accounts for the use of **eternal** words in the language of love, since time either stands still when lovers are together or drags by with excruciating slowness when they are apart. 'I must hear from thee every day in the hour,' says a passionate Juliet to her Romeo, 'for in a minute there are many days.'

---○---

'Always! That is a dreadful word. It makes me shudder when I hear it. Women are so fond of using it. They spoil every romance by trying to make it last for ever. It is a meaningless word, too. The only difference between a caprice and a life-long passion is that the caprice lasts a little longer.'

Oscar Wilde The Picture of Dorian Gray

---○---

Just as forever has become a single word, so 'always' looks back to a time when it was **all ways**. The original

reference was perhaps spatial, but it is easy to see how the basic idea of infinity was transferred to time. As it happens, 'I love you in all ways' is certainly as interesting a statement as 'I will always love you.'

EXIT

---○---

JAQUES:
All the world's a stage,
And all the men and women merely players:
They have their exits and their entrances;
And one man in his time plays many parts . . .

William Shakespeare As You Like It

---○---

We are familiar with the use of **exit** on signs that mark the way out of public buildings. The American showman Phineas Barnum is said to have thought that the word was *too* familiar. Visitors lingered in one of his exhibitions until he put up a sign 'To the **egress**.' No one knew what this meant, but it suggested yet another curiosity. Only when people found themselves outside did they realise that egress meant exit.

---○---

'I learned long ago that the most important and valuable of acting techniques is the exit.'
    'But I'd like to ask more questions.'
    'All the more reason for the exit. Keep them asking and exit clean and sharp.'

John Steinbeck Travels with Charley

---○---

Exit began as a Latin stage-direction. It is from the verb ire 'go' and means 'he/she goes', i.e. 'leaves the stage'. As an English verb, exit is treated as if it meant 'leave' and a new third person ending is added: 'he exits'. Used in that way the word is the tip of a linguistic iceberg: it belongs to a separate professional language of the theatre.

There are enough special words used by actors and others connected with the theatre, film industry and radio and television drama to have inspired at least two dictionaries. Wilfred Granville produced *A Dictionary of Theatrical Terms* in 1952. Walter Parker Bowman and Robert Hamilton Ball published their *Dictionary of Terms in English of the Drama and Stage from Medieval to Modern Times* in 1961. The latter deals not only with historical terms but is especially strong on American usage.

---○---

Mr Nooks had merely overplayed — 'hoked' is the technical word — the role of the Apothecary, which is a pretty easy role for anyone to hoke, if he has been born an earnest, congenital ham.

Sinclair Lewis Bethel Merriday

---○---

This special language, or professional slang, soon becomes evident in novels which have actors as principal characters. Bethel Merriday was Sinclair Lewis's contribution to such literature, and he is at pains to get the language right. At one point he specifically comments on the deep resentment of actors who hear laymen refer to **practising** a play instead of **rehearsing** it, and he clearly does not want to be classed as a layman himself. Today it is difficult to imagine even a layman not knowing that actors rehearse a play, but Lewis's novel was published in 1940, before chat-shows with actors talking about their craft had become a daily event on television. Before that happened, the general public was far less exposed to such words.

┌─────────────────────────────┐
│ **ERUDITE   RUDE** │
│   │
│ Latin rudis 'raw, untaught'. An │
│ erudite person is ex-rudis 'no longer │
│ untaught'. │
└─────────────────────────────┘

Lewis tries both to use the terms and explain them to his non-actor readers. 'She had, by stage usage, "**blown**"; she had "blown higher than a kite",' is his comment after describing what an English actor would call **drying** 'forgetting one's lines'. 'Will you read for it?' asks one of his characters, addressing a newcomer to the profession. 'You mean, try and see if I can act one of the parts?' asks the novice. 'Professionally, we call it "read for a part",' says the actor, condescendingly.

---○---

'The only thing is, he won't feed. I never struck a worse feed.' And Mr Nunn paused impressively.

Miss Trant stared. This seemed a curious complaint to make. 'Do you mean that he won't eat?'

'This feeding I'm talking about,' Mr Nunn went on, 'is a name in the profession for working up to gags. The chap that feeds has to ask the comedian questions and get angry with him and all that.'

J.B. Priestley The Good Companions

---○---

Elsewhere Lewis comments on actors' use of vocatives: 'He had never addressed her by any more intimate form than "Oh, darling — look here, sweetest," and in the world of the theatre, that constitutes ignoring a person.' Further comment on this point was later made by Tallulah Bankhead in her autobiography *Tallulah*: 'Rarely was I able to catch the names of the dowagers and drinkers I met at parties, in dressing rooms, or in Bond Street. **Darling** has implications of affection, or, at least, friendliness. It cannot disturb the recipient. Did I try to pin the correct caption on every clown I encounter I'd make embarrassing blunders. They're all darlings to me.'

Most of the words that occur in stage language are like **darling**, in that they are normal words used in a special way. Actors can even make **actor** itself into a

'I suppose you think acting is an art, don't you? It isn't even an art, it's just entertainment at its highest and prostitution at its lowest.'

Margaret Drabble The Garrick Year

special word by putting a heavy pronunciation on the second syllable and rolling the final r. It then designates an actor of the old school who proclaims rather than speaks every word he says, both on and off stage.

It is fitting that a language of the theatre should exist, since actors are often word-buffs. If they are involved with drama from Shakespeare onwards they can find themselves asked to make sense to a modern audience of words which have often changed their meaning greatly. They can only do so if they have thoroughly understood what a line meant when it was written. The research they are obliged to do often makes them more interested than most in the history of language.

EXPERT

Expert is a word that has been over-used by chat-show hosts, faced with the task of introducing someone who is not well-known to the viewers or listeners. The word is supposed to establish the guest's credentials, though few such guests would use the word of themselves. It would sound pretentious, even though its basic meaning is seen in words like **experience**, **experiment**, which also derive from Latin *periri* 'to go through'. The expert is simply someone who has 'tried things out', often in a very narrow field. Nicholas Murray Butler pointed out that 'an expert is one who knows more and more about less and less'.

We all learn by experience, but some of us have to go to summer school.

Peter de Vries Tunnel of Love

Journalists now seem unable to use the word expert without sneering at the person to whom the word is applied. They imply that the expert is a self-important publicity seeker, simply because he or she has been the victim of media shorthand. Those who are regularly called upon as experts — **heavies**, as they are sometimes known in the slang of production offices — therefore try to avoid the label. **Authority** looks well in print: **pundit**, from a Hindi word meaning 'learned', is less hackneyed when spoken. American journalists occasionally use **mavin** or **maven**, a Yiddish word based on Hebrew 'understanding'.

Teaser: What is curious about the word 'excellency'?
(Answer page 230) **??**

FOR VEST

FENCE

'Are you suggesting our friend Deacon is really a "fence"?' asked Gossage giggling, as if coy to admit knowledge of even this unexotic piece of thieves' jargon.

Anthony Powell *Casanova's Chinese Restaurant*

Anthony Powell is right to refer to **fence** as an unexotic slang-word. It has been used in the sense of 'one who buys and sells goods that have been stolen' since the late 17th century and is very generally known. In literature one of the best known fences is Fagin, in Dickens's *Oliver Twist*. At one point he is even addressed as 'you insatiable old fence'.

Fence provides a good example of aphesis, the linguistic process by which the first syllable of a word is lost. In this case the original word was **defence**, the idea of a wooden fence being to defend whatever or whoever was behind it. Since one function of the fence who received stolen property was to protect both the thief and his loot, this may be why the word was applied to him.

To fence in the sense of 'use a sword' is doubly suitable. The weapon is wielded both for **offence** and defence. Both words look back to a Latin *-fendere, fensus*

FELLOW

'How many cops you ever hear say "fellows"? Cops say "guys" or "dudes" or "studs" or "cats", but no cop in the history of the Los Angeles Police Department ever said "fellows". Nobody but you, Baxter Slade.'

Joseph Wambaugh *The Choir Boys*

---

which had a basic meaning of 'strike'. To fence in its swordplay sense is first found in Shakespeare, who also uses the word as a noun. When the Bastard in *King John* says 'Teach us some fence!' he means 'teach us the art of fencing'.

FIREPOT

In Kashmir a firepot is the poor man's fire, a small earthenware pot in a wickerwork container like a basket; it is filled with live charcoal and held pressed to the stomach; every poor man, woman and child carries one under their robes so that they all look pregnant; sometimes they burn themselves terribly but the firepots save them at least from death by cold.

Rumer Godden *Kingfishers Catch Fire*

From time to time novelists are likely to pause in their story-telling in order to look closely at a particular word. They do so for a variety of reasons. The word may be one which they know will be unfamiliar to their readers. It may even be one which would defeat any dictionary that was there, waiting to be consulted. None of the usual English dictionaries, for instance, offers a definition of **firepot** as defined by Rumer Godden in the passage quoted above.

A definition within the narrative is justified in this case for other reasons. The object referred to helps to set the scene, providing authentic local colour. Rumer Godden is also a wordsmith who recognises a curious word when she sees one. The word-story is simply a different kind of story which it falls to her to relate. Almost inevitably, because she is a natural story-teller, she does much better than would the average lexicographer. No writer of a dictionary entry would have made that remark about 'they all look pregnant' which immediately conjures up a vivid picture of a Kashmiri street scene.

Rumer Godden uses another glossing device in the same novel. A character in the book, rather than the author as narrator, pauses to define a particular word: 'Sophie was then thirty-five; afterwards she often wondered how she had managed to reach that age and remain as insouciant as she was. "Insouciant is the right word," said Sophie. "Careless and indifferent."'

---○---

'You go round by the pleached walk.'

He was not precisely sure what a pleached walk was, but when he came upon it there was no mistaking it and, smiling to himself, he descended a flagged step and passed into a green tunnel. The trees whose branches met and interwove above his head were apples and pears.

Ruth Rendell The Best Man to Die

---○---

Ruth Rendell is more subtle in the passage quoted above. Her character is said to be as uncertain about the meaning of **pleached** as readers are likely to be, but the problem is overcome without fuss. Readers, along with the character, learn what the word means. By contrast a distinct lack of subtlety is shown by Peter de Vries in Comfort Me with Apples. The narrative is interrupted for the author, thinly disguised, to say: 'Deduction, he pointed out on the basis of the dictionary definition which he had taken the trouble to acquaint himself with since embarking on this intel-

---

FINANCE   PARAFFIN

Latin finis 'end, border'. Finance is something that puts an end to a debt. Paraffin has little affinity to other substances, no common 'borders' with them.

---

lectual *étude*, deduction was reasoning from generalities to particulars, induction from particulars to generalities. In the light of which facts mystery writers, going on about the "deductive feats" of their protagonists, were misusing the word on a scale unparalleled in the history of poor English; what they meant was induction.'

This comes over as academic pedantry, and is not necessarily very accurate. Whatever difference there may be between **deduction** and **induction** in specialised contexts, the fact is that **deduce** in general terms means 'to reach a logical conclusion' by whatever means. Anyone who has deduced something has made a deduction.

---○---

The word 'party' indicated, in that ultimate climax of civilisation, 1930 in New York, many things. To the artistic, it meant gin and necking. To the raucously inartistic it meant gin and necking. To persons so rich and respectable that they had not yet begun to whimper about the 'Depression' that was just begun, it meant contract bridge and gin. But to the forward-looking group, it meant just Talk.

Sinclair Lewis Ann Vickers

---○---

Sinclair Lewis is an especially 'linguistic' novelist who often comments on particular words. He is aware that dictionary-style definitions do not necessarily get at the heart of words, that at a particular time and in a particular place they can mean different things to different groups of people. His **party** example illustrates the point well. Lewis also frequently adds a parenthetic comment to the effect that a speaker really did use this word on that occasion. He does so especially when the word has since gone out of fashion or has changed its meaning, as is often the case with ephemeral slang. He is insisting on the accuracy of his verbal reporting. In this respect he is usually very convincing, remarkably good at capturing the idiolect, or personal dialect, of an individual.

In *Ann Vickers*, however, Lewis does something very different. A long essay interrupts the narrative, based on the supposed definition of a single word. In a dictionary, **penology** would be described as 'the branch of criminology that deals with the management of prisons'. Lewis is highly subjective about the topic: 'Penology! The science of torture! The art of locking the stable door after the horse is stolen! The touching faith that neurotics who hate social regulation can be made to love it by confining them in stinking dens, giving them bad food and dull work, and compelling them to associate with precisely the persons for associating with whom they have first been arrested. The credo that it is sinful for an individual to commit murder, but virtuous in the State to murder murderers. The theory that men chosen for their ability to maul unruly convicts will, if they be shut up in darkness, away from any public knowledge of what they do, be inspired to pray and love these convicts into virtue. The science of penology!'

There is much more along these lines, but the novel is probably more successful when it exemplifies the points Lewis wants to make in fictional scenes. *Ann Vickers* is, after all, a novel and not a collection of sociological essays.

———————O———————

Jacob stooped to the God-forgive-me, which was a two-handled tall mug. Such a class of mug is called a God-forgive-me in Weatherbury and its vicinity for uncertain reasons; probably because its size makes any given toper feel ashamed of himself when he sees its bottom in drinking it empty.

Thomas Hardy Far from the Madding Crowd

———————O———————

Thomas Hardy's description of the **God-forgive-me** takes us back to the

FIX

'Will you try,' said my opposite neighbour, handing me a dish of potatoes, broken up in milk and butter — 'will you try some of these fixings?'
There are few words which perform such various duties as this word 'fix'. It is the Caleb Quotem of the American vocabulary. You call upon a gentleman in a country town, and his help informs you that he is 'fixing himself' just now, but will be down directly: by which you are to understand that he is dressing. You inquire, on board a steamboat, of a fellow-passenger, whether breakfast will be ready soon, and he tells you that he should think so, for when he was last below, they were 'fixing the tables': in other words, laying the cloth. You beg a porter to collect your luggage, and he entreats you not to be uneasy, for he'll 'fix it presently'; and if you complain of indisposition, you are advised to have recourse to Doctor So-and-So, who will 'fix you' in no time. One night, I ordered a bottle of mulled wine at an hotel where I was staying, and waited a long time for it; at length it was put upon the table with an apology from the landlord that he feared it wasn't 'fixed properly'. And I recollect once, at a stage-coach dinner, overhearing a very stern gentleman demand of a waiter who presented him with a plate of underdone roast-beef, 'whether he called that, fixing God A'mighty's vittles?'

Charles Dickens American Notes

miniature word-story which can legitimately interrupt a narrative. Maie Casey provides something similar in *An Australian Story*: 'Another object of interest lived in this room. It was Grannie's best **voniklos**. You may well ask what that was. A voniklos is a small round cushion filled with swansdown; its covering, in this case of saffron and grey striped satin, was joined together in the manner of a football with careful attention to the stripes. These delicious little cushions — there were several less elegant in the house — were placed behind the head, the neck or the small of the back when one reclined in armchair or sofa.'

This is all very well, but for word-buffs it is not enough. The meaning of a word is only half the story. Miss Casey makes no attempt to explain why these 'little cushions' bore such a strange name. The word looks as if it is Greek or Russian, but the Oxford Dictionary Word and Language Service was unable, when consulted, to say more than that.

'What do you mean, precisely, by organic?' he demanded . . .

'Well, it's no use our talking in the way we have been doing if the words we use mean something different to each of us . . . and nothing,' he added with a wet grin, 'to some of us. It's all very well using these coins, as long as we know what their value is, and agree on it.' . . . 'Yes, but is this let's-define-our-terms academicism really important at this early stage?'

Malcolm Bradbury *Eating People is Wrong*

In *Moby Dick* Herman Melville writes a treatise on whaling practices at the same time as telling a story. By supporting his fictional passages with a great many factual details, he aims to convince his readers that everything he relates is true. The following demonstrates his treatise style: 'What does the whaler do when she meets another whaler in any sort of decent weather? She has a *'Gam'* . . . But what is a *Gam*? You might wear out your index-finger running up and down the columns of dictionaries, and never find the word. Dr Johnson never attained to that erudition; Noah Webster's ark does not hold it. Nevertheless, this same expressive word has now for many years been in constant use among some fifteen thousand true born Yankees. Certainly, it needs a definition, and should be incorporated into the Lexicon. With that view, let me learnedly define it.
'GAM Noun — *A social meeting of two (or more) Whale-ships, generally on a cruising-ground; when, after exchanging hails, they exchange visits by boats' crews; the two captains remaining, for the time, on board of one ship, and the two chief mates on the other.'*

EXCISE — *a hateful tax levied upon commodities and adjudged not by the common judges or property, but wretches hired by those to whom excise is paid.*

Samuel Johnson
Dictionary of the English Language

[The Commissioners of Excise seriously considered bringing an action for libel against Johnson because of this definition.]

Elsewhere in the novel, Melville writes: 'Regarding the sperm-whale's head as a solid oblong, you may, on an inclined plane, sideways divide it into two quoins.' He adds a footnote to the effect that **'Quoin** is not a Euclidean term. It belongs to the pure nautical mathematics. I know not that it has been defined before. A quoin is a solid which differs from a wedge in having its sharp end formed by the steep inclination of one side, instead of the mutual tapering of both sides.'

This comes very close to true dictionary style and helps Melville in his drive towards authenticity, but some readers might have appreciated the rather more subjective approach that is open to the novelist. The writer, after all, is not obliged to be as disciplined as the modern lexicographer. (Dr Johnson occasionally allowed himself a much-prized subjective comment.) Nevertheless, the variety of ways in which imaginative writers define special words is interesting in itself. The writers are also capable of making ordinary words rather special by the way they define them. Oliver Wendell Holmes demonstrates the art when he deals with **prologue** in The Autocrat of the Breakfast Table:

What is a Prologue? Let our Tutor teach:
Pro means beforehand; logos stands for speech.
'Tis like the harper's prelude on the strings,
The prima donna's courtesy ere she sings.

That certainly sets a challenge for a budding lexicographer. Perhaps one day we will see a versified dictionary.

FORBID

───────○───────

Her father forbade her. 'Forbid' is a husk of a word today, but at that time, in that quaint province, in the mouth of an 'indulgent father', it apparently was still viable, for the great moist weight of that forbidding continued to be felt in the house for years.

John Updike Flight

───────○───────

Bid is a thoroughly mixed-up little word. Old English had the separate verbs beodan and biddan, the first of which meant 'announce, command, offer', the second 'to request'. The two have been confused since the 16th century in both form and meaning, but the main

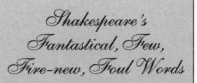

Shakespeare's Fantastical, Few, Fire-new, Foul Words

BENEDICK:
He was wont to speak plain and to the purpose, like an honest man and a soldier, and now is he turn'd orthography [i.e. pedantic in his use of words]; his words are a very fantastical banquet, just so many strange dishes.

Much Ado About Nothing

BOY:
He hath heard that men of few words are the best men, and therefore he scorns to say his prayers lest 'a should be thought a coward.

Henry V

BEROWNE:
Armado is a most illustrious wight,
A man of fire-new words, fashion's own knight.

Love's Labour's Lost

BEATRICE:
What hath passed between you and Claudio?
BENEDICK:
Only foul words; and thereupon I will kiss thee.
BEATRICE:
Foul words is but foul wind, and foul wind is but foul breath, and foul breath is noisome; therefore I will depart unkiss'd.
BENEDICK:
Thou hast frighted the word out of his right sense, so forcible is thy wit. But, I must tell thee plainly, Claudio undergoes my challenge.

Much Ado About Nothing

FOUNDER

The seamen every now and then
cried out she would founder.
It was my advantage, in one
respect, that I did not know
what they meant by founder,
till I inquired.

Daniel Defoe *Robinson Crusoe*

modern sense of bid is 'make an offer',
as when we bid for something at an
auction. Occasionally we bid someone
good day.

Forbid makes use of a prefix which
was once common, but which would no
longer suggest prohibition or exclusion
if attached to a word. Used with bid in
the sense of 'command' it gave a basic
sense of 'command not to do something'. The German equivalent of the
prefix is *ver-*, seen in *verboten* 'forbidden',
a word that Germans traditionally tended
to take seriously. As Heinrich Heine
said: 'No revolution will take place in
Germany, because revolutions are forbidden there.' The English attitude to
'forbidden' is decidedly less reverential.

Many would agree that 'forbidden fruit
tastes sweetest'.

———————○———————

*The water began boiling and she put in some tea,
wishing that tea bags weren't verboten at the
farm because of the chemicals in the paper.*

Judith Rossner *Any Minute I Can Split*

———————○———————

The German word is well known and is
sometimes used jokingly in English. It
falls into a very special category of
'national words', single words which in
themselves invoke a stereo-typed image
of a country and its people. *Verboten* has
been a word that foreign visitors to
Germany have noticed because of its
constant appearance on public signs. *Tea*
is probably a national English word;
l'amour 'love' is perhaps a French member of the group.

> *Teaser: What is the 'word
> of fear / Unpleasing to a
> married ear' according to
> Shakespeare?*
> (Answer page 230) **??**

FOR
POLICE

GAIN

○

The education of Mr Jonas had been conducted from his cradle on the strictest principles of the main chance. The very first word he learned to spell was 'gain', and the second (when he got into two syllables), 'money'. From his early habits of considering everything as a question of property, he had gradually come to look, with impatience, on his parent as a certain amount of personal estate, which had no right whatever to be going at large, but ought to be secured in that particular description of iron safe which is commonly called a coffin, and banked in the grave.

Charles Dickens Martin Chuzzlewit

○

Ernest Weekley remarks in his *Etymological Dictionary of Modern English* that the word **gain** should never have been adopted into English. It was an unnecessary addition to the vocabulary since **win** already existed. The two words are no longer fully synonymous, of course. English does seem to have gained rather than won by taking over the word, though Jonas Chuzzlewit (whose personal credo was 'do other men; for they would do you') was thus obliged to cope with four rather than three letters.

Gain derives immediately from French *gagner* 'earn, win', but ultimately has to do, as Professor Weekley expresses it, with 'the most ancient human occupations'. The postulated early Latin word from which *gagner* derives, *gwadaniare*, also led to German *Weide* 'pasture'. At one time, the word reminds us, to gain one's living meant to survive, obtain enough to eat by cultivation, hunting and fishing.

Teaser: What does 'girlcott' mean?

(Answer page 230) **??**

GALA

○

Gala is an odd-looking word. It has to do with Old French *galer* 'make merry', Modern French *se régaler* 'to amuse oneself'. There is a connection also with **gallantry**, based on the idea of merrymaking in female company. Beyond that the word becomes obscure. Some would derive it from the ancient Germanic word that led also to **well**, **weal**, **wealth** and link it eventually with Latin *hilaris* 'cheerful', but this is tentative speculation.

In *Duck Soup*, Groucho Marx gave the word a new twist. When Rufus T. Firefly is told that it is a gala day, he replies: 'A gal a day is enough for me. I don't think I can handle any more.' **Gala night** would have been an even more appropriate phrase for the pun, and is perhaps more frequently used. The kind of local gala day described at length in Elizabeth Gaskell's *Wives and Daughters* is now more likely to be called a **fête**.

○

When money had to be raised in our village, the committee (we loved forming committees) decided on a fête. The locals never did understand the circumflex e and these functions were known as 'feets'.

Fred Archer Under the Parish Lantern

○

Fred Archer's locals, referred to in the above quotation, lived in Worcestershire. The circumflex accent may have bothered them, but it is difficult to see why they could not cope with the pronunciation *fate*. *Fête* was borrowed from French in this special sense of an outdoor entertainment, usually for charitable purposes. The word looks back beyond that to Latin *festa* 'feast'. **Feast** itself is obviously from the same source, as are **festivity**, **festival**. **Festoon** also belongs to the group, though it passed through Italian *festone* on its way into English. It described the chain of flowers or ribbons used as a decoration at a festival. These various words may be almost identical etymologically, but their distinctions of meaning contribute greatly to the richness of the English language.

GATE

---○---

And I say also unto thee, That thou art Peter, and upon this rock I will build my church; and the gates of hell shall not prevail against it.

New Testament (Authorised Version)
St Matthew

---○---

A **gate** of the hinged variety takes its name from a Germanic word with the basic sense 'opening'. A different Old Norse word led to the *gate* 'way, street' which occurs in English street names, mostly in the North and Midlands. The *-gates* with which journalists have been bombarding us since 1972 are a curious off-shoot of the first of these two words.

Journalistic usage of the suffix *-gate* began while the hearings connected with the **Watergate** scandal of 1972 were still in progress. The name of a place with *-gate* attached managed to imply that a scandal and cover-up, similar to the Watergate affair, had occurred there. Watergate itself, incidentally, is not an unusual place name; London, for example, has a Watergate which marks the site of a gate which led to the Thames from the Bridewell Palace. There is also a Watergate Walk where there was once an entrance from the river to York House.

Examples of journalistic *-gate* inven-

tions include **Volgagate** (a supposed Russian scandal), **Motorgate** (fraud enquiry at General Motors), **Oilgate** (North Sea Oil). **Billygate** or **Cartergate** was used of Billy Carter's Libyan connections, **Contragate** or **Irangate** of the 1986 Iran-contra affair. Humour was pleasantly displayed in **Pearlygate**, in which American televangelists were accused of fraud.

---○---

I caught a cold in the park. The gate was open.

James Joyce *Ulysses*

---○---

Both *The Oxford Dictionary of New Words* and *Neologisms*, by Jonathon Green, give further examples of such word formation, which continues apace. An issue of the *Observer* newspaper (December 1992) had a headline: 'Now it's **Grottogate** as store chiefs accused of spying on sacked Santa.' There followed a lengthy story about the sacking of a man who acted as Father Christmas after store managers had eavesdropped on some of his conversations with children. In the same issue another journalist began an article by saying: 'I do hope we have not heard the last of **Threshergate**.' The reference was to the alleged visit of Mr Norman Lamont to one of Thresher's off-licences.

This use of *-gate* has clearly become a journalistic cliché, as newspaper readers have noticed. Mrs Betty Stout, writing to *The Times* in January 1993, remarked: 'It seems that every time there is some new scandal, revelation, titillation or whatever we have to have the word "gate" tacked on to the end of it. I am sick and tired of all these gates that keep opening. How about shutting some of them?'

GIFT

VALENTINE:
Win her with gifts, if she respect not words:
Dumb jewels often in their silent kind
More than quick words do move a woman's
  mind.

William Shakespeare Two Gentlemen of Verona

Gift is clearly connected with the verb **give**. The synonym **present** looks exactly the same as its associated verb, but noun and verb are homographs with very different pronunciations. We normally avoid that oddity by saying that we will present someone with a gift rather than a present.

In Old English 'gift' always meant 'payment for a wife'. Gifts still often have to do with an expression of sexual interest, but clearly the meaning has become more general. In German, where Gift once had the same meaning as in English, the sense-development has been more bizarre. Das Gift was used as a euphemism for 'poison, venom' and now has only that sense.

'The only thing a man like me can do for a woman is buy her things and love her a hell of a lot at night. I'm different from your literary boy-friends and your artistic boy-friends. I can't write you a poem or paint your picture. The only way I can show you that I love you is to spend money on you.'

Mary McCarthy
The Man in the Brooks Brothers Shirt

As Shakespeare and Mary McCarthy point out in their different ways, gifts can be said to constitute a kind of silent language. It is one employed especially by those who feel that they cannot use words as they should, and there is a parallel with normal language. Words, apart from explaining our thoughts, reveal much about our social background and educational level. The gifts of the man in the Mary McCarthy story — 'several pieces of glamour-girl un-

Shakeaspeare's
Gentle, Good, Gracious
Words

AUMERLE:
Let's fight with gentle words
Till time lend friends, and friends their
  helpful swords.

Richard II

CAIUS:
Peace-a your tongue. Speak-a your tale.
SIMPLE:
To desire this honest gentlewoman, your
  maid, to speak a good word to Mistress
  Ann Page for my master, in the way
  of marriage.

The Merry Wives of Windsor

ROSALINE:
The King was weeping-ripe for a good word.

Love's Labour's Lost

LEWIS:
Be plain, Queen Margaret, and tell thy
  grief;
It shall be eas'd, if France can yield relief.
QUEEN:
Those gracious words revive my drooping
  thoughts,
And give my tongue-tied sorrows leave to
  speak.

Henry VI Part Three

derwear and a topaz brooch' — say things about him that deeply disappoint the woman concerned.

———————○———————

However mysterious his words might seem, his presents spoke his affection in a more homely and convincing language.

Mary Russell Mitford Our Village

———————○———————

Eric Linklater, in *Magnus Merriman*, makes perceptive comments on the subject of gifts between the sexes. His hero regrets that his own gifts have had too deep an influence: 'his presents had obviously encouraged her affection for him'. He is still more worried by the gifts he has received. 'She presented him with a book, a silk muffler, and a pair of cuff-links. These presents Magnus accepted with more embarrassment than pleasure, for though a young man may bestow gifts in a mood of lightest dalliance, a young woman seldom gives anything away except under the compulsion of serious intentions. Woman's nature is conservative, and her presents to a man are tainted with a suspicion that they are ultimately destined for the enrichment of her own household.'

———————○———————

GLOAMING

———————○———————

'Excuse me, Dr Robert Shannon, what is precise meaning of Scottish 'gloaming'? A wood, forest, nullah or concealed place, probably, suitable for love?'

A.J. Cronin Shannon's Way

———————○———————

It is an Indian student who is asking the question about **gloaming** in the passage quoted above. He has heard the song

'Roamin' In The Gloamin'', made famous by Sir Harry Lauder. His various guesses about gloaming are logical, given the context, and show how easy it is for us to misunderstand the meaning of a word. For example, what does **nullah** mean? As used above it appears to be equated with 'wood, forest'. In fact it adapts a Hindi word which means 'river, stream' or the 'ravine' through which a river runs. The Indian student presumably has the latter sense in mind.

As for 'gloaming', it means 'evening twilight'. The word looks as if it is closely related to **gloom** and **gloomy**, but the experts say not. It has more to do with the **glow** of the setting sun. 'Gloaming' is, in a sense, a Scottish equivalent of **twilight**, where the twi- is related to **two** but is probably a reduction of an earlier word meaning '(be)tween'.

———————○———————

GREAT-GRANDMOTHER

———————○———————

'Your great-great-great-great-grandmother had these cups when she was married,' said Hephzibah to Phoebe.

Nathaniel Hawthorne
The House of the Seven Gables

———————○———————

The **great-great-great-great-grand-mother** in the above passage shows a very curious English adaptation of a French expression. **Grandmother**, to begin with, is a half-translation of French *grand-mère*, with the *grand* being left intact. The French themselves had imitated the Roman example of *avunculus magnus* 'great uncle', *amita magna* 'great aunt', where *magnus/magna* meant 'old'. As it happens, the Anglo-Saxon word for a grandmother was *oldmother* (*oldfather* for **grand-**

GENTLE

SERVANT:
Save you, gentlemen!
STEPHEN:
Nay, we do not stand much on
our gentility.

Ben Jonson Every Man in his Humour

father), so in theory the word was merely replaced by a hybrid of the same meaning. 'Grand', however, has other meanings and associations which are rather flattering, something that cannot be said of 'old'.

When it came to indicating a grandmother's mother, English resorted to a translation of French grand to arrive at **great-grandmother**. The French themselves refer to an arrière-grand-mère, literally a 'rear-grandmother'. Great-grandmother, then, begins with a translated French word, followed by the same French word pronounced in an English way.

---○---

'This is Ben's great-granddaughter,' she said. 'Beth Farber.'

'Great is right,' I said, taking her hand. 'What do you do in the world, Beth — other than upset men?'

Garson Kanin Moviola

---○---

English is by no means consistent in its use of great and grand to indicate relationships. Logically we should speak of grand-uncles and grand-aunts, for instance, instead of **great-uncles**, **great-aunts**, since they are of the same generation as grandparents. It is also illogical to speak of **grandchildren** and **great-grandchildren**, since grand and great both refer to advanced age. French uses a different system to refer to the younger

generations: a grandchild is a petit-enfant, a 'little-child', while great-grandchild is arrière-petit-enfant 'rear-little child'. In favour of the English way of doing things, which includes adding great as many times as is necessary to take a relationship back by further generations, is the simple fact that the system works, causing no confusion. The use of grand for both young and old members of a family also creates a special verbal link between them.

---○---

Time's glory is . . .
To show the beldam daughters of her daughter,
To make the child a man, the man a child.

William Shakespeare The Rape of Lucrece

---○---

In the 17th century it was possible to refer to a great-grandmother as a **beldam**. The word reflects the early use in polite terms of address of words like **good** in English, beau 'handsome' and belle 'beautiful' in French. It would now be thought condescending to address someone as 'my good man' or 'my good woman', but that was not always so. **Goodman** was formerly as respectful a form of address as **Mister**. **Goodwife**, later contracted to **goodie**, was the female equivalent. The 'good' was merely part of a ritual formula, not a genuine comment on the real goodness of the person concerned.

That was true also of French beau and belle, which gave rise to beau-père 'father-in-law' and belle-mère 'mother-in-law'. French people do not necessarily think that their in-laws are handsome or beautiful, even though they appear to say so. 'Beldam', then, which appears to be modelled on French belle dame 'beautiful lady', was merely a conventional way of referring at first to a grandmother, later a great-grandmother. Clear evidence that the bel was not thought of as meaning 'beautiful' is seen in the word's rapid decline in meaning. By the late 16th century it could be used to describe any loathsome old woman. Shakespeare, for example, uses it in both its family relationship sense (*Henry IV Part One*) and as a word for 'hag' (*Macbeth*).

'Great-grandmother' has avoided such semantic humiliation. It is difficult to see how anyone who is both great and grand could be other than a person of dignity, to whom all respect is due.

GUINNESS

———————○———————

As we read in the first chapter of Guinness'es.

James Joyce *Ulysses*

———————○———————

Guinness is of course a name rather than a word, but proper names can become words very easily. Eric Partridge listed a great many examples in his *Name Into Word*, a discursive dictionary published in 1949. Earlier works on the theme include *Lives Enshrined in Language* (1922) by the Rev. T. Stenhouse and *Names of Places in a Transferred Sense* (1909) by Carl Efvergren. The words derived from the names of people, usually known as eponyms, form the more interesting group. A **bowie knife** commemorates the American soldier James Bowie: a **boycott** recalls Charles Boycott, a **land-agent** in Ireland who was ostracised for refusing to reduce rents. Other individuals are responsible for **colt**, **lynch**, **macintosh**, **ohm**, **pasteurise**, **sandwich**, **watt** and many more.

In modern times a personal name may first become a trade name, then a word. W.H. Hoover gave his family name to the vacuum cleaner that he manufactured, which led to **hoover** becoming a verb meaning 'to vacuum

clean a carpet'. The name of the Hungarian inventor L. Bíró has travelled a similar route to become a **biro**, any kind of ball-point pen.

———————○———————

'What makes you so Park Avenue today? Or are you being English?'

Sinclair Lewis *Gideon Planish*

———————○———————

Hoover and biro were no doubt used allusively before becoming recognised words: many other proper names never get past the allusion stage. **Park Avenue**, in the passage quoted above, is an *ad hoc* transfer of a name to adjectival status. Sinclair Lewis relied on the fact that readers would know not only that Park Avenue was a street in New York City but that it was a symbol of wealth and luxurious living. Mention of the name was also supposed to suggest the kind of behaviour associated with the very rich. A modern writer or speaker might still allude to Park Avenue in this way, but the name of the street has by no means been accepted as a normal word.

———————○———————

A great man coming up, Tom Eaves's hat would drop off his head, and he would rush forward with a bow and a grin, which showed that he knew the world too — in the Tomeavesian way, that is.

William Thackeray *Vanity Fair*

———————○———————

In ordinary conversation we are all likely to make allusion to proper names if we think that our audience will grasp our meaning. The allusion may be to a public figure whose character is generally known, or the name of someone who is merely a mutual friend can be used. Within the confines of a novel, the novelist may feel that a character has been well enough delineated to allow a character's name to become what might be called 'an allusive conversion'. **Janian**,

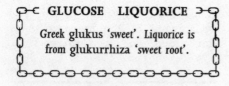

GLUCOSE LIQUORICE

Greek glukus 'sweet'. Liquorice is from glukurrhiza 'sweet root'.

for example, is not a word or allusion that means anything out of context, but when Rochester remarks in Charlotte Brontë's *Jane Eyre* that the heroine has made a 'truly Janian reply', the reader understands what he means.

William Golding in *Darkness Visible* refers to 'the Toni-ness of Toni': John Wain says in *The Contenders* that 'Myra was certainly more **Myra-ish**, or **Myresque**.' Once again, such allusive conversions remain mysterious unless a reading of the novels has made the people concerned familiar. **Podsnappery**, for this reason, stands a better chance of being meaningful out of context. *Our Mutual Friend* has been widely read, and many will remember the 'school of thought or religion' which Dickens linked with the name of Mr Podsnap. Its articles of faith included 'getting up at eight, shaving close at a quarter past, breakfasting at nine, going to the City at ten, coming home at half-past five, dining at seven'.

What, then, of 'Guinness' in a modern context? The family name was long ago transferred to the product, and is more widely known in that connection. The product has certain well-known associations which make restricted allusions possible. 'Guinness socks' would normally be a puzzling phrase, but it causes no difficulty when Joyce Cary uses it in *The Horse's Mouth*: 'He had a complete new colour scheme, all in browns. Brown suit, the colour of old ale. Golden brown tie like lager. Brown boots shining like china beer handles. Guinness socks. And a new brown bowler, the colour of bitter beer, over his left eye.' The passage shows how easy it would be for Guinness to become a colour word.

That long lustrous dark brown hair . . . and those perfectly curved lips . . . with brown lipstick! Yes! She had it on again! The brown lipstick, the color of caramel, hellish, rebellious, perfectly elegant.

Tom Wolfe Bonfire of the Vanities

The name Guinness has also on at least one occasion been called upon to inject a little humour into the teaching of English grammar. A text-book published in 1840 dealt with the use of apostrophe s after a noun to indicate possession. 'When the singular terminates in -ss,' the author explained, 'the final s is sometimes dispensed with: as "for goodness' sake!" Nevertheless, we have no objection to Guinness's Stout.'

FOR
HIMSELF

HALLELUJAH

Here lies my wife
Here lies she;
Hallelujah!
Hallelulee!

Epitaph at Leeds, quoted in
Faber Book of Comic Verse

Hallelujah is an exhortation, usually translated as 'praise the Lord!' The word is sometimes found in its Latin form **alleluia**, but an exact transcription from Hebrew would give *hallelu-Yah*. **Yah** in turn is an abbreviation of **Yahweh**, the proper name of the God of Israel. The Jewish scholars known as the Massoretes, wishing for reverential reasons to prevent this sacred name from being uttered during the reading of scripture, combined its consonants and the vowels of another word meaning 'lord' to arrive at the artificial form **Jehovah**.

The meaning of Yahweh is explained in Exodus. Moses asks the 'God of the fathers' what his name is and is told: 'I *am who I am*. Say this to the people of Israel, "I AM has sent me to you".' O. Odelain and R. Séguineau, in their *Dictionary of Proper Names and Places in the Bible*, therefore explain that, since God speaks of himself as I AM,'in speaking of God, men will follow Moses' lead and say "He is" (*Yahweh*)'. They add that this account 'links the name of God to an ancient form of the verb *hayah* "to be"'.

JIMMY PORTER:
How I long for a little ordinary enthusiasm. Just enthusiasm — that's all. I want to hear a warm, thrilling voice cry out Hallelujah! Hallelujah! I'm alive!

John Osborne Look Back in Anger

This is the name, then, that forms part of Hallelujah. Yahweh also occurs in various other forms, such as Yahu, Jo, Jeho, which are concealed in many proper names. **John**, for example, is **Yohanan** or **Yehohanan** 'Yah has shown favour' in Hebrew. **Ann(e)** may seem to be a very different name: curiously it means the same as John. Ann(e) is from **Hannah**, which in turn abbreviates **Hananiah**, Hebrew *Hananyah*, another way of saying 'Yah has shown favour'.

HANDKERCHIEF

IAGO:
*Have you not sometimes seen a handkerchief
Spotted with strawberries in your wife's hand?*
OTHELLO:
I gave her such a one; 'twas my first gift.
IAGO:
*I know not that; but such a handkerchief -
I am sure it was your wife's — did I today
See Cassio wipe his beard with.*

William Shakespeare Othello

It is difficult to imagine a literary work which makes more dramatic use of a **handkerchief** than Shakespeare's *Othello*. For a modern reader or play-goer, difficulties are imposed by the item itself. A handkerchief today is so ordinary, so unpleasantly associated with blowing one's nose, that it is hard to take it seriously. It is hardly a prized personal possession, something to be sentimental about. Handkerchiefs were far more important in the 17th century, when they were expensive, fashionable accessories, but Othello's first gift to Desdemona was valuable to him in a different way. To give it to her was a meaningful symbol of his love because it was the most precious thing in his possession, an irreplaceable family heirloom, the same handkerchief that his father had given to his mother. When Iago convinces him that Desdemona has given this handkerchief to Cassio, his sense of betrayal is overwhelming. She could find no better way to rub salt into the wound that thoughts of her infidelity have inflicted.

'I'm so afraid you'll catch cold, aunt — have a silk handkerchief to tie round your dear old head — you really should take care of yourself — consider your age.'

Charles Dickens The Pickwick Papers

Nor would this fatal handkerchief have been used for nose-wiping. In the passage quoted above Isabella is maliciously reminding the maiden aunt that she is no longer young, but notice the use to which the handkerchief is put. Mr Pickwick himself later goes to sleep in a chair, but before doing so he pulls 'his silk handkerchief over his head'. For some this will recall working-men having a day at the English seaside, sitting in deckchairs with their trousers rolled up and knotted handkerchiefs on their heads, but from an etymological point of view, this is the true use of the handkerchief, or **kerchief**, which is carried in the hand. 'Kerchief' is a form of French couvre-chef 'cover-head', and the item to which it referred was originally a cloth used as a woman's head-dress.

This idea of covering was extended to the **neck-kerchief**, also known as a **neckerchief** or **neck-handkerchief**. For women this was used to cover the shoulders and breast. Leigh Hunt, describing the typical maidservant of the early 19th century, says that she has 'black stockings, a stuff gown, a cap, and a neck-handkerchief pinned corner-wise behind. On Sundays . . . she lays aside the neck-handkerchief for a high-body, which, by the way, is not half so pretty. There is something very warm and latent in the handkerchief, — something easy, vital, and genial. A woman in a high-bodied gown, made to fit her like a case, is by no means more modest, and is much less tempting.'

The 'tempting' aspect of the neck-handkerchief and its necessity for reasons of modesty is commented on by 18th century novelists. In Henry Fielding's Joseph Andrews, for instance, the young hero rescues Fanny from a would-be ravisher who has torn her handkerchief from her neck. Joseph is then injured in a fight with the villain and Fanny attends to him.

Fielding continues: 'This modest creature, whom no warmth in summer could ever induce to expose her charms to the wanton sun, a modesty to which perhaps they owed their inconceivable whiteness, had stood for many minutes bare-necked in the presence of Joseph, before her apprehensions of his danger, and the horror of seeing his blood would suffer her once to reflect on what concerned herself; till at last, when the cause of her concern had vanished, an admiration at his silence, together with observing the fixed position of his eyes, produced an idea in the lovely maid, which brought more blood into her face than had flowed from Joseph's nostrils. The snowy hue of her bosom was likewise changed to vermilion at the instant when she clapped her handker-

> ## HAVILDAR
>
> On the trolley were Colonel Savage, me, a sergeant (they call them havildars in the Indian Army) and five sepoys — called riflemen in Gurkha regiments.
>
> **John Masters** Bhowani Junction

Teaser: The longest word used by Shakespeare in his plays and poems begins with 'h'. What is it?

(Answer page 230)

chief round her neck. Joseph saw the uneasiness which she suffered, and immediately removed his eyes from an object, in surveying which he had felt the greatest delight which the organs of sight were capable of conveying to his soul.'

'Who could have withstood their exhortations to subscribe to our noble society for providing the infant negroes in the West Indies with flannel waistcoats and moral pocket-handkerchiefs?'

'What's a moral pocket-ankercher?' said Sam. 'I never see one o' them articles o' furniter.'

'Those which combine amusement with instruction, my young friend,' replied Mr Stiggins, 'blending select tales with wood-cuts.'

Charles Dickens The Pickwick Papers

Dickens was later to have fun with handkerchiefs in his own way, as with the absurdly inappropriate 'moral pocket handkerchiefs' described above. The passage also gives some indication of how handkerchief was commonly pronounced in former times. **Hankercher** was normal in the 16th and 17th centuries, and is no doubt how Shakespeare pronounced the word. **Handkercher** and **kercher** are also found as written forms, but long after 'handkerchief' had become the normal written form, the -cher pronunciation was used. By the 19th century, however, the spelling pronunciation had come into its own amongst the educated. Sam Weller's version of the word was now considered to be vulgar or dialectal.

Dickens frequently comments on the handkerchiefs borne by individuals, such as the 'pink checked gingham handkerchief about six inches square' flourished by Job Trotter. The silk handkerchiefs carried by the gentry, items of some value, are important in Oliver Twist, where the members of Fagin's gang are trained to steal them. In that same novel Dickens refers to a woman's **ridicule**, a popular corruption of **reticule**. While men now used 'pocket handkerchiefs', women still needed somewhere to put them. The reticule, a small bag carried in the hand or on the arm, was suitable for the purpose. The word is derived ultimately from Latin rete 'net'.

A woman might in theory choose instead to drop her handkerchief. A gentleman in whom she was interested could then retrieve it and legitimately begin a conversation. Women tend to be more subtle than this when they are inviting courtship, and the original allusion was no doubt to the children's game in which a girl threw her handkerchief at the boy of her choice. He would then chase her to demand the reward of a kiss.

All this takes 'handkerchief' a long way from its original use as a kind of scarf. The French word couvre, incidentally, which leads to the ker- of 'kerchief', also appears as the first element in **curfew**, which originally meant 'cover-fire'. In medieval Europe a bell was rung each evening as a reminder that domestic fires were to be 'covered' or extinguished. It was a primitive kind of fire-prevention scheme, to ensure that unattended fires did not spread during the night. In English the word 'curfew' was merely applied to the ringing of an evening bell, for whatever reason. As for

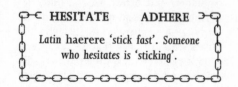

HESITATE   ADHERE

Latin haerere 'stick fast'. Someone who hesitates is 'sticking'.

the -chief of handkerchief, it is found again in **mischief** (see page 115).

Shakespearean scholars are interested in the handkerchief used by Iago to such appalling effect for reasons other than its significance in the plot of *Othello*. Literary detectives have in the past wondered about its strawberry motif. Shakespeare invented the name Othello for the un-named '*Capitano Moro*' in his source — Giraldi Cinthio's *Hecatomithi* — but why 'Othello'? It was possibly suggested by a noble Venetian family known as the *Otelli del Moro*, who originally came from Morea (now Peloponnese), southern Greece. Their heraldic device is said to have been a mulberry, not a strawberry, but the change is a small one. It would certainly be fitting if the strawberries on Othello's handkerchief were meant to refer to a heraldic bearing, adding weight to his description of it as 'an antique token'.

HIDING

○

'My husband gave him a good hiding, but Master Charlie came up smiling, as usual.'

'I don't think', remarked Marina coldly, 'that you would be well-advised to trust my husband to give people "hidings".' She delicately isolated this word.

Doris Lessing *A Home for the Highland Cattle*

○

Adults have been threatening to **tan the hides** of children since the 17th century. The children presumably understand that their backsides are at risk, though tanning a hide really means to convert it into leather, usually by soaking it. 'To give someone a good hiding' is to beat or thrash him. The original reference was no doubt to beating the hide of an animal with a whip.

'Hide' in the sense of 'conceal' appears to link ultimately with 'hide' in its 'skin' sense. The original meaning of the verb may have been to 'conceal something or someone with hides'.

HOAR

. . . Whose beard with age is hoar.

Samuel Taylor Coleridge *The Ancient Mariner*

Hoar is now only used to describe a 'hoar frost', which whitens the landscape. This whiteness is very much a secondary meaning of the word, which originally meant 'old, august', but our ancestors closely associated venerable

HONOUR

FALSTAFF:

Honour pricks me on. Yea, but how if honour pricks me off when I come on? How then? Can honour set to a leg? No. Or an arm? No. Or take away the grief of a wound? No. Honour hath no skill in surgery, then? No. What is honour? A word. What is in that word? Honour. What is that honour? Air. A trim reckoning! Who hath it? He that died o' Wednesday. Doth he feel it? No. Doth he hear it? No. 'Tis insensible, then? Yea, to the dead. But will it not live with the living? No. Why? Detraction will not suffer it. Therefore I'll none of it. Honour is a mere scutcheon.

William Shakespeare
Henry IV Part One

old age with grey or white hair.

'Hoar' has not survived well in English because of the sound clash with **whore**. Elizabethan playwrights could usually be relied upon to pun on the two words, as Shakespeare does in *Romeo and Juliet*. By contrast, the German word related to 'hoar' has remained in daily use as the polite form of address to a man — Herr. Similar references to distinguished seniority are found in such titles as **monsieur**, **senator**, **señor**, **signor**, **sire**. (Our own Mr is ultimately from master, Latin *magister* from *magnus* 'great'.)

HOBBLEDEHOY

Such young men are often awkward, ungainly, and not yet formed in their gait; they straggle with their limbs, and are shy; words do not come to them with ease, when words are required, among any but their accustomed associates. Social meetings are periods of penance to them, and any appearance in public will unnerve them. They go about much alone, and blush when women speak to them. In truth, they are not as yet men, whatever the number may be of their years; and, as they are not boys, the world has found for them the ungraceful name of hobbledehoy.

Anthony Trollope The Small House at Allington

Whatever happened to the **hobbledehoy**? The word has curiously dropped out of use since Trollope's time, though surely such young men still exist? Hobbledehoy first appeared in the 16th century, applied to a youth who was 'neither a man nor a boy'. As Trollope suggests in the passage quoted above, the exact age to which this applies varies with each individual. Traditionally, however, **hobbledehoydom** occurred between the ages of 14 and 21. An old rhyme says:

The first seven years bring up as a
    child,
The next to learning, for waxing too
    wild,
The next keep under Sir Hobbard de
    Hoy,
The next a man, no longer a boy.

Early forms of the word mostly began with **hobbard** rather than **hobble**. The change was due to folk etymology, 'hobble' suggesting clumsy movement — appropriate for the young men concerned. As to the word's origin, it has been the subject of much learned discussion that has yielded no satisfactory results. The word remains an etymological mystery.

His office was that of page to the dame; an office which, after long remaining in abeyance, has been of late years revived, as may well be seen in the persons of sundry smart hobbledehoys, now constantly to be met with on staircases and in boudoirs, clad, for the most part, in garments fitted tightly to the shape, the lower moiety adorned with a broad strip of crimson or silver lace, and the upper with what the first Wit of our times has described as 'a favourable eruption of buttons'.

Richard Harris Barham The Ingoldsby Legends

Trollope uses the word in more than one novel, but in *The Small House at Allington* he really gets his teeth into it. He discusses at great length the difference between young men who mature early and those who pass through a sometimes lengthy period of awkwardness. In abridged form he says: 'When I compare the hobbledehoy of one or two and twenty to some finished Apollo of the same age, I regard the former as unripe fruit, and the latter as fruit that is ripe. Then comes the question as to the two fruits. Which is the better fruit, that which ripens early — which is, perhaps, favoured with some little forcing apparatus, or which, at least, is backed by the warmth of a southern wall; or that fruit of slower growth on which the sun operates in its own time? I like the smack of the natural growth.'

───────◯───────

From boyhood until hobbadyhoyhood (which I take to be about the sixteenth year of the life of a young man, and may be likened to the month of April when Spring begins to bloom) — from fourteen until seventeen, I say, I remained at home, doing nothing — for which I have ever since had a great taste.

William Thackeray *The Fatal Boots*

───────◯───────

Trollope then describes the life led by the hobbledehoy in his own imagination. He takes 'long walks, in which he dreams of those successes which are so far removed from his powers of achievement. Out in the fields, with his stick in his hand, he is very eloquent, cutting off the heads of the springing summer weeds as he practises his oratory with energy'. There is much more along these lines. Trollope writes on the subject in a way that suggests he has powerful memories of his own time as a hobbledehoy. His insights into what it means to be passing through hobbledehoydom, or **hobbledehoyhood** as he also calls it, would certainly strike a chord in the memory of anyone who has suffered in a similar way.

───────◯───────

He was at that age when young men admire a formed beauty more than a face with any amount of future capability of loveliness, and when they are morbidly conscious of the difficulty of finding subjects of conversation in talking to girls in a state of feminine hobbledehoyhood.

Elizabeth Gaskell *Wives and Daughters*

───────◯───────

Hobbledehoy is used only of gangly young men and there seems to be no

HOSPITALITY

'Hospitality', she speculated, 'is a mutual affair, as the French word *hôte* indicates. Here in America, I think, we tend to overemphasize the obligations of the guest, as though he entered a hotel where the rules were pasted over the wash-basin.'

Mary McCarthy *The Groves of Academe*

corresponding word for one who is 'neither a woman nor a girl'. Trollope himself playfully suggests a suitable term when he writes of John Eames: 'He had a younger sister who loved him dearly, who had no idea that he was a hobbledehoy, being somewhat of a **hobbledehoya** herself.' The word was not taken up, though it would have been a useful addition to our vocabulary. Its very awkwardness reflects the type of person it describes.

────────────────

HOUSE

───────◯───────

HOSTESS:
He hath eaten me out of house and home; he hath put all my substance into that fat belly of his.

William Shakespeare *Henry IV Part Two*

───────◯───────

No word could seem more ordinary than **house**, but it has its curious aspects. In certain contexts, for example, it can suddenly demand a different pronunciation or definition. The inner change of sound to -z- that occurs in the plural 'houses' can occur with 'house' itself when it becomes a verb: 'the Tate Gallery will house the exhibition'. Tech-

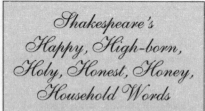

Shakespeare's Happy, High-born, Holy, Honest, Honey, Household Words

ROSALINE:
In that hour, my Lord,
They did not bless us with one happy word.

Love's Labour's Lost

FERDINAND:
This child of fancy, that Armado hight,
For interim to our studies shall relate,
In high-born words, the worth of many a
    knight
From tawny Spain lost in the world's debate.

Love's Labour's Lost

ROMEO:
Do thou but close our hands with holy words,
Then love-devouring death do what he dare.

Romeo and Juliet

BEROWNE:
Honest plain words best pierce the ear of grief.

Love's Labour's Lost

ANNE:
Within so small a time, my woman's heart
Grossly grew captive to his honey words.

Richard III

KING:
Then shall our names,
Familiar in his mouth as household words —
Harry the King, Bedford and Exeter,
Warwick and Talbot, Salisbury and
    Gloucester —
Be in their cups freshly remember'd

Henry V

nically, then, the noun and verb are homographs.

As for its definition, house frequently describes something other than a building where people live. It refers to the people themselves in a sentence like: 'he came home late and woke the whole house'. In a phrase like 'the House of Windsor' it describes people both living and dead who have lived in many different houses. By metonymy, a rhetorical figure of speech that most of us use every day without thinking, it also refers to the American presidency in the phrase 'a statement from the White House'. Incidentally, how long will that 'White' survive, one wonders, in these politically correct times? The British equivalents 'Number Ten' and 'Downing Street' manage to avoid the problem. 'Chequers', the name of the official country residence of the Prime Minister, is racially tactful, hinting at a multicultural society.

Michael Hurst sat in the house-place. House-place is a sort of better kitchen, where no cookery is done, but which is reserved for state occasions.

Elizabeth Gaskell Half a Life-Time Ago

In some English dialects, house could formerly refer to one or two specific rooms rather than a farmhouse in its entirety. In Wuthering Heights Emily Brontë writes: 'One step brought us into the family-sitting room, without any introductory lobby or passage: they call it here "the house" pre-eminently. It includes kitchen and parlour generally; but I believe at Wuthering Heights the kitchen is forced to retreat altogether into another quarter.'

In another context, house provides a good example of folk etymology. Folk etymology is the process by which ordinary people alter a word to make it more 'logical' or more understandable.

Thus **shamefast**, which meant something like 'held fast in shame', was assumed to be **shamefaced**, which made more immediate sense. **Penthouse** was originally **pentice** or **pentis**, from Old French *appentis*, ultimately from Latin *appendere*, literally to 'hang to', from *pendere* 'hang, be suspended'. The medieval pentis was a subsidiary structure attached to the wall of a main building, a **lean-to** annex. Sometimes the word was applied to the eaves of a roof if they projected a considerable distance.

---○---

MOTH:

. . . with your hat penthouse-like o'er the shop of your eyes, with your arms cross'd on your thin-belly doublet, like a rabbit on a spit . . .

William Shakespeare Love's Labour's Lost

---○---

By the end of the 17th century it seems to have been assumed that a **pentis** had been given that name because it had a sloping roof (French *pente* 'slope') and had originally leaned against a house. Pentis was perhaps also seen as a vulgar pronunciation, like the later **workis** (**vurkis** in Dickens) for **workhouse**. Penthouse was therefore 'restored' as the supposedly correct form. The modern penthouse apartment originally occupied the space immediately beneath a sloping roof. Later developments have associated it with luxurious living accommodation at the top of an apartment building, but it is still not a real house because it is not a separate building.

The novelist Jane Duncan, in My Friends the Miss Boyds, tells a more personal story about 'house'. She describes the daughter of a friend, 'who between the ages of four and five worried her parents a good deal by her preoccupation with the word. Jay-ell refused to accept a great number of words common in the English language, and replaced them by "house" words of her own construc-

tion. A match-box was a "matches house", a handbag a "money house" inside which there might be a "lipstick house", the stable was a "horse house", and the cutlery drawers of the sideboard were "spoon houses". The principle seemed to be that any container for anything was a "house", so that a book was a "story house", which led to the complication of a "story house's house" for bookshelf.'

This little girl, says Jane Duncan, 'would invite you, if she liked you, to "let a story out of its house" for her at bedtime, and at the end would say: "Finished now. Put it back in the house for next time."' Jay-ell — Janet-Lydia on formal occasions — reverted to normal vocabulary after the age of five, but had demonstrated with simple logic how many languages construct their vocabularies.

---○---

'What has elegance or prettiness to do with the affair? Did you ever know a widower marry again for such trifles as those? It's always from a sense of duty of one kind or another — isn't it, Mr Gibson? They want a housekeeper; or they want a mother for their children; or they think their last wife would have liked it.'

Elizabeth Gaskell Wives and Daughters

---○---

'House' continues to offer scope for novelty. There is, for example, the cynical modern joke which redefines **housekeeper**. He or she has become the person who manages to keep the house in the divorce settlement.

FOR A
PRETTY
GIRL

I

Mark wasn't interested in others and their affairs. His favourite word was 'I', John's father had once said, with 'me' a close second.

Ruth Rendell Talking to Strange Men

The personal pronouns are amongst the most interesting words in the language. **I** is obviously of special importance, since it is probably the most frequently used word of all in ordinary social conversations. It is difficult to avoid using it, even if one is not an **egotist**. (**Egotism**, like **egoism**, is based on Latin *ego* 'I', and the two words are frequently confused. It is the egotist who talks about himself all the time and is described in slang as 'the big **I-am**'. Egoism is an ethical theory that bases morality on self-interest. An **egoist** is one who believes in that doctrine.)

I in Old English was *ic*. The word was clearly related to the same pronoun in other Germanic languages, such as Old High German *ih*, modern German *ich*. The similar Old Norse *ek*, *eg* led to Norwegian *eg*, Swedish *jag*, Danish *jeg*. All these forms are linked through a common ancestor to Latin *ego*. The so-called oblique forms of the word, **me**, **my**, **mine**, together with the words to which they are linked in various languages, derive from a different Indo-Germanic root.

```
⚓ ILLUSION    PRELUDE ⚓
Latin ludere 'to play'. An illusion is
something that 'mocks, plays with'
the beholder. A prelude is 'before the
playing' of the main musical work.
```

'Will you tell Miss Everdene that somebody would be glad to speak to her?' said Mr Oak. (Calling one's self merely Somebody, without giving a name, is not to be taken as an example of the ill-breeding of the rural world: it springs from a refined modesty, of which townspeople, with their cards and announcements, have no notion whatever.)

Thomas Hardy Far from the Madding Crowd

Many people consciously try to avoid using I too often, but that can cause problems. In some languages a word meaning **someone** or **somebody** replaces I. The English equivalent of this would be **one**, but comments that 'one seldom watches television' and suchlike sound not only pompous, but perhaps even more egotistical than the use of I. Writers sometimes use authorial **we**, which suggests the arrogant assumption of royal prerogative and can lead to peculiar syntax. Dickens, for example, in chapter 38 of *The Pickwick Papers*, writes: 'The case is not a peculiar one, as we ourself can testify.' In the 18th century it was at least possible to avoid constantly saying 'I think . . .' by throwing in an occasional **Methinks**.

But she was assiduous with her thank you notes: 'You have always been on hand to cheer Denis and I up when things were not going well' — nobody ever had the courage, he [Sir Ronald Millar, Mrs Thatcher's speech-writer] says, to tell her it should be 'Denis and me'.

Valerie Grove Interview, The Times 7.5.93

Then again, 'me' is clearly a word that troubles modern speakers. 'They didn't do it just to upset you and I' said a contributor to a recent BBC radio programme. This avoidance at all cost of 'you and me' is becoming more common by the minute in awful phrases like 'between you and I'. Speakers have at the back of their minds the idea that it is wrong to say 'you and me' (or 'me and you') in certain situations, so they over-correct themselves. 'You and I' sounds posher, even though it may be gram-matical nonsense. A very simple test can be applied to decide whether 'you and I' or 'you and me' is the correct form. If the phrase can be replaced by us, then 'me' is correct; if it can be replaced by 'we' then 'I' should be used. The sen-tence quoted above would become 'They didn't do it just to annoy us,' so it should have been 'you and me'. 'You and I' is nevertheless correct as the subject of a sentence: 'You and I are going to Spain this year, not Italy.'

'That is what I say,' returned Mrs Mawmsey, who habitually gave weight to her speech by loading her pronouns. 'Does he suppose that people will pay him only to come and sit with them and go away again?'

George Eliot Middlemarch

We is a flexible little word, capable of meaning not only I when used by authors, but you when used by doctors. 'We must turn over a new leaf, Sir Roger; indeed we must,' says a doctor to a patient who drinks too much, in Trollope's Doctor Thorne. Margaret Atwood, in Bodily Harm, says of a woman who is in hospital after an operation that she was 'hooked like a junkie on those pats of the hand and Rotarian words of cheer and collective first-person plurals ("We're

Teaser: The phrase 'pound and dollar' suggests a word beginning with 'i'. Which one?

(Answer page 230) **??**

Shakespeare's Ill Words

HERO:
I will go to Benedick
And counsel him to fight against his passion;
And, truly, I'll devise some honest slanders
To stain my cousin with. One doth not know
How much an ill word may empoison liking.

Much Ado About Nothing

coming along nicely") and in a feeble rage because of it.'

In Good as Gold, Joseph Heller humor-ously claims that 'we' can have yet another meaning. Pomeroy says: '"We is a plural pronoun. You've fallen into this disgusting, jingoistic habit of saying we, us and our when talking about the coun-try, the government, our forefathers. . . . Who is this we that must stand ready to make the sacrifices and suffer casual-ties?" "By we", said Gold, "he means them."'

Touchingly they expounded their views in the first person plural . . . 'We don't despise the Eclectics,' said he. And — 'We prefer the Lombardic architecture to the purely Venetian,' said Doria. And 'we' found good Italian wines and 'we' found nothing but hideousness in Murano glass.

William J. Locke Jaffery

Old English had **wit**, a dual form of the first person pronoun, as well as 'we', the normal plural. 'Wit' has disappeared because English can get along perfectly well without it. Two people can be specified when necessary by saying 'We would both like to thank you' or 'Both of us would like to thank you'. Often the extra words are unnecessary because the we is all too obviously dual. The quotation above concerns a newly married couple, thrilled to have merged their individual identities into a partnership. A similar use of dual 'we' can be what Nina Bawden refers to, in *George Beneath a Paper Moon*, as 'a display of territorial aggro': 'She was a little proprietary, saying "we" all the time. "We" thought that. "We" did this. And making their relationship clear: "Do you remember those ducks at that little pub near Rouen, George? We thought we'd found such a quiet place, off the road, and they started up about three in the morning and kept us awake for the rest of the night!"'

The Latin word for 'we' is *nos*, which leads to *noster* 'our'. This in turn has given us the word **nostrum**, a remedy that will cure everything. The word is also applied to political or social reforms that will supposedly have that effect. Quack doctors peddled these wonderful medicines, always insisting that their composition was based on 'our own' secret formula.

INCREASE

I'll tell you a plan for
gaining wealth,
Better than banking, trade,
or leases;
Take a bank note and fold
it across,
And then you'll find your money
IN-CREASES.
This wonderful plan, without
danger or loss,
Keeps your cash in your hand,
and with nothing to trouble it;
And every time that you fold
it across
'Tis plain as the light of the day
that you double it!

Anon

a young man of her own class who was being too forward. Sam Weller, in *The Pickwick Papers*, more forward than most, is duly addressed as 'Imperence' by a cook.

IMPERENCE

○

'Imperence!' was my Magdalen's only exclamation, as she flounced by.

W.M. Thackeray *The Fatal Boots*

○

Imperence has regretfully disappeared from the language. In the 19th century it was commonly addressed to someone who was demonstrating both **impudence** and **impertinence**. The speaker was usually a female servant addressing

IMPOSSIBLE

○

In two words — im-possible.

Samuel Goldwyn

○

Various people have tried to make **impossible** their own. Samuel Goldwyn made his claim with the gem quoted above. Arthur Wellesley, Duke of Wellington, asked: 'Is anything impossible? Read the newspapers.' Fridtjof Nansen is credited with: 'The difficult is what takes a little time; the impossible is what takes a little longer.' Variations of that saying are displayed in many a modern workplace.

In *The Beryl Coronet*, Sherlock Holmes is made to utter the famous words: 'When you have excluded the impossible, whatever remains, however improbable, must be the truth.' Less known is Dr Johnson's irritated comment on a violinist's playing: 'Difficult do you call it, Sir? I wish it had been impossible.'

INSINUATE

───○───

Shall I then drop the needle of insinuation and pick up the club of statement?

James Elroy Flecker *Hassan*

───○───

To **insinuate** something is to introduce it into someone's mind in an indirect way. The word is based on Latin *sinuare* 'winding' from *sinus* 'curve'. One of the special meanings of *sinus* for the Romans was the concave fold formed at the front of a woman's toga, in which she carried her baby. This led to the idea of a 'recess' or 'cavity'. The sinuses of the skull which connect with the nostrils are so-called because they are bone cavities. The Latin word could also refer to the mother's breast itself, a sense passed on to modern French as *sein* 'breast'. **Sinuous** 'curved' is another member of this word-family. Mathematicians will also recognise their **sines** and **cosines**, Latin *sinus* having been used to translate an

IT

'Stigand, the patriotic Archbishop of Canterbury, found it advisable — '
'Found *what*?' said the Duck.
'Found it,' the Mouse replied rather crossly; 'of course you know what "it" means.'
'I know what "it" means well enough, when I find a thing,' said the Duck; 'it's generally a frog or a worm. The question is, what did the Archbishop find?'
The Mouse did not notice this question, but hurriedly went on.

Lewis Carroll
Alice's Adventures in Wonderland

Arabic word of similar meaning.

In *The Darling Buds of May* Mariette does not bother to insinuate herself into Mr Charlton's affections; she simply sits on his lap and allows her **sinuosity** to do its work. It produces a powerful effect. H.E. Bates says that 'the illusion of being caressed in a silken, sinuous, maddening way by the goose's neck returned to Mr Charlton as he felt her silken legs cross his own. A sensation that for the second time his blood was turning white, while being at the same time on fire, coursed completely through him. The soles of his feet started tingling. The scent of gardenia overwhelmed him like a drug'.

FOR
ORANGE

JARGON

○

With beast and bird the forest rings,
Each in his jargon cries or sings.

Henry Wadsworth Longfellow
The Return of Spring

○

Jargon is related to **gargle**, both words imitating an inarticulate sound. In the 14th century, jargon was applied both to the twittering and chattering of birds and to unintelligible speech. The word now mainly refers to technical language, used amongst professionals to the consternation of any laymen who happen to be listening. If such language is directly addressed to a layman he may feel that an attempt is being made to 'blind him with science'.

○

The apothecary from over the way came to his assistance. This gentleman, as sometimes happens to those of the learned professions, had rather more lore than knowledge, and began to talk of the sinciput and the occiput, and cerebum and cerebellum, until he exhausted David Ramsay's brief stock of patience.

'Bell-um! bell-ell-um!' he repeated, with great indignation; 'what signify all the bells in London, if you do not put a plaster on the chield's crown?'

Sir Walter Scott The Fortunes of Nigel

○

When Rip Van Winkle returns to the village after his long sleep the words that are a 'Babylonish jargon' to him include: 'rights of citizens — elections — mem-

bers of Congress — liberty — Bunker's Hill — heroes of seventy-six — and other words'. They are meaningless to him because when he went to sleep America was still a British colony.

JERRY

○

We called 'em 'Fritzies' at that time. Afterwards they were 'Jerries', on account of their tin hats.

Robert Graves Christmas Truce

○

Jerry is now outdated slang for a German. The word was mostly used by British soldiers during the 1914–18 War. Robert Graves's explanation of its origin (above) is interesting, since most people would assume that it was based on an abbreviation of **German** itself. In the 19th century 'jerry' was a slang term for a round felt hat, but Graves presumably refers to another of the word's slang meanings, 'chamber-pot'. This once-common domestic object had earlier been known as a **Jeroboam**; it was also called a **Jordan**, with a possible punning reference — as Eric Partridge once suggested — to the 'waters of Jordan'.

○

After all, what were those Jerries? A bunch of goddam Huns. 'Huns' sounded like a funny word now.

Ernest Hemingway The Torrents of Spring

○

The original **Huns** were not Germans, but an Asiatic nomadic race who invaded Europe in the fifth century. Their leader was Attila, known as the Scourge of God. Applied to a German soldier, Hun was a general term of abuse. It alluded to the appalling reputation for savagery gained by Attila's followers.

Teaser: How long should a 'journey' take?
(Answer page 231) **??**

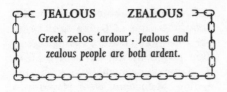

JEALOUS   ZEALOUS

Greek *zelos* 'ardour'. Jealous and zealous people are both ardent.

JIGGERED

○

'Hollo!' he growled, 'where are you two going?'
   'Where should we be going, but home?'
   'Well then,' said he, 'I'm jiggered if I don't see you home!'
   This penalty of being jiggered was a favourite suppositious case of his. He attached no definite meaning to the word that I am aware of, but used it to affront mankind, and convey an idea of something savagely damaging. When I was younger, I had a general belief that if he had jiggered me personally, he would have done it with a sharp and twisted hook.

Charles Dickens *Great Expectations*

○

There are probably still speakers who express surprise or determination with the help of **jiggered**. Robert L. Chapman lists it in his *Dictionary of American Slang* as a variant of 'I'll be **damned/danged/ darned/ding swizzled/jig-swiggered/ hanged/hornswoggled/a monkey's uncle**'. These are mostly nonsensical euphemisms and **jiggered** itself may be, as Eric Partridge suggested, a meaningless replacement for **buggered**. In this case, the Dickensian remark quoted above becomes unintentionally even nastier than intended.
   Quite a different explanation of the word is possible. In the West Indies jigger is a form of **chigoe**, a small flea which burrows into the foot. In former times it could have severe consequences, leading to deformity. *The Dictionary of Jamaican English*, by F.G. Cassidy and R.B. Le Page, comments on the insect itself as

well as words like **jigger-foot** and **jig-ger-nit**, but makes no mention of being jiggered, in the sense of being irritated by a flea. This is nevertheless a tempting explanation of the expression, which possibly originated in the USA. *The Oxford English Dictionary* reports that jigger is also used there, applied to various harvest-ticks 'which fasten on the human skin and cause great irritation'. A farm-hand attacked by such a tick would have good reason to say that he was jiggered.

JUKEBOX

○

'You mean you'd put in one of those horrors and throw out the nickelodeon?'

Peter de Vries *Comfort Me with Apples*

○

The 'horror' referred to in the above conversation is a **jukebox**. The curious part of that word, it might be supposed, is **juke**, but **box** is not without interest. Perhaps we should begin, though, with the **nickelodeon** mentioned by Peter de Vries. It was an early form of jukebox, though the word had previously de-

Shakespeare's Word of Joy

JULIET:
What say'st thou? Hast thou not a word of joy? Some comfort, nurse.

Romeo and Juliet

> ## JUDGEMENT
>
> 2nd Murd. What, shall I stab him as he sleeps?
> 1st Murd. No, he'll say 'twas done cowardly, when he wakes.
> 2nd Murd. Why, he shall never wake until the great judgement-day.
> 1st Murd. Why, then he'll say we stabb'd him sleeping.
> 2nd Murd. The urging of that word judgement hath bred a kind of remorse in me.
> 1st Murd. What, art thou afraid?
> 2nd Murd. Not to kill him, having a warrant, but to be damn'd for killing him, from the which no warrant can defend me.
>
> **William Shakespeare** *Richard III*

scribed a cinema which had an admission price of a **nickel**, or five cents. The coin name came about because the first American coin of that value contained 25 per cent nickel.

It is worth asking why the metal received that name in the first place, though the story is fairly complex. A Swedish mineralogist, Axel von Cronstedt, first obtained nickel from the copper-coloured ore niccolite in 1754. The mining name of niccolite was German *Kupfernickel*, where *Kupfer* meant 'copper'. Von Cronstedt used only the second part of the German name, which is a pet form of **Nikolaus (Nicholas)**. Just as **Old Nick** in English refers to the devil, so **Nickel** in German was the name used for a mischievous demon. The early miners who called niccolite *Kupfernickel* did so because they thought that the ore itself was 'mischievously deceptive'. Its colour wrongly suggested that it would yield copper.

The *-odeon* of nickelodeon is thought to have been an abbreviation of **melodeon**, the name of both a small organ like a harmonium and a German accordion played by folk musicians. Melodeon was simply melody with a fanciful ending. Melodeons were played at a music-hall type of entertainment which had a nickel as entry fee, and **nickelmelodeon**, then **nickelodeon**, became a more general term for 'entertainment'. The word was retained when the entertainment became a film show. Later still, when inflation had made the name inappropriate for a movie theatre, it was applied to the early jukebox. It now had the sense: 'melodies obtained for a nickel'.

The history of 'jukebox' is quite different. Juke is a word in Gullah, the Creole language spoken by blacks who live in the sea-islands and coastal districts of South Carolina, Georgia and northeastern Florida. (**Gullah** is probably a corruption of *Angola*.) The word was brought to America from Africa and originally meant 'disorderly'. A **juke house** in the American south became another term for a brothel.

Brothels were not merely 'houses of horizontal entertainment', as they were once described. It was also possible to drink and dance there. **Juking** acquired the sense of going on a kind of pub crawl, dancing and drinking at various establishments. Chapman's *Dictionary of American Slang* lists the further sense-developments that then occurred. Amongst college students, to juke meant to 'have a good time', especially at a party. In college slang juke later came to have the specific meaning 'to dance'. **Jukebox** was therefore an excellent name for something that provided dance

The pilgrims now gathered round the figure of Eliza on her soap box as if to form the audience at a play.

Virginia Woolf *Between the Acts*

music and helped create a party atmosphere.

Boxes come in all shapes and sizes, and owe their origin to the small evergreen box tree, Latin name *buxus*, Greek *puxos*. The first kind of box in which it was possible to put things was a small case made of boxwood in which drugs and ointments were kept. Once the word had come to mean a wooden container, it was ready for a further change of meaning. The money given to servants and tradesmen at Christmas was handed to them in a money-box. It was soon possible to refer to the money itself as a **Christmas box**. The day on which it was given became **Boxing Day**.

To box in the sense of strike someone with the fist is not recorded until the 16th century. It seems most unlikely that a totally new 'box' word, unconnected in any way with the first one, should appear on the scene at such a late stage with a different meaning. The more plausible explanation is that **boxing** in its fighting sense was yet another extended meaning of the original word. The connection between the two probably lies in the 'gift' meaning of box, which was established by the 14th century. To give someone a box on the ear, to rough humorists then as now, would be to give him a present.

Human beings become boxes when described as **chatterboxes** or **sauceboxes**. Children who talked too much were known in the 17th century as **prattlebaskets** or **prattleboxes**. In local dialect they later became **chatterbags**

JUSTICE

There is no weapon like words, no armour against words, and with words the Master Philologist has conquered me. It is not at all equitable: but the man showed me a huge book wherein were the names of everything in the world, and justice was not among them. It develops that, instead, justice is merely a common noun, vaguely denoting an ethical ideal of conduct proper to the circumstances, whether of individuals or communities. It is, you observe, just a grammarian's notion.

James Branch Cabell *Jurgen*

and **chatterbaskets**, but chatterbox has been the more usual word since the beginning of the 19th century. The -box version of the word was probably influenced by saucebox, already being used of an impertinent person in the 16th century. In Henry Fielding's *Joseph Andrews* a boy tells his father that he loves a certain young lady more than his sisters because she is better-looking than any of them. 'Is she so, saucebox?' says one of the sisters. She translates part of the word into action by 'giving him a box on the ear'.

FOR A
DRINK

KINDLE

———○———

Nabir had never heard of a kindle of kittens but that is what his house was filled with.

Rumer Godden *Kingfishers Catch Fire*

———○———

Kindle is a pleasant word for a number of kittens. It is quite distinct from the kindle which means 'set fire to', connected with Old Norse **kyndill** 'candle'. The feline kindle means something like 'catkind' as opposed to 'mankind' and links closely with German *Kind* 'child'. Breeders of hares, it is said, use a similar term when they say that a pregnant doe is **in kindle**.

Once the kittens reach maturity they can, if we wish to display our esoteric knowledge, be referred to as a **clouder** or **cludder** of cats. Both forms are variants of **clutter** and **cluster**, and would certainly need to be explained if used in modern times. They are examples of the many group terms for animals which appeared mainly in the 15th century. An attempt was made at the time to create almost an artificial vocabulary known only to the initiated — those who were rich enough to be able to indulge in hunting and fishing.

———○———

STEPHEN:
Unless a man have not skill in the hawking and hunting languages now-a-days, I'll not give a rush for him: they are more studied than the Greek, or the Latin. He is for no gallant's company without them.

Ben Jonson *Every Man in his Humour*

———○———

Sir Arthur Conan Doyle comments fully on the subject in his historical novel *Sir Nigel*. The hero goes to consult Sir John Buttesthorn, head huntsman to the king, and is tested on his knowledge:

'Answer me now, how would you say if you saw ten badgers together in the forest?'

'A **cete** of badgers, fair sir.'

'Good, Nigel — good, by my faith! And if you walk in Woolmer Forest and see a swarm of foxes, how would you call it?'

'A **skulk** of foxes.'

'And if they be lions?'

'Nay, fair sir, I am not like to meet several lions in Woolmer Forest.'

In spite of his objection, Nigel is pressed on the lions question. He has to be told that the correct word is **pride**. This is odd, since the latter term is one of the few that most people actually know. **Cete** is a fanciful form of **set**, which describes both the badgers' home and a group of them. **Skulk** is hardly a group term, though it correctly describes the fox's stealthy prowling. In transferring to group usage an action associated with the noun, it is typical of many such words.

———○———

GUILDFORD:
Ladies, a general welcome from his Grace
Salutes ye all; this night he dedicates
To fair content and you. None here, he hopes,
In all this noble bevy, has brought with her
One care abroad.

William Shakespeare *Henry VIII*

———○———

The invention of words for special groups of humans may seem to be

---

KITCHEN   COOK

Latin coquus 'cook' and derivative coquina 'kitchen', the latter taken into Old English as cycene, then cicen.

---

modern, but is not. The so-called *Book of St Albans*, printed in that city in 1486, already refers to a **herd** of harlots, a **host** of men, a **charge** of curates, a **dignity** of canons, a **drift** of fishers, a **bevy** of ladies, a **worship** of writers. The last of these is an ironic comment on writers of the time, who tended to seek the patronage of the rich in fulsome dedications.

Many other terms which were suggested at an early date now seem strange because words have either changed their meanings, or are no longer used as they once were. A **charge** of curates made more sense, for instance, when the word could be used of 'moral weight, impor-

tance'. Shakespeare had that meaning in mind in *Romeo and Juliet*, when Friar Laurence says: 'The letter was not nice, but full of charge/Of dear import; and the neglecting it/May do much danger.'

From time to time the topic of group terms is raised in newspaper correspondence columns and new terms are suggested. Some, such as a **den** of gamblers, a **school** of artists, seem worthy of permanent adoption. Others, such as a **giggle** of girls, an **exaggeration** of fishermen, have become fairly well-known jokes. A select list of these words appears on page 101. Longer lists are to be found in works such as C.E. Hare's *The Language*

GROUP TERMS

ANIMALS

(Some animals are described by a number of terms)

Army of frogs
Barren of mules
Bevy of roes
Bury of conies
Business of ferrets
Cartload of monkeys
Cete of badgers
Clowder of cats
Cowardice of curs
Crash of rhinoceros
Down of hares
Dray of squirrels
Drove of asses, cattle, hares
Earth of foxes
Flock of camels, goats, sheep
Gang of elk
Haras of horses
Herd of antelopes, asses, buffaloes, cattle, deer, elephants, giraffes, goats, swine
Husk of hares
Kennel of dogs
Kindle of kittens
Knot of toads
Labour of moles
Leap of leopards

Litter of cubs, pigs, pups, whelps
Mob of cattle (Australian)
Mute of hounds
Nest of mice, rabbits
Pace of asses
Pack of hounds, stoats, weasels, wolves
Rag of colts
Rake of mules
Set of badgers
Shrewdness of apes
Skulk of foxes
Sloth of bears
Sounder of boars, swine (wild)
Stable of horses
String of racehorses
Stud of mares
Sute of bloodhounds
Team of oxen
Trace of hares
Trip of goats, hares
Troop of kangaroos
Troupe of monkeys

BIRDS

Band of jays
Bevy of quails, swans
Brood of chickens
Building of rooks
Charm of finches
Chattering of starlings
Clamour of rooks
Clattering of choughs
Coil of teal (on land)
Colony of gulls
Company of widgeon
Convocation of eagles
Covert of coots
Covey of grouse, partridges
Crowd of redwings
Deceit of lapwings
Descent of woodpeckers
Exaltation of larks
Fall of woodcock
Flight of birds, cormorants, doves, pigeons, plovers, swallows, widgeon, woodcock
Flock of birds, fieldfares, parrots, pigeons, swifts
Flush of mallard (on land)
Gaggle of geese
Herd of cranes, curlews, swan wrens
Host of sparrows
Murder of crows
Murmuration of starlings
Muster of peacocks
Mustering of storks
Mutation of thrush
Nye of pheasants
Ostentation of peacocks

of *Field Sports* and especially *An Exaltation of Larks*, by James Lipton.

For those who like to play with language in this way, there is a great deal of territory to explore. The language of hunting was concerned not just with group terms. In speaking of the fox, for example, it was necessary to distinguish between the male **dog-fox** and the female **vixen**, to refer to their mating as **clickitting**, their offspring as **cubs**, their excrement as **billitting**, their tail as a **brush**, their cry as a **bark**. A parallel set of terms for the hare would be **buck, doe, bucking, leverets, crotiles, scut** and **beat** or **tap** for the special noise.

The horses snorted again and one of them nickered shrilly.

John Steinbeck To a God Unknown

Many of the words that describe animal noises are familiar because we learn them as children. We may never use the words in adult life, but we know (or should do) which animal **barks, bays, bellows, bleats, brays, chatters, grunts, mews, neighs, roars, squeaks, trumpets.** We could also say which bird **caws, coos, crows, gobbles, honks,**

Paddling of ducks (on water)
Peep of chickens
Pride of peacocks
Puddling of mallard
Rafter of turkeys
Run of poultry (domestic)
Scry of fowls
Sedge of herons
Siege of herons
Skein of geese (flying)
Spring of teal (on water)
Team of ducks (flying)
Tidings of magpies
Tribe of sparrows
Trip of dotterel, wildfowl
Unkindness of ravens
Walk of snipe
Watch of nightingales
Wing of plovers

Fishes are mostly **schools** and **shoals**, but a **family** of sardines, a **smuck** of jellyfishes, a **hover** of trout, a **bale** of turtles. Seals and whales, being mammals, are **herds**.

Insects are mostly **swarms** and **clouds**, but an **army** of caterpillars, a **flock** of lice, a **nest** of ants.

PEOPLE

Argument of bridge-players
Bevy of ladies
Blast of hunters
Blather of generals
Blush of young boys
Cackle of colonels
Charge of curates
Click of chorus-girls
Condescension of actors
Congregation of people
Conversion of preachers
Corpulence of councillors
Dash of captains
Dawdling of waiters
Dearth of domestics
Debauchery of bachelors
Den of gamblers
Dignity of cannons
Diligence of messengers
Discretion of priests
Disguising of tailors
Draught of butlers
Drift of trawlermen
Drove of tourists
Eloquence of lawyers
Epidemic of doctors
Epidermic of dermatologists
Erudition of editors
Exaggeration of fishermen
Execution of officers
Fleece of punters

Flutter of spinsters
Gaggle of gossips, women
Galaxy of film-stars
Gargle of golfers
Guffaw of clowns
Gush of poets
Hastiness of cooks
Heckle of Socialists
Herd of harlots
Hubbub of husbands
Knot of astrologers
Lash of carters
Malapertness of pedlars
Melody of harpers
Mischief of urchins
Muddle of mayors
Obeisance of servants
Pity of prisoners
Psalter of bishops
Rascal of boys
Saunter of loafers
School of clerks
Sentence of judges
Simplicity of subalterns
Skinful of scotches
Slink of mannequins
Spray of damsels
State of princes
Stodge of Conservatives
Thrust of gate-crashers
Trance of virgins
Unemployment of graduates
Worship of writers

hoots, quacks. It is less obvious, perhaps, that an eagle **screams**, an ostrich **wails**, a woodpecker **yaffles**. Some of these words are applied at times to humans, but there are many types of people who (perhaps) deserve special terms for the sound that characterises them. Nor need it end there: not all of the categories mentioned above would be of interest if applied to politicians, say, or plumbers, but it is clear that there is scope for invention.

KNOWLEDGE

'Sexual love is knowledge, both in etymology and in cold fact; "he knew her" as the Bible says! Sex is the joint or coupling which unites the male and female ends of knowledge merely — a cloud of unknowing!'

Lawrence Durrell Clea

KINE

———○———

Kine, and horses, and little humorous donkeys, browse together in the meadows, and come down in troops to the river side to drink.

R.L. Stevenson *An Inland Voyage*

———○———

Stevenson's **kine** is a grammatical fossil, an archaic plural form of **cow**. The plural suffix concerned normally occurs as -*en*, and was formerly attached in northern English to words like **tongue** and **ear**. In modern English it survives in only three common words, making it useful for a game of linguistic Trivial Pursuit. In **children** the -*en* was added to what was already a plural, **childer**. Something similar happened with **brethren**, formed from the plural **brether** to make the double plural *bretheren*, short-

ened to brethren. In this case two plurals now exist, **brothers** and brethren, and are used in different contexts. The final word in this group, as no word buff needs to be told, is **oxen**.

———————

KNIGHT

———○———

So faithful in love, and so dauntless in war,
There never was knight like the young Lochinvar.

Sir Walter Scott *Marmion*

———○———

The k of English words beginning with kn- has not been pronounced since the middle of the 17th century. Before that a word like **knight** would have sounded quite different from **night**. Loss of the initial k sound happened gradually over a long period. Ultimately it has to be explained in term of linguistic laziness.

The word from which knight derives gave rise to similar words in several Germanic languages. In English the word originally meant 'boy', then 'attendant, servant'. Those who attended the king as personal servants eventually became knights in the modern sense. By the Middle Ages knights had become independent enough to be described as **knight-errants**, wandering the world in

Teaser: In Sir Walter Scott's The Fortunes of Nigel, *a man talks of 'knapping, Fulhams, bristles, topping, slurring and stabbing.' What subject is he discussing?*
(Answer page 231) **??**

search of chivalrous adventures. Later they were the butt of literary jokes, above all in Don Quixote, by Miguel Cervantes. To this 'Knight of the Woeful Countenance' we owe our word quixotic, used of anyone who has romantic and unrealistic ideas.

At that time their conversation when alone together was tinged with the language of their favourite romances. Sometimes Edmund would amuse his sister and himself by translating, when a battered old zinc bucket became 'ye antique pail', or a tree slightly damaged by the wind 'yon lightning-blasted pine', while some good neighbour of theirs whom they could see working in the fields would have given Edmund what he would have called 'a darned good bommicking' if he had heard himself referred to as 'yon caitiff hind.'

Flora Thompson Over to Candleford

The first part of Don Quixote was published in 1605. Four years later Beaumont and Fletcher amused themselves with a similar theme in The Knight of the Burning Pestle. When Ralph, a grocer, decides to become a knight-errant he tells the elder apprentice who is to be his squire, 'that you never call any female by the name of a woman or wench, but "fair lady", if she have her desires, if not, "distressed damsel"; that you call all forests and heaths "deserts", and all horses "palfreys".'

A gentle knight was pricking on the plain.

Edmund Spenser The Faerie Queene

He then gives Tim, the apprentice, a vocabulary test: 'Admit this were a desert, and over it a knight-errant pricking, and I should bid you inquire of his intents, what would you say?' 'Sir, my master sent me to know whither you are riding?' 'No, thus: "Fair sir, the right courteous and valiant Knight of the Burning Pestle commanded me to inquire upon what adventure you are bound, whether to relieve some distressed damsel, or otherwise?"'

This conversation takes place in the grocer's shop. When a woman customer appears, the second apprentice who has been listening to the conversation puts the grocer in his place by saying: 'Right courteous and valiant Knight of the Burning Pestle, here is a distressed damsel to have a halfpenny-worth of pepper.'

Shakespeare's Keeping One's Word

POINS:
Jack, how agrees the devil and thee about thy soul, that thou soldest him on Good Friday last for a cup of Madeira and a cold capon's leg?

PRINCE:
Sir John stands to his word — the devil shall have his bargain; for he was never yet a breaker of proverbs; he will give the devil his due.

POINS:
Then thou art damn'd for keeping thy word with the devil.

PRINCE:
Else had had been damn'd for cozening the devil.

Henry IV Part One

FOR
LEATHER

LALLYGAG

———○———

Teaser: What is curious about the word 'latchstrings'? (Answer page 231) **??**

Annixter pretended to be a woman-hater, for no other reason than that he was a very bull calf of awkwardness in feminine surroundings. 'Feemales!' Rot! There was a fine way for a man to waste his time and his good money, lallygagging with a lot of feemales.

Frank Norris The Octopus

———○———

Lallygag is a variant of **lollygag**, according to Webster's *New Collegiate Dictionary*. The meaning of the word can be surmised from the above quotation; it has to do with 'fooling around, being frivolous instead of serious'. On the subject of why the word has this meaning, and how it originated, the dictionary editors prefer to remain silent, leaving room for amateur speculation.

By the early 19th century, **gag** in colloquial slang already meant to hoax, pull someone's leg. An early commentator explained that **gagging** in this sense derived from the idea of thrusting absurdities down the throat of an incredulous person. The way was open for gag to take on the meaning of 'indulge in light-hearted conversation'.

Words with an l-ll structure exist in various languages (e.g. Danish *lalle*, Dutch *lullen*) with a sense of 'to prattle'. The source of such words is clearly the natural sound made by an infant before it learns to speak. Latin had a verb *lallare*, based on a child's babbling of 'la-la'. From this was derived French *lallation* 'child's babbling', though **lallation** in English was later used to describe the Chinese habit of pronouncing l for r, as when saying lum for rum.

The first part of lallygag/lollygag may therefore have a 'prattling' sense, but words like **loll** suggest a lazy passing of time which are also appropriate to the

meaning. **Lollop** can also mean 'to lounge, flop about, sprawl'.

Frank Norris's Annixter would not have indulged in such etymological speculation, of course, when speaking of lallygagging, nor would his audience have needed to do so. The word somehow manages to suggest its meaning. It describes an activity which Annixter pretends to condemn, though he later discovers what delights it holds in store.

LEAP-FROG

———○———

They were townsmen out for a lark, and, after partaking of refreshment at the hotel, they would play leap-frog or kick an old tin about the green.

Flora Thompson Lark Rise to Candleford

———○———

The earliest reference in English literature to the game of **leap-frog** occurs in Shakespeare's *Henry V*. Henry is telling Princess Katharine of his personal strengths and weaknesses. He is not a poet or a dancer, he says, but: 'if I could win a lady at leap-frog, or by vaulting into my saddle with my armour on my back, under the correction of bragging be it spoken, I should quickly leap into a wife'.

Shakespeare obviously did not invent the word leap-frog; there had simply been no reason previously for the game to be mentioned in serious literary works. Later writers were to allude to it figuratively. Of the battle between the flesh and the spirit Jonathan Swift says:

'There is a perpetual game at leap-frog between both; and sometimes the flesh is uppermost, and sometimes the spirit.'

———————○———————

'Can you play leap-frog?'
  'Yes!' She loosened her duffle coat.
  I moved a few paces farther on and leaned over to make a 'back'. A moment later I heard the crunch crunch of her running steps and with the lightest possible tap of her fingers upon my spine she soared lightly over me and bounded onwards, her toes dabbing the frosted grass in a line of little round holes. She leaned over for me. I ran and went over with a light spring, touching the stuff of her coat with the gentlest flying caress of one hand. There seemed to be no gravity in the park that morning.

Iris Murdoch A Word Child

———————○———————

Leap-frog is no doubt played by children throughout the world, but surely there is something curious about the English name for the game? The 'frog' part of it is apt, conjuring up a better image than the French equivalent saute-mouton, even though that translates rather neatly as 'leap-sheep'. Nor is German Bock-springen, literally 'buck-leap', an improvement as far as the animal is concerned, but at least it does get the word-order right. For surely the English word should be 'frog-leap', not 'leap-frog'? It is a simplified form of 'frog's leap', not 'leap the frog'. We have a similar word **frog-march** which would suggest something quite different if we inverted it to 'march-frog'.

  The English word, then, is curious, but we can be sure that children in various other countries have given the game many a strange name in their different languages.

———————————————

LIMB

———————○———————

FALSTAFF:
Care I for the limb, the thews, the stature, bulk, and big assemblance of a man! Give me the spirit.

William Shakespeare Henry IV Part Two

———————○———————

In his Diary in America Captain Frederick Marryat relates that in 1837 he was escorting a young American lady who slipped and grazed her shin. Marryat asked her whether she had hurt her leg much, only to have her turn away from him in shocked horror. Eventually he was able to discover what had caused her displeasure. The word **leg**, she said, was never uttered in the presence of ladies, the word **limb** was preferred. She went on to say that amongst her acquaintance there were even those who spoke of 'the limb of a table or piano'.

———————○———————

'Parents are incomprehensible. You would think it was the nineteenth century. A hundred years ago they used to put frilly covers on piano legs because they thought legs were rude.'

Clifford Hanley The Taste of Too Much

———————○———————

Marryat says that some time later he visited a seminary for young ladies where he saw a piano with its four limbs. The mistress of the establishment was determined to protect the delicacy of her charges to the utmost degree. She had therefore dressed all four piano limbs 'in modest little trousers, with frills at the bottom of them!'

○━ **LIQUID**   **PROLIX** ━○

Latin liquere 'be fluid'. A prolix person 'pours out' speech.

> ## LIFE
>
> He put his heavy, cheery, needing-to-be-reassured hand on the shape under the sheet and said, 'It's not such a bad life, Trixy. Is it now? Not a bad life?' But he could feel her stiffen: the word 'life' was taboo: it reminded you of death. She turned her face away from him towards the wall and then hopelessly back again — the phrase 'turn to the wall' was taboo too.
>
> **Graham Greene** *The Power and the Glory*

This anecdote became widely known and gave rise to many a British laugh at the expense of American prudery. Those acquainted with Marryat's broad humour, displayed in his novels and children's stories, will wonder just how much truth there was in the tale. He may well have been pulling his readers' limbs, while making a satirical comment on the verbal evasion that we know as euphemism.

The leg/limb example smacks of hypocrisy and would now be considered absurd, yet even in these far more relaxed times most people regularly use euphemisms. Their use of vague terms for more precise ones might be explained away as social tact; whatever its motive it leads to an avoidance of direct reference to such subjects as old age, race, copulation, death, defecation, farting, genitalia, lavatories, menstruation, sweat and similarly embarrassing topics. A surprising number of people would still ask for the **white meat** of a chicken in order to avoid saying **breast** at the dinner table. Many more examples are to be found in such works as *The Faber Dictionary of Euphemisms*, by R.W. Holder and *A Dictionary of Euphemisms*, by Judith S. Neaman and Carole G. Silver.

Commercial euphemism is at the heart of advertising. Estate agents have become especially notorious for managing to find positive ways of describing negative features. A 'basement flat' sounds much better as a 'garden flat'; 'miles away from any shops or public transport' is likewise more palatable as 'secluded'. It goes without saying that all those concerned with selling products of any kind use language in a similar way, skirting round disagreeable truths.

'What are you doing there, you limb?'

Harriet Beecher Stowe *Uncle Tom's Cabin*

To return to 'limb' for a moment, there may still be children who hear themselves addressed as 'you young limb'. The expression occurs, for example, in *Oliver Twist* and was formerly common. It meant much the same as 'you little devil', since the allusion was to an old saying that mischievous people were the 'devil's limbs'. They were the means by which he did his foul deeds.

LOO

'Don't bother to hop on one foot and then the other like a three-year-old who's got to go to the Lou.'

Norman Mailer *An American Dream*

Norman Mailer demonstrates in the passage above the unfamiliarity of many Americans with the British word loo, unless he believed an absurd story that connects the origin of the word with the name of Lady Louis Hamilton, said to have been written on a lavatory door in Dublin in the 19th century. Americans are certainly used to the idea of a first name — **John** — being used for 'lavatory'. This usage arose, incidentally, because Americans used to remark that they were going to visit 'cousin John'.

'H. Dean had to go to the john — '
'The loo,' Stevie translated.

Sumner Locke Elliott Edens Lost

The origin of 'loo' seems obvious enough — **Waterloo** as a jokey variation of **water-closet**, then 'Waterloo' being abbreviated. British people are familiar with the name Waterloo for one reason or another. Even if they could say little about the Battle of Waterloo they know that it is the name of a huge London railway terminus. There is not the same general familiarity with French words such as l'eau 'the water' or lieu 'place', both of which have been suggested as sources for 'loo'.

Waterloo is a small town in Belgium. The Water- of the place-name means the same as in English; loo in Flemish means 'marsh', but there is no marsh in the area. Adrian Room, in his Place Names of the World, therefore suggests that the -loo may represent Old High German losi 'ditch'.

She kept saying these very corny, boring things, like calling the can the 'little girls' room'.

J.D. Salinger The Catcher in the Rye

In The Faber Dictionary of Euphemisms, R.W. Holder lists about 140 other substitutes for the word 'lavatory', but there are likely to be many more. He does not record **summer houses**, for example, though it is said that guides on some coach tours are likely to tell a group at a stopping place that 'the summer houses

are over there'. The pun is then explained as: 'Some are for men and some are for women.'

LORD

None of them had ever seen a person bearing a title of nobility before, and none had been expecting to see one now, consequently the title came upon them as a kind of pile-driving surprise and caught them unprepared. A few tried to rise to the emergency, and got out an awkward 'My lord', or 'Your lordship', or something of that sort, but the great majority were overwhelmed by the unaccustomed word and its dim and awful associations with gilded courts and stately ceremony and anointed kingship, so they only fumbled through the handshake and passed on, speechless.

Mark Twain Pudd'nhead Wilson

People react differently to titles, whether they be social or professional. There are those, like the citizens of Dawson's Landing described by Mark Twain, who are thrown into a state of confusion when introduced to someone who is not a normal Mr, Mrs or Miss. Some admit to no problem, but stick resolutely to a neutral you throughout a conversation. There is a third group which goes to the other extreme, dropping a title into the conversation at every opportunity. They are not necessarily honouring the person concerned — it is more a matter of reflected glory.

Writers have long been commenting on the subject. In Vanity Fair, for example, Thackeray describes George Osborne's father, a merchant: 'Whenever he met a great man he grovelled before him, and my-lorded him as only a free-born Briton can do. He came home and looked out his history in the Peerage; he introduced his name into his daily conversation, he bragged about his Lordship to his daughters.' Jane Austen comments on a military title in *Persuasion*: '"I have let my house to Admiral Croft" would sound extremely well; very much better than to any mere Mr—; a Mr (save, perhaps, some half-dozen in the nation), always needed a note of explanation.'

In ordinary life, the titles that most people come across are medical, religious or academic. In a medical context, doctor has reassuring qualities in itself for a patient. Just as Mark Twain talked of 'the dim and awful associations' of the word lord, using awful in its original sense of 'awe-inspiring', so 'doctor' immediately suggests years of specialised training and the passing on of accumulated knowledge.

Religious titles such as **Father**, conventionally used to a Catholic priest, may have the same kind of distancing effect as the clerical collar. The priest himself may not welcome this, but use of the title is probably a help to parishioners. They need to feel that the priest is a special person: the title verbally signals that fact.

'It's good to have you back, Professor Waltz,' she said. I had given up trying to make her understand that I was only an instructor, realizing that the dignity of the house, as well as her own ego, were nourished by use of the more prestigious title.

Peter de Vries Let Me Count the Ways

In the academic world, **professor** is the most prestigious title, when it is properly applied to a teacher of the highest rank in a university. In the US the title is often used to teachers of lower rank. Marian Castle, in *Deborah*, has a conversation in which a young man is addressed as professor, 'the title by which the local teacher — if male — was always known'. In this instance the

conversation continues: 'Don't call me professor,' he snapped. 'Why not?' 'Because I'm nothing but an underpaid, unnoticed, unimportant instructor at the new University of Chicago. Maybe,

Shakespeare's Large, Loving, Lowly Words

CLAUDIO:
If I have known her,
You will say she did embrace me as a husband,
And so extenuate the 'forehand sin.
No, Leonato,
I never tempted her with word too large
But, as a brother to his sister, show'd
Bashful sincerity and comely love.

Much Ado About Nothing

[After tearing up a love-letter from Proteus]
JULIA:
O hateful hands, to tear such loving words!
Injurious wasps, to feed on such sweet honey
And kill the bees that yield it with your stings!
I'll kiss each several paper for amends.

The Two Gentlemen of Verona

GLOUCESTER:
Why, 'tis well known that whiles I was Protector
Pity was all the fault that was in me;
For I should melt at an offender's tears,
And lowly words were ransom for their fault.

Henry VI Part Two

after another twenty years and a couple more degrees and a book or so, I might really have become a full professor.'

In Lucky Jim, Kingsley Amis describes the head of the history department: 'no other professor in Great Britain set such store on being called Professor'. Many who hold an academic doctorate seem to feel a similar need to be reassured constantly by the sound of the title.

In the English-speaking world, professional titles are in restricted use. The situation is different in a country like Sweden, where professional descriptions such as company director are far more frequently used, both in direct address and in third-person reference.

'You're here as a breadwinner. Breadwin or get out.'

James Purdy Eustace Chisholm and the Works

Of the titles mentioned above, the most curious etymologically is lord. In Anglo-Saxon times a lord was a hlafweard, literally 'loaf-ward'. He was the master of a household, in other words, who provided loaves of bread for his dependents. **My lord** would now only be used humorously to a husband by his wife, but if he happens to be the **bread-winner** of the family then there is some historical justification for its use.

The **lady** of the household in Anglo-Saxon times was the hlæfdige, where hlæf is again from hlaf 'loaf'. The -dige part of the word is related to **dough** and seems to have been a verb meaning 'to knead'. If the lady of the household did not knead the dough herself, she would have supervised the servants who did so. A servant at the time, incidentally, was a hlafæta 'loaf-eater'. That word did not survive, though the later contemptuous term for a particularly well-fed servant, **beef-eater**, is still with us as a nickname for a Yeoman of the Guard.

LOST

I once was lost but now am found . . .

Amazing Grace

There is a very curious use of the word lost in the phrase 'lost property office'. The items that are stored there, awaiting collection from their absent-minded owners, were admittedly 'lost' at one time, but their presence in the lost property office can only mean that they were subsequently found. 'Found property office' would therefore be a more logical description, as is recognised, for example, in Polish.

As for the expression 'no love is lost' between two people, this is ambiguous. While it normally means that neither likes the other, in the past it could mean that two people gave all their love to each other so that none was lost or wasted. Thomas Percy's Reliques of Ancient English Poetry has the following:

No love between this two was lost,
Each was to other kind:
In love they lived, in love they died,
And left two babes behind.

LOVE

Love! sure the word is formed on purpose out of the prettiest soft vowels and consonants in the language.

William Thackeray Barry Lyndon

Thackeray is joking, of course, in the above quotation, but he has a point. The word used to describe 'an intense feeling of deep affection' needs to be soft-sounding in itself. Not that **love** always has that meaning; the word is frequently used of lesser passions. Already in the 18th century Henry Fielding was commenting in *Tom Jones*: 'She was in love, according to the present universally received sense of that phrase, by which love is applied indiscriminately to the desirable objects of all our passions, appetites, and senses, and is understood to be that preference which we give to one kind of food rather than to another.'

Hah, all we poets write a deal about love: but none of us may grasp the word's full meaning until he reflects that this is a passion mighty enough to induce a woman to put up with him.

James Branch Cabell Jurgen

Aware of this debasement of meaning, other authors have felt the need to define the word in their own way. Thomas Hardy, in *Far from the Madding Crowd*, takes a highly realistic view: 'They spoke very little of their mutual feelings; pretty phrases and warm expressions

LUCK

'I thought when Uncle Oscar said filthy lucker, it meant money.' 'Filthy lucre does mean money,' said the mother. 'But it's lucre, not luck.' 'Oh!' said the boy. 'Then what is luck, mother?' 'It's what causes you to have money. If you're lucky you have money. That's why it's better to be born lucky than rich. If you're rich, you may lose your money. But if you're lucky, you will always get more money.'

D.H. Lawrence The Rocking-Horse Winner

being probably unnecessary between such tried friends. Theirs was the substantial affection which arises (if any arises at all) when the two who are thrown together begin first by knowing the rougher sides of each other's character, and not the best till further on, the romance growing up in the interstices of a mass of hard prosaic reality.

'This good-fellowship — *camaraderie* — usually occurring through similarity of pursuits, is unfortunately seldom added to love between the sexes, because men and women associate, not in their labours, but in their pleasures merely. Where, however, happy circumstance permits its development, the compounded feeling proves itself to be the only love which is as strong as death — that love which many waters cannot quench, nor the floods drown, beside which the passion usually called by the name is evanescent as steam.'

Love — a temporary insanity cured by marriage.

Ambrose Bierce The Devil's Dictionary

Hardy would no doubt have drawn a moral conclusion from the fact that 'love' is from the same Germanic root as the -lief in **belief**. For the etymologist, as for anyone else, to love someone is to believe in that person. Another word of the same family is **leave**, as used in the phrase 'ask leave to do something'.

GRACE:
Love! why the very word is breathing satire upon a man's reason — a mania, indigenous to humanity — nature's jester, who plays off tricks upon the world, and trips up common sense.

Dion L. Boucicault London Assurance

'Love' became the key-word of the 1960s with the hippie movement. In The

> ## LUMBER
>
> Lumber! Lumber! What a queer word, especially when said over and over beneath the bed-clothes. It meant odds and ends of old rubbish, her mother had explained, but, to her, it sounded more like black shadows come alive and ready to bear down on one.
>
> **Flora Thompson** *Over to Candleford*

Selling of the President, Joe McGinniss gives an example of the effect this had on the American public at the time. During the Nixon presidential campaign, a commercial was shown which ended with a shot of a soldier who had the word LOVE on his helmet. The advertising agency had been especially pleased with this, thinking how lucky they had been to find such an interesting soldier.

Unfortunately, when the commercial was shown, complaints started to pour in. The word was thought to be inappropriate in such a context, and the association of soldiers with hippies was not liked. The shot of the soldier was hastily removed. Amongst those who had seen the commercial, however, was the soldier's mother. She wrote to say what a thrill it had been to see her son's face on the screen. The letter was signed: Mrs William Love.

I am armour-proof against old discouragements. I forgive, or overcome in fancy, old adversaries. I play over again for love, as the gamesters phrase it, games for which I once paid so dear.

Charles Lamb *Essays of Elia* 'New Year's Eve'

For many people, the word 'love' is seen at its most curious when it is used during a game of tennis to mean 'no points, nil'. This has long been explained by bar-room philologists as a corruption of French l'oeuf 'the egg'. Attention is often drawn to the analogous **duck** in cricket, which is certainly an abbreviation of **duck's egg** and a joking reference to the 0 shape.

The problem with ingenious etymology is that it is seldom true. Charles Lamb hints at the true explanation of the tennis term in the quotation above. 'Play for love' was already being used by 17th-century gamblers to mean 'play for nothing', picking up on the expression 'love or money'. For at least 300 years — and moralists must make of this what they will — it has been at least partly true to say that 'love means nothing'.

FOR
SIS

METICULOUS

---○---

She gave no impression of observing the room meticulously (at least not with the implication of fear pedantic use of the term implies)

Anthony Powell Casanova's Chinese Restaurant

---○---

In *Something About Words*, Ernest Weekley remarks that he had recently come across the sentence: 'He selected a cigarette with meticulous care.' This, he thought, was an example of an unthinking and unjustified use of the word **meticulous**. The cigarettes in a packet, after all, would presumably be exactly the same, so why would the choice of one rather than another require 'great attention to detail'? A better use of the word is demonstrated by Graham Greene in *The Quiet American*: 'He was very meticulous about small courtesies.' Social behaviour is indeed something that at times has to be thought about carefully.

The 'pedantic' use of meticulously which Anthony Powell speaks about in the passage quoted above would be restoring a meaning to the word that has been obsolete since the 17th century. When 'meticulous, meticulously' first came into English there was a far greater awareness of their derivation from Latin *metus* 'fear'. 'Meticulous' itself at first meant 'fearful, timorous', but it is easy to see how hesitant behaviour and reluctance to make a choice because of timidity led to a reinterpretation of the word's meaning.

What is curious about 'meticulous' is that it appears to be the only English word derived from Latin *metus*. There was another Latin word *pavidus* 'fearful', but this too has been unproductive. **Pavid** has only on rare occasions been used in English to mean **timid** — itself a word which, like **timorous**, is ultimately from Latin *timere* 'to be afraid'. Latin *trepidus* 'uneasy, alarmed' led to **trepidation** 'fearful agitation' and **intrepid** 'fearless'. *Trepidus* belongs to a family of words which includes Latin *terrere* 'frighten', seen in words like **terrible, terrify, terror, terrorise, terrorist**. Latin *tremulare* is another family-member, leading to **tremble**.

In spite of all these 'fearful' words derived from Latin, the learned English words which describe a fear of something specific make use of -*phobia*, from Greek *phobos* 'fear'. A list of such words (see page 116) makes an interesting comment on the complexity of modern life.

MIEN

---○---

'If a woman is momentarily melted by softness in a man, she is for ever subdued by boldness and bravery of mien.'

George Meredith Evan Harrington

---○---

Mien is a peculiar word that occurs in literature but never in a normal conversation. It has to do with a person's general appearance and manner, which seems to connect it with French *mine*, of similar meaning. Scholars believe that it was probably influenced by that word, but may at first have been a shortened form of **demean**, an earlier form of **demeanour**.

George Meredith's comment (above) is put into the mouth of a caring sister

Teaser: What is curious about the word 'month'?
(Answer page 231) **??**

who is advising her brother on how to win a young lady's affections. 'I must make you angry before her,' she tells him. 'You have your father's frown.' That, she thinks, is a distinct advantage. Her unusual view is that an angry frown will make a far greater impression than smiles and charm.

Shakespeare's Magical, Medicinal, Mildest, Moving Words

SILIUS:
Thou wilt write to Antony?
VENTIDIUS:
I'll humbly signify what in his name,
That magical word of war, we have effected.

Antony and Cleopatra

PAULINA:
. . . I
Do come with words as medicinal as true,
Honest as either, to purge him of that humour
That presses him from sleep.

The Winter's Tale

COUNTESS:
Ah! what sharp stings are in her mildest words.

All's Well that Ends Well

PROTEUS:
Nay, if the gentle spirit of moving words
Can no way change you to a milder form,
I'll woo you like a soldier, at arms' end,
And love you 'gainst the nature of love —
    force ye!

The Two Gentlemen of Verona

MISCHIEF

Since the days of Adam, there has been hardly a mischief done in this world but a woman has been at the bottom of it.

William Thackeray Barry Lyndon

There can be no better example of a **mischievous** opening sentence to a novel than the one quoted above. Thackeray is displaying his own well-developed sense of **mischief**.

The word looks curious, as if it refers to an unsuccessful **chief**. While that is not true, there is nevertheless a direct connection between 'chief' and 'mischief'. Both are also linked through French chef 'head' to **achieve**, which has a basic meaning of bringing something to a successful head or conclusion. The obsolete verb **mischieve** meant exactly the opposite, to come to a bad end. 'Mischief' and mischievous clearly derive from the verb.

---

*She is gentle, she is shy,
But there's mischief in her eye,
She's a flirt!
With her dimples and her curls
She exasperates the girls
Past belief;
They hint that she's a cat,
And delightful things like that
In their grief.*

Samuel Minturn Peck The Flirt

To **do someone a mischief** can still mean to do that person real harm, just as a **mischief-maker** is not merely 'mischievous'. In former times the two descriptions would have meant much the same. In *Julius Caesar*, for instance, Brutus tells himself how he must think of Caesar:

'And therefore think him as a serpent's egg,
Which, hatch'd, would as his kind grow mischievous,
And kill him in the shell.'

In modern times we might describe a mischievous child as **naughty**. This is another word that had a far stronger meaning for Shakespeare and his contemporaries. A naughty person was originally worth **naught**, or nothing. When Dogberry tells Conrade, in *Much Ado About Nothing*, that he is a 'naughty varlet' he is telling him quite seriously that he is utterly worthless and contemptible. Words of this type perhaps come to have watered-down meanings because they are applied inappropriately in an exaggerated way. To tell someone that she is

---

PHOBIAS

A hundred and one things which cause fear.

Aelurophobia — cats
Agoraphobia — crowds, open spaces
Algophobia — pain
Amathophobia — dust
Androphobia — men
Anemophobia — draughts, wind
Anthophobia — flowers
Apiophobia — bees
Arachnophobia — spiders
Ataxiophobia — disorder
Bactrachophobia — toads
Bathmophobia — walking
Batrachophobia — frogs
Belonephobia — needles
Bogyphobia — demons
Cardiophobia — heart disease
Catoptrophobia — mirrors
Cherophobia — germs
Chrematophobia — wealth
Chromophobia — colours
Cibophobia — food
Coitophobia — sex
Cremnophobia — precipices
Demophobia — people
Dipsophobia — drinking
Dysmorphophobia — deformity
Emetophobia — vomiting

Entomophobia — insects
Eremiophobia — solitude
Ergophobia — work
Erythrophobia — red
Galeophobia — sharks
Gamophobia — marriage
Gerascophobia — ageing
Geumophobia — tastes
Gynophobia — women
Haphephobia — touching
Heliophobia — sun
Hippophobia — horses
Hydrophobia — water
Hypengyophobia — responsibility
Hypnophobia — sleep
Hypsophobia — heights
Iatrophobia — doctors
Ichthyophobia — fish
Kakorrhaphiophobia — failure
Kenophobia — open spaces
Keraunophobia — lightning, thunder
Kleptophobia — thieves
Kopophobia — examinations
Laliophobia — talking
Maniaphobia — insanity
Molysomophobia — infection
Mythophobia — lying
Necrophobia — death
Nudophobia — nakedness
Nyctophobia — darkness, night
Odontophobia — teeth
Oinophobia — wine
Olfactophobia — smells
Ombrophobia — rain
Ommatophobia — eyes
Ophidiophobia — reptiles

Osmophobia — odours
Panophobia — everything
Papaphobia — the Pope
Pathophobia — disease
Peccatophobia — sinning
Pedophobia — children
Peladophobia — baldness
Peniaphobia — poverty
Phagophobia — eating
Pharmacophobia — drugs
Phengophobia — daylight
Phonophobia — noise
Photophobia — light
Phthisiophobia — tuberculosis
Pnigophobia — choking
Ponophobia — fatigue
Potamophobia — rivers
Psychrophobia — cold
Pyrophobia — fire
Scatophobia — excrement
Siderodromophobia — railways
Siderophobia — stars
Spectrophobia — ghosts
Taphophobia — funerals
Teratophobia — monsters
Thalassophobia — sea
Theophobia — God
Thermophobia — heat
Tomophobia — surgery
Toxicophobia — poisons
Traumatophobia — war
Triskaidekaphobia — thirteen
Uranophobia — homosexuality
Urophobia — urinating
Vermiphobia — worms
Xenophobia — foreigners
Xerophobia — deserts, dryness
Zoophobia — animals

wicked, for instance, may now mean only that she is 'playfully malicious'.

MISLED

---○---

The first time she'd seen that word, in a Toronto newspaper when she was eight, she'd thought a molester was someone who caught moles.

Margaret Atwood Bodily Harm

---○---

Many people would be able to match Margaret Atwood's story of **molester** with a misunderstanding of their own. One of these days the subject will be raised in a newspaper correspondence column and the misleading words will be exposed. 'Misleading' is the right word, since **misled** has managed to **mislead** many a young reader into thinking that a word which is pronounced *mizzled* exists.

MONKEY-ROPE

---○---

Monkey-rope is an unlikely word on which to base a philosophy or establish a principle, but Herman Melville does so in *Moby Dick*. He is describing the whaling process in detail and explains that the harpooner is protected by 'what is technically called in the fishery a monkey-rope'. This is a safety line, one end of which is normally attached to the ship, the other to the harpooner as he stands on the back of a dead whale.

On board the *Pequod* things are different. The monkey-rope — 'an elongated Siamese ligature' as Melville describes it — is attached instead to another member of the crew. This, says Melville, is 'in

> ⊶ **MERCY   COMMERCE** ⊷
>
> *Latin merces 'reward', originally price paid for merx, mercis, 'merchandise'.*

order to afford to the imperilled harpooner the strongest possible guarantee for the faithfulness and vigilance of his monkey-rope holder'. The point is that if the harpooner is dragged under, the rope-holder goes with him, since tradition does not allow him to cut the rope.

When Melville becomes the bowsman and takes charge of the monkey-rope, it raises thoughts about mutual dependability in a more general way. 'I saw that this situation of mine was the precise situation of every mortal that breathes; only, in most cases, he, one way or other, has this Siamese connection with a plurality of other mortals. If your banker breaks, you snap; if your apothecary by mistake sends you poison in your pills, you die.' The problem with life, he adds, is that you can only have the management of one end of the rope.

MORTGAGE

---○---

And then with tears, and sighs, and some slight kisses,
They parted for the present — these to await
According to the artillery's hits or misses,
What sages call Chance, Providence, or Fate —
(Uncertainty is one of many blisses,
A mortgage on Humanity's estate).

Lord Byron Don Juan

---○---

Byron demonstrates in the passage above how to make brilliant literary use of a very unpoetic piece of legal jargon. **Mortgage** has become a familiar word

MODESTY

'I should say that kindness, and sincerity, and — if I may say so — modesty are worth far more to a man, to a husband, than all the wit and beauty in the world.' I was not sure what he meant by modesty. It was a word I had never understood. I always imagined it had something to do with minding meeting people in a passage on the way to the bathroom.

Daphne du Maurier Rebecca

in modern times, now that house ownership is more common. In Byron's day it was a word which plagued mainly the owners of large country estates. It came into English from French and literally means 'dead pledge'. In the 17th century lawyers explained it by saying that if the mortgagor did not repay the money he had borrowed within the stipulated time, his property was taken from him and was thereafter 'dead' to him. If the money was repaid, then the debt itself was 'dead'.

Your place is mortgaged; the bank owns it.'

But, like the dark water underneath, his words did not disturb me. They had nothing to do with me; neither the words nor the water; or so I thought as I said goodbye to him and climbed the hill towards the school. 'Mortgage,' I thought, 'now what does that mean?' and still puzzling it over I decided to ask Miss Moriarty or better still to look it up in the big black dictionary. It was kept in the school press.

Edna O'Brien The Country Girls

The mort- of mortgage occurs again in English words like **mortal**, **immortal**, mortify, mortuary, all of which are based on Latin mors, mortis 'death'. Gage is a Germanic word from a postulated waddi 'pledge'. Associated words etymologically include **engage**, **wage**, **wager**, **wed**, **wedding**, some of which have strong connections with mortgage in other ways.

MYRIAD

I suppose that, in the literal and unrhetorical use of the word myriad, I must, on my different visits to London, have looked into many myriads of female faces, in the hope of meeting Ann.

Thomas de Quincey
Confessions of an English Opium Eater

One wonders exactly what de Quincey meant in the sentence quoted above. He is referring to his search for the girl who saved his life when he was young, and stresses that he is using **myriad** in its 'literal and unrhetorical' sense. In the Greek numeral system a myriad was 10 000. Does he really mean that he looked into many 10 000s of faces?

Myriad was also used in Greek to mean 'countless, an indefinitely great number'. That was probably the intended meaning, but in this sense 'myriads' is illogical; the word should be in the singular. English writers nevertheless show a distinct preference for the plural form. Milton has it in Paradise Lost; Tennyson, in The Princess, has:

Myriads of rivulets hurrying thro'
   the lawn,
The moan of doves in immemorial
   elms,
And murmuring of innumerable
   bees.

FOR
A DIG

NATCH

As a pseudonym for correspondence with the Chief, he chose Armada — natch!

Kim Philby My Silent War

The above passage refers to a Royal Navy captain, Naval Attaché in Spain, who had what Kim Philby calls 'illusions' rather than 'delusions' of grandeur. Naturally, therefore, he chose Armada as a pseudonym. That last sentence rather tamely paraphrases Philby's original. His use of the colloquial abbreviation **natch** for **naturally**, something he is able to do because of the way the sentence is constructed, happens to be quite effective. It catches the reader's attention and has a personalising effect, making us aware of Philby as an individual who is speaking to us.

That rather suggests that Philby is consciously applying literary skills with his use of 'natch'. His book, as it happens, makes it clear that he was by no means a writer in any real sense of the word. His writing style is a mishmash of the literary and colloquial and shows little sign of artistic control.

I will knit you a wallet of forget-me-not blue, for the money to be comfy.

Dylan Thomas Under Milk Wood

The use of abbreviated words is widespread, but is governed by curious conventions. **Oft** and **ne'er**, for example, are thought to be acceptable within a poem because they are given fancy names and are said to be rhetorical devices. No speaker would use either of them in a normal conversation. By contrast, a person who says that he has just had an **op** is allowed no rhetorical excuse: it is assumed that he is too lazy to say **operation**. Words like **phone** are known to be abbreviations, but do not normally expose anyone who uses them to accusations of laziness. Other abbreviations have become so usual that they are now words in their own right. Only a pedant would talk about an **omnibus** or manufactory instead of a **bus** and **factory**.

'I want you to move your stuff out as soon as poss, today if you can.'

Iris Murdoch Under the Net

Abbreviations in poetry were the subject of Harry Graham's Poetical Economy:

What hours I spent of precious time,
What pints of ink I used to waste,
Attempting to secure a rhyme
To suit the public taste,
Until I found a simple plan
Which makes the lamest lyric scan!

When I've a syllable de trop,
I cut it off, without apol.:
This verbal sacrifice, I know,
May irritate the schol.;
But all must praise my dev'lish cunn.
Who realise that Time is Mon.

I gladly publish to the pop.
A scheme of which I make no myst.,
And beg my fellow scribes to cop.
This labour-saving syst.
I offer it to the consid.
Of ev'ry thoughtful individ.

There are several more verses on this theme of suppressing 'all syllables that are unnec', as Harry Graham expresses it. He is merely having fun, but provides serious food for thought to those who are interested in linguistic redundancy. It is also hard to say why his 'playful clippings', as they are sometimes called, are not as valid as those which occur in genuine poetry. 'Oft' is surely as absurd as 'individ'?

---○---

'What's the diff? You're a right champ.'

Clifford Hanley *The Taste of Too Much*

---○---

Harry Graham's abbreviations are mostly examples of apocope, as rhetoricians would have it. This Greek word has been used in English since the 16th century and means 'a cutting off' of a letter or syllable at the end of a word. If the cut is made in the middle, as with his ev'ry and dev'lish, it is known as syncope, where again the basic meaning has to do with 'cutting off'. There is a word (natch!) which refers to the cutting of the first syllable: aphesis. It applies to the poet's **'twixt** and the **plane** of everyday conversation. Needless to say, these technical terms are words which one might use in an English examination paper (or **exam**), but which have little use elsewhere. One does not remark to a football spectator who is abusing the **ref** that he has just apocopated 'referee'.

---○---

Leah is simply a wiz at chemistry . . .

Sinclair Lewis *Ann Vickers*

---○---

Some abbreviations work in a specific context but would flounder outside it. In *The Groves of Academe* Mary McCarthy makes a character say: 'No one will

> ### NECROMANCY INNOCENT
>
> Indo-European nek — *'cause someone's death'*. Greek nekros *'death'*, Latin nocere *'harm'*. An innocent person is *'not harming'*.

> ### NEGRO
>
> We dislike both terms [Negroes\coloured people] intensely, but we consider them slightly less ruffling than 'nigger' or 'coon' or 'jig' or 'spade' or 'smoke' or any of the other labels by which white ditch-diggers indicate their superiority to Negro bishops. We expect it to take a few more decades before we're simply called 'Americans' or 'human beings.'
>
> **Sinclair Lewis** *Kingsblood Royal*

protect us **exes** in America unless we also become **antis**.' **Ex** would now normally refer to an ex-wife or husband. Here the reference is to being an ex-member of the Communist Party, or ex-believer in Communism. Sumner Locke Elliott, in *Edens Lost*, has: 'A refugee. One of the **reffos**, as they were called, although no one meant it to be a slight.' A speaker in Herman Melville's *Moby Dick* says: 'I'll give ye a **glim** in a jiffy.' The curious glim means a glimmer of light. A television review in *The Times* by Peter Barnard, September 1992, suddenly refers to **hoolis**. This might well confuse but for the earlier mention in the article of hooligans.

---○---

'Let's go to the good pull-up and get a cut off the joint with two veg.'

Joyce Cary *The Horse's Mouth*

---○---

It would be difficult to compile a full list of words that are regularly abbreviated. The examples given on page 125 have been noted during casual reading and merely hint at the range of such words in use. Thousands of similar abbreviations are no doubt used in professional or social environments where special vocabularies are shared and certain words are frequently used. In ordinary conversations, a great many speakers lean naturally towards a verbal shorthand that from time to time produces new words. Harry Graham would say that they are all part of **lang's** rich **pat.**

NEUROTIC

───────○───────

They are not long, the days of wine and roses.

Ernest Dowson
Vitae Summa Brevis Spem Nos Vetat Incohare Longam

───────○───────

Neurotic is a learned word that has slipped into everyday speech. Anyone who shows signs of being mildly obsessive or oversensitive about something is told that 'there's no need to be neurotic about it'. In the medical profession the word refers to **neurosis**, a mental illness caused by a disorder in the nervous system which leads to depression and irrational behaviour.

───────○───────

Days of Wine and Neuroses for Rome MPs

Article headline *The Times* 12.3.93

───────○───────

There are a number of similar medical words, mostly beginning with neuro-, which are based on Greek *neuron* 'nerve' and usually have something to do with **neurology**, **neuropathology** or **neurophysiology**. **Neuralgia**, which refers to an intense intermittent pain along the course of a nerve, is one of the more familiar members of this word-family. Likely to become better known in future is **neural** 'relating to a nerve',

NESTLEDRAFF

'This little doggie is a sweet thing. What do you call him?'
'Oh, that's Billjohn. He was the nestledraff.'
'The nestledraff?'
'The baby of the litter, you know. The Devon folk pronounce it "nissledraff". It is usually the most affectionate.'

Henry Williamson
The Dream of Fair Women

long in use as a medical term but recently borrowed by the computer boffins. Their so-called 'neural networks' or 'nets' will have an ever-increasing effect on our lives.

Learned words of the *neuro-* type soon get their come-uppance, as it were, if they drift into common parlance. In his novel *The Island*, for example, Peter Benchley records a discussion about a party of **neurosurgeons** who have hired a boat for a fishing trip. The crew-members are soon referring to the **nooros**, using an *ad hoc* abbreviation which is quite clear in context but would look very odd out of it.

NINCOMPOOP

───────○───────

Rawdon Crawley paid scarcely any attention to Dobbin, looking upon him as a good-natured nincompoop and underbred City man.

William Thackeray *Vanity Fair*

───────○───────

Samuel Johnson suggested that **nincompoop** might derive from Latin *non compos (mentis)* 'not of sound mind'. This is an attractive theory if one considers only the modern form of the word: unfortunately in all its earliest occurrences it was written, and no doubt pronounced, as **nickumpoop**. The change to nin- may have come about by association with **ninny**, a word which was in use by the 16th century with the meaning 'simpleton, fool'. The likely origin of 'ninny' is from **innocent**, either the personal name or the word.

How many Caesars and Pompeys, he would say, by mere inspiration of the names, have been rendered worthy of them! And how many, he would add, are there who might have done exceeding well in the world, had not their characters and spirits been totally depressed and Nicodemus'd into nothing.

Laurence Sterne Tristram Shandy

For the origin of nickum- it may be necessary to look to another name, **Nicodemus**. As Sterne makes clear in the above quotation, this had a poor reputation by the 18th century. It is possible that it had earlier led to **noddy**, yet another name for a fool. Noddy is certainly the nickname of Nicodemus Boffin, in Dickens's Our Mutual Friend, though there is no evidence that this was always the pet form of the name. The word 'noddy', together with its synonyms **noddypeak**, **noddypoll** and the significant **noddypoop** were in use by the 16th century. The original allusion, however, could have been to the involuntary nodding of the head which accompanies certain illnesses. Possible support for this view is to be found in The Two Gentlemen of Verona, where a dialogue runs:

Proteus: What said she?
Speed: (nodding) Ay.
Proteus: Nod-ay. Why, that's noddy.

Whether a pet form of Nicodemus does or does not account for noddy, there is still a strong case for it to be seen as responsible for the first element of 'nickumpoop'. **Poop** was in independent existence by the 17th century, when nickumpoop first appeared, with various slang meanings. One of these was to do with the buttocks, the poop being the backside of a person in the same way that it was the stern of a ship. Another meaning of the noun was 'fool', since the verb seems to have meant 'make a fool of'. Shakespeare has a reference in Pericles to a prostitute who 'quickly poop'd him; she made him roast meat for worms'. The Elizabethan audience would probably have understood by this that the woman concerned had made a fool of her client by infecting him with syphillis.

As Professor Weekley pointed out in his Etymological Dictionary, the explanation of 'nincompoop' as 'Nicodemus the poop' makes it a parallel construction to the 'Tom the fool' which became **tomfool**. There need have been no special reason for one name rather than another being attached to -poop, though Nicodemus, as we have seen, does not seem to have been in high standing.

NIRVANA

I looked at him, installed in his deep chair and already half-way back to Nirvana, putting pipe and beer alternately to lip.

Peter de Vries Comfort Me with Apples

Nirvana has a specific meaning in Buddhist theology, a much looser one in ordinary English usage. For the Buddhist it refers to the extinction of individual existence, the absorption into the supreme spirit. It describes a state where

Teaser: What is curious about the word 'notepaper'?

(Answer page 231)

??

human desires and passions are no longer troublesome and one is completely at peace. In English the word is used more generally of 'a blissful state', one which has not necessarily been reached by meditation.

Robert Louis Stevenson, in *An Inland Voyage*, gives what is perhaps the fullest comment on the word — which derives fron a Sanskrit word meaning 'blowing out, extinction' — from a Western point of view. He is talking about the state of mind into which he drifts while on a canoeing holiday, mechanically paddling for hours on end, though his comments could probably be applied more generally to the effect of any highly repetitive work:

'What philosophers call *me* and *not me*, *ego* and *non ego*, preoccupied me whether I would or no. There was less *me* and more *not me* than I was accustomed to expect. I looked on upon somebody else, who managed the paddling; I was aware of somebody else's feet against the stretcher; my own body seemed to have no more intimate relation to me than the canoe, or the river, or the river banks. Nor this alone: something inside my mind, a part of my brain, a province of my proper being, had thrown off allegiance and set up for itself, or perhaps for the somebody else who did the paddling. I had dwindled into quite a little thing in the corner of myself. I was isolated in my own skill.

'Thoughts presented themselves unbidden; they were not my thoughts, they were plainly someone else's; and I considered them like a part of the landscape. I take it, in short, that I was about as near *Nirvana* as would be convenient in practical life; and if this be so,

I make the Buddhists my sincere compliments; 'tis an agreeable state, not very consistent with mental brilliancy, not exactly profitable from a money point of view, but very calm, golden and incurious, and one that sets a man superior to alarms. It may be best figured by supposing yourself to get dead drunk, and yet keep sober to enjoy it. I have a notion that open-air labourers must spend a large portion of their days in this ecstatic stupor, which explains their composure and endurance.

'This frame of mind was the great exploit of our voyage, take it all in all. It was the farthest piece of travel accomplished. Indeed, it lies so far from beaten paths of language, that I despair of getting the reader into sympathy with the smiling, complacent idiocy of my condition; when ideas came and went like motes in a sunbeam.'

NONCE

———◯———

KING:
When in your motion you are hot and dry —
As make your bouts more violent to that end —
And that he calls for drink, I'll have preferr'd him
A chalice for the nonce; whereon but sipping,
If he by chance escape your venom'd stuck,
Our purpose may hold there.

William Shakespeare Hamlet

———◯———

The original editors of The Oxford English Dictionary introduced the concept of **nonce** words, words seemingly invented for or on a specific occasion. It is possible to record and comment on such words when they are used by writers, but they occur in conversation and may have a life span of milliseconds. The BBC disc jockey Jimmy Young, for example, interrupted his programme one day to allow a colleague to trail a Christmas **carolathon**, presumably a 'marathon carol concert'. Once the trail had ended Mr Young referred to his own programme by saying: 'Meanwhile, back here at the **Jimathon** . . .' In the immediate context this 'nonce word', or instant neologism, was both under-standable and apt, but it is doubtful whether the average listener to the programme, or for that matter, Jimmy Young himself, remembered the word an hour later.

When not describing such words, 'nonce' usually occurs in the phrase **for the nonce** 'for the specific occasion', as

---

IN BRIEF

Ad — advertisement

Auto — automobile

Baccy — tobacco

Beaut — beauty (especially in Australia, New Zealand)

Bicarb — bicarbonate (of soda)

Biccies — biscuits

Bike — bicycle

Biz — business (show-biz)

Bod — body (miserable looking bod)

Brill — brilliant

Bunk — bunkum

Cab — cabriolet

Canter — Canterbury

Cert — certainty (dead cert)

Champers — champagne

Chev/Chevvy — Chevrolet

Cig/ciggy — cigarette

Circs — circumstances (under the circs)

Con — confidence (man)

Condo — condominium (in USA only, a block of flats)

Cop — copper, 'one who cops or seizes someone'

Cos — because

Crim — criminal (Australia, New Zealand)

Demo — demonstration

Demob — demobilisation

Doc — doctor

Dorm — dormitory

Fab — fabulous

Fan — fanatical follower or supporter

Flu — influenza

Frank — frankfurter

Gely — gelignite

Gent — gentleman

Gran — grandmother

Gym — gymnasium

Hack — hackney

Hanky — handkerchief

Hi-fi — high fidelity

Hols — holidays

Incog — incognito

Intro — introduction

It — Italian vermouth (gin and It)

Jag — Jaguar

Jiff — jiffy (half a jiff)

Jog — jogtrot

Lab — laboratory

Lat — latrine

Limo — limousine (USA)

Lit — literature (as in lit crit)

Mac — mackintosh

Mag — magazine

Memo — memorandum

Merc — Mercedes

Mo — moment (be with you in a mo)

Mob — Latin *mobile vulgus* 'excitable crowd'

Mod — modern

Navvy — navigator (labourer)

Nympho — nymphomaniac

Para — paragraph

Patter — Paternoster

Pervie — pervert

Photo — photograph

Pleb — plebeian

Porn/porno — pornography, pornographical

Pram — perambulator

Preggers/preggo — pregnant

Prelim — preliminary

Prep — preparation

Pro — professional

Prof — professor

Prom — promenade (concert)

Prop — propeller

Pub — public house

Recap — recapitulate

Rev — revolution (revs of an engine)

Sarcy — sarcastic

Sec — second (just a sec)

Soccer — Association (football)

Spec — speculation (on spec)

Specs — spectacles

Soc Sci — Social Science

Talc — talcum powder

Taxi — taximeter

Thesp — Thespian

Tick — ticket (on tick)

Trig — trigonometry

Tux — tuxedo (USA)

Van — caravan

Vet — veterinary surgeon

Wig — periwig (corruption of peruke)

in the *Hamlet* quotation above. The word is clearly connected with both **once** and **one**.

NOSE-THRILL

'When Stalky blows out his nostrils like a horse he's on the warpath.'

Rudyard Kipling *Stalky and Co.*

A **nose-thrill** sounds as if it should be an exciting perfume or odour. The word is in fact a recorded form of **nostril**, one which is etymologically justified. The thrilling story of the word begins with the word **thorough**, an older form of **through**, used as if it meant 'a thoroughfare, a way through, a hole'. The diminutive ending -el was added to 'thorough' to give **thoroughel**, 'small hole'. 'Thoroughel' was then elided to **thirl**, and the combination 'nose-thirl' came into being. This eventually led to 'nostril' after further elision had occurred. The process known as metathesis had also caused the interchange of sounds within 'thirl' to give the -tril of 'nostril' and the independent word **thrill**.

The verb thrill originally meant 'pierce, penetrate, make a hole in'. Later it came to mean 'penetrate the mind emotionally', especially with joy, fear or pleasure. For some reason we have never applied it to anger, which is the one emotion which nostrils are able to reveal.

When Mr Pickwick is in a rage at Jingle, Dickens says: 'He could have been almost induced to wonder that the indignant fire which flashed from his eyes did not melt the glasses of his spectacles — so majestic was his wrath. His nostrils dilated, and his fists clenched involuntarily. . . .' *Down Among the Women*,

by Fay Weldon, has: '"I think babies are rather sweet," says Scarlet bravely, and watches for Wanda's nostrils to flare, as she has since she was a tiny child. Tormenting Wanda was never without its pleasures.'

NOVEL

Imagine dying from a fractured skull delivered by a hysterical parent swallow. A novel death. In a novel, who'd believe it? Novel. Odd word.

Margaret Laurence *The Diviners*

Not especially, is the comment that springs to mind when reading the comment of the distinguished Canadian writer Margaret Laurence, quoted above.

Shakespeare's Not One Word

CELIA:
Why cousin! why, Rosalind! Cupid have mercy! Not a word?

ROSALIND:
Not one to throw at a dog.

CELIA:
No, thy words are too precious to be cast away upon curs; throw some of them at me.

As You Like It

Miss Laurence uses **novel** in two distinct senses — 'strange, not previously known' and 'fictional story'. Both have straight-forward explanations.

Underpinning them is Latin *novus* 'new', which also led to words like novice (from *novicius* 'recently acquired slave'), **novelty**, **renovate** and **innovate**. In astronomy a **nova** is so called because it is a *nova stella* 'new star'. The Greek word which is a member of this family is *neos* 'new', leading to **neologism** 'new word' and many other words which begin with *neo-*.

In common with the ancient Athenians and the modern Americans, Magnus had a great liking for novelty, and would adopt a new fashion — in thought, in clothes or in behaviour — not only with enthusiasm but with such conviction that often it appeared to have been his own discovery.

Eric Linklater *Magnus Merriman*

It was the Italians who first applied *novella* to a tale, such as one of the short stories in Boccaccio's *The Decameron*. The word was then adopted as Spanish *novela*, French *nouvelle*. When the English began to use the word it was with the French pronunciation, which put the stress on the second syllable. They also contrasted the word with a **romance**, as Nathaniel Hawthorne was to explain very fully in the Preface to *The House of the Seven Gables*:

'When a writer calls his work a Romance, it need hardly be observed that he wishes to claim a certain latitude, both as to its fashion and material, which he would not have felt himself otherwise entitled to assume had he professed to be writing a Novel. The latter form of composition is presumed to aim at a very minute fidelity, not merely to the possible, but to the probable and ordinary course of man's experience. The former — while, as a work of art, it must rigidly subject itself to laws, and while it sins unpardonably so far as it may swerve aside from the truth of the human heart — has fairly a right to present that truth under circumstances, to a great extent, of the writer's own choosing or creation.'

A **novelist** in the 17th century was an innovator or a person who favoured novelty. The word then came to mean someone who passed on newsworthy stories. When a writer in 1728 used novelist in its modern sense, he felt obliged to add: 'I mean novel-writers.'

At that time novelists did not have a high social standing, but things have changed. In modern times writers who do not produce novels, but are perhaps the harmless drudges who toil away on books about words and names, are compelled to be apologetic when explaining their profession to strangers. They define themselves by what they do not do. The description 'writer of non-fiction' is usually interpreted by hearers as 'not a writer of fiction', and the disappointment is made clear. It should not be otherwise. In a world of often harsh reality, those who can produce imaginative works of quality should be highly prized.

FOR THE RAINBOW

OBSCENE

○

The great sugar figurines too of the Delta folklore — Yuna and Aziz the lovers interlocked, interpenetrated. They were splendidly obscene — surely the stupidest word in our language?

Lawrence Durrell Clea

○

Lawrence Durrell is presumably saying in the passage above that it is stupid to call depictions of the sexual act **obscene**. It is difficult to see in what way the word itself is 'stupid'. Shakespeare, one of the first to use it in English, gives it the same meaning as Latin *obscenus* 'disgusting, repulsive' in *Richard II* and other plays. As a new word to English, however, it was clearly capable of being misunderstood and misused by those who knew no Latin. In *Love's Labour's Lost* Costard the clown is made to misuse **obscenely** when he says: 'O' my troth, most sweet jests, most incony vulgar wit, / When it comes so smoothly off, so obscenely, as it were, so fit.'

In *A Midsummer Night's Dream* Bottom

ODDMEDODD

'I suppose I'm the most disreputable person present,' he said suddenly. 'A real oddmedodd!'
'What is an oddmedodd?'
'One of those creatures whom the winds roughen, on whom the rains fall. A scarecrow — whom men fix on a cross as a warning, but which even the thieving crows despise.'
'In Devon we call them mommets.'

Henry Williamson
The Dreams of fair women

has misunderstood the same word. He announces to his companions: 'There we will meet; and there we may rehearse most obscenely and courageously.'

Obscène began to be used in French in the mid-16th century, and no doubt came into English from that immediate source. The ultimate origin of the word is a mystery, though Professor Weekley tentatively linked it with Latin *caenum* 'mud'.

OBUMBRATED

○

This retort lighted up the countenances of his friends, which had begun to be a little obumbrated.

Tobias Smollett The Adventures of Peregrine Pickle

○

Obumbrated is a Johnsonian way of saying 'over-shadowed'. It is the Latin prefix *ob-* 'over' which momentarily causes the word to look strange. When it is stripped away, one is immediately in the familiar world of Latin *umbra* 'shade', a word used in English to describe the shadow projected on the earth by the moon during a solar eclipse. A **penumbra** is an 'almost shadow' or 'partly shaded region'.

In his *Glossary of Terms and Phrases*, the Rev. H. Percy Smith mentions that in ancient Rome *umbra* took on the slang meaning of 'gate-crasher, uninvited guest'. The word was also applied to any companions who were brought along by those who had been invited.

○

The rain it raineth on the just
And also on the unjust fella:
But chiefly on the just, because
The unjust steals the just's umbrella.

Lord Bowen
(quoted in Walter Sichel *Sands of Time*)

○

In English, the many other words in this group include the botanical **umbel** 'flower cluster' (Latin *umbella*, creating a 'little shadow'.) It was this that led, through Italian, to the later **umbrella**. A tree is **umbriferous** if it 'provides shade'. The natural pigment **umber** and its colour may also belong here, though a reference to the region of Umbria in central Italy is possible.

------○------

The whole quarter lay drowsing in the umbrageous violet of approaching nightfall.

Lawrence Durrell *Clea*

------○------

When we **take umbrage** at something we are overshadowed by the suspicion that we have been insulted. **Umbrageous** has the more literal meaning 'abounding in shade' but the word is mainly poetic. **Adumbrate** means to indicate something faintly, 'foreshadow' it, represent it in outline. To be **sombre** is to be *sub-umbra* 'under a shadow' and therefore 'gloomy'. Sombre, in fact, is the more straightforward way of saying obumbrated.

OCCUPY

------○------

DOLL TEARSHEET:
You a captain! you slave, for what? For tearing a poor whore's ruff in a bawdy house? He a captain! hang him, rogue! He lives upon mouldy stew'd prunes and dried cakes. A captain! God's light, these villains will make the word as odious as the word 'occupy'; which was an excellent good word before it was ill sorted.

William Shakespeare *Henry IV Part Two*

------○------

The comment above seems extraordinary, but there is negative evidence, as it were, to show that **occupy** was at one time as offensive as the four-letter word which means to copulate. Because it had come to have precisely that meaning, the word almost disappeared from 17th- and 18th-century literature. It had become indecent when men stopped speaking of being 'occupied with a woman' and spoke instead of 'occupying a woman'.

Ben Jonson, in 1640, had this to say on the subject in his *Timber: or Discoveries Made upon Men and Matter*: 'Many, out of their own obscene apprehensions, refuse proper and fit words; as *occupy*, *nature* and the like.' Both examples that he mentions are once again 'fit words'. Modern readers are aware of words like **gay**, which once had innocent meanings but have become ambiguous. They are less likely to notice the absence in former times of words that were once dangerous but are now completely acceptable.

As a footnote to this subject, someone has probably made a study of the words that Shakespeare, especially, does *not* use, though he might have been expected to do so. As an example, nowhere does he mention **tobacco**, or the kind of **pipe** that one **smokes**. In most of the plays any such references would have been anachronistic, but some depict Elizabethan life in which tobacco played its part.

OMELETTE

------○------

'Certain words, those ending with "ette" for example, gave him physical discomfort.'

Hesketh Pearson *The Life of Oscar Wilde*

------○------

We shall never know why the suffix *-ette* offended Oscar Wilde so much. Unattractive modern coinages in English,

ON

Jim was born in Gulgong, New South Wales. We used to say 'on' Gulgong — and old diggers still talked of being 'on th' Gulgong — though the gold-field there had been worked out for years. The expression 'on' came from being on the 'diggings' or gold field — the workings or the gold-field was all underneath, of course, so we lived (or starved) *on* them — not in nor at 'em.

Henry Lawson
Brighten's Sister-in-Law

SIR HARCOURT:
But etiquette! Max, remember etiquette!
MAX:
Damn etiquette! I have seen a man who thought it sacrilege to eat fish with a knife, that would not scruple to rise up and rob his brother of his birthright in a gambling-house.
SIR HARCOURT:
Pardon me, — etiquette is the pulse of society, by regulating which the body politic is retained in health.

Dion L. Boucicault London Assurance

---

such as luncheonette and leatherette, had not appeared in his time. He would have been familiar with words like cigarette, statuette, rosette, toilette, etiquette, roulette, palette, all borrowed from French and regularly formed in that language, but it is difficult to see how these could cause him 'physical discomfort'.

The *-ette* in such words is the modern French form of a suffix common to Romance languages. It occurs in Spanish as *-ito, -ita*, occasionally *-ete, eta*: in Italian it is *-etto, etta*. In early French it had the forms *-et* and *-ete*. One would expect such a suffix to be of Latin origin, but it is thought to be Celtic. Normally it acts as a diminutive, identifying something that is small of its kind. A **cigarette** is a small **cigar**, a **statuette** a small **statue**, a **rosette** a small **rose**, and so on. English-speakers recognise this meaning of the suffix and have no difficulty with words like **diskette, novelette** or the chemist's **pipette**. A slight knowledge of French explains **maisonette** as a small *maison* 'house', and suggests that the ubiquitous **cassette**, in its video or audio form, is a small *casse* 'case'. **Roulette** can similarly be linked with *rouelle*, then *roue* 'wheel'; **palette** is from *pale* 'blade, paddle'.

Some of the French -ette words are more puzzling and lead us into the fascinating worlds of comparative philology and semantic change. By **etiquette**, for instance, we now understand the conventional rules of polite social behaviour, or the unwritten rules which dictate how members of the same profession behave to one another. This is very much a secondary meaning of French *étiquette* 'label,' which also gave us the word **ticket**. The acute accent on the initial letter of the French word is a clue to the fact that its earlier form was *estiquet(te)*, derived from a verb *estiquer* 'to stick'. The original *estiquet* was presumably 'a small piece of paper stuck to something else' — what we might now call a 'sticker'. It seems to have been a notice showing the prescribed ceremonial order of events in a royal court, stuck to a wall, that was responsible for the modern meaning of 'etiquette'.

'Europe! Little vignettes about life there? How human nature is the same all over?'

Peter de Vries Comfort Me with Apples

The **vignettes** that Peter de Vries has in mind in the above quotation are 'short descriptive essays and character sketches'.

This is again a metaphorical extension of a word's original meaning, since vignette literally means 'little vine'. The word was first used to describe the trailing vine that formed a decorative border on the page of a book (see page 3). In either of its senses the word is relatively rare, especially in spoken English. Because of that, it has retained its Frenchified pronunciation of *vinyet*, avoiding the hard *g* sound. In this respect it has been more fortunate than the name Agnes, for example, though the latter sounds far more pleasant as *Anyes*.

Toilette appears to be a simple word, since it refers to a little *toile* 'cloth'. What is curious in this case is how the word has changed its meaning. The cloth concerned was placed on a table which then became a *table de toilette*. On this table were placed the hair-brushes and cosmetic items, *articles de toilette*, with which a woman could beautify herself. Making use of these led to the phrase 'make one's toilet(te)', which meant to go through the whole process of applying make-up, brushing one's hair and getting dressed. Later came a separate dressing room, equipped with a toilet table, washing facilities and a lavatory. It was a 'toilet room' where one literally went to 'powder one's nose', but it is easy to see how *toilet* became a euphemism for 'lavatory'. The word toilette has been retained in English for anything to do with toiletry, but even here the notion of a 'little cloth' has been left far behind.

While -*ette* words, in spite of occasional complications, are generally recognised as diminutives, words which use the earlier form of the French suffix often pass unnoticed. **Islet** is self-ex-

planatory, but the fact that a **bullet** is a small *boule* 'ball' (*boulet* in modern French is 'cannonball') is less obvious. Similarly, a **hatchet** is a small *hache* 'axe'; **pocket** represents *poket* or *poquet*, a small **poke**. Poke in its turn was once a standard word meaning a 'bag' or 'sack'; it is now restricted to the fossilized expression 'a pig in a poke'. **Gullet** is from *goulet*, a diminutive of *gueule* 'mouth' with links to *gorge* 'throat'; **fillet** originated as a *filet*, a small *fil* 'thread', used metaphorically of a narrow strip of meat. **Pullet** is clearly a *poulette*, a small *poule* 'hen', while a **turret** is a diminutive of **tour** 'tower'.

He remembered one fellow, during the 1928 boomlet, who had tried to get him interested in some new idea for burglar-proof bicycle pumps.

Stuart Brown Contango

More interesting in some ways is **corset**, from Old French *cors*, modern French *corps* 'body'. The French word serves as a reminder that originally our own word **corpse**, from Latin *corpus*, also meant 'body', not 'dead body'. The King James Bible, at 2 Kings 19.35, therefore talks of 'dead corpses'. In the Revised Standard Version the translators have amended this to 'dead bodies'.

Not all words with suffix -*et*(*te*) have come into English from French. **Sonnet**, for example, is from Italian *sonetto*, a diminutive of *suono* 'sound'. Similarly, **gazette** has an Italian rather than French origin. The *Gazeta della Novita* was a Venetian newspaper which could be bought for a *gazeta*, a 'small coin'. The coin name is of obscure origin, but may link with a Greek word meaning 'treasure'. As for the small frigate known as a **corvette**, it is said to derive from Dutch *korf*, a 'kind of ship'.

At an early stage -*et* (later -*ette*), was used as a suffix to form feminine forms

OFFER   SUFFER

Latin ferre 'carry'. Offer is from ob-ferre 'bring before one'; suffer is from sub-ferre 'bear (up) under'.

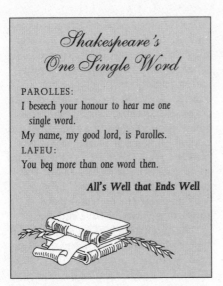

Shakespeare's One Single Word

PAROLLES:
I beseech your honour to hear me one
   single word.
My name, my good lord, is Parolles.
LAFEU:
You beg more than one word then.

All's Well that Ends Well

of names — Antoinette, Bernadette, Claudette, Georgette, Juliet, Paulette, and the like. Such a name might then become a word, as with **marionette**, a double diminutive of Maria, where the original representation was of the Virgin Mary. The 'little' meaning is still present in these examples, perhaps in an affectionate rather than a derogatory way. In any case, the association of smallness with femininity allowed -ette to become a suffix that converted words as well as names into their feminine forms.

Dorothy Minto was an adorable 'soubrette', then a label for the cheeky daughter, perhaps coquettish, certainly comical.

Ivor Brown *A Charm of Names*

An early example of such a word is **brunette**. This was applied in the 18th century to a girl or woman who was a 'nut-brown maid' either because she had a dark complexion or brown hair. The word is a diminutive of French *brun* 'brown'. Later in the same century, **coquette** appeared. It seems illogical

that this should refer to a woman since it is based on *coq* 'cockerel', and indeed the earliest form of the word was *coquet*. This was used to describe a man who was thought to display the amorous nature and strutting gait of a cock. The feminine word was formed later and applied to an amorous woman, a flirt. Rather similar is **soubrette**, the 'pert maidservant' of period comedy or the actress who plays such parts. The word is a feminine form of Provençal *soubret* 'one who causes problems', usually by doing something reluctantly.

Pray Sir,' said Adams, 'What is a Coquette? I have met with the word in French authors, but never could assign any idea to it. I believe it is the same with une Sotte, Anglice a Fool.' 'Sir,' answer'd the gentleman, 'perhaps you are not much mistaken: but as it is a particular kind of folly, I will endeavour to describe it. Its characteristic is affectation, and this led and governed by whim only. Its life is one constant lie; and the only rule by which you can form any judgement of them is, that they are never what they seem. If it was possible for a Coquette to love (as it is not, for if ever it attains this passion, the Coquette ceases instantly) it would wear the face of indifference, if not of hatred, to the beloved object; you may therefore be assured, when they endeavour to persuade you of their liking, that they are indifferent to you at least.

And indeed this was the case of my Sapphira, who no sooner saw me in the number of her admirers, than she gave me what is commonly called encouragement; she would often look at me, and, when she perceived me meet her eyes, would instantly take them off, discovering at the same time as much surprise and emotion as possible. These arts failed not of the success she intended. To detain you no longer, after I had gone through a sufficient course of gallantry, as I thought, and was thoroughly convinced I had raised a violent passion in my mistress, I sought an opportunity of coming to an éclaircissement with her. I will not describe all the particulars of this interview; let it suffice, that when she could no longer pretend not to see my drift, she first affected a violent surprise, and immediately after as violent a passion: she wondered what I had seen in her conduct, which could induce me to affront her in this manner: and breaking from me the first moment she could, told me, I had no other way to escape the consequence of resentment than by never seeing, or at least speaking to her more.

Henry Fielding *Joseph Andrews*

---○---

Suffragette was coined in the early years of the 20th century for a woman who demanded suffrage, the right to vote. The word was meant to be a put-down, probably having been suggested by French *midinette*. It was the girls who poured on to the Parisian streets from their shops or offices at midi 'midday' who were derisively known as *midinettes*. Other words of this type may also have been jokingly formed, though the cinema **usherette** and the American drum **majorette** seem to have established themselves permanently.

By no means all such coinages survived. In his *Words and Ways of American English*, Thomas Pyles records the short-lived **farmerette**, **guidette** and **tusslerette**, the last-named being a female wrestler. Pyles also points out that a group of chorus girls were known as The *Rockettes*. In Britain the girls who worked in ammunition factories during World War One were briefly known as **munitionettes**.

---○---

. . . the tea parlours that were by no means luncheonettes.

John Updike *Still Life*

---○---

There is a further, minor use of the suffix -*ette* where it indicates an imitation material. **Leatherette** is artificial leather; **flannelette** is a napped cotton fabric which tries to pass itself off as flannel. In spite of such occasional variants, the familiarity of -*ette* in its meaning of 'small' mostly leads to neologisms where it has this meaning. The American **luncheonette** is a place where light lunches are sold to be eaten on the premises. **Dinette** usually refers to a small space attached to a kitchen where people eat. Garson Kanin, in his novel *Moviola*, says: 'They had lived originally in a dinette apartment.' In the same book he talks of 'a tiny kitchenette', which appears to be tautologous — 'a tiny kitchen' would have sufficed.

One of the most familiar words of this type came into being when self-operated laundries appeared. They were dubbed **launderettes** by the company that originally operated them, a term which it tried to protect as a trademark. Competitors were forced to find alternative descriptions, and high streets soon displayed names like *Clean-a-Matic*, *Kwikwash* and *Launderwite*. Faced with these, Oscar Wilde might well have had second thoughts about words ending in -*ette*, acknowledging that launderette was a reasonable word. Ordinary people certainly thought so. They talked of 'going to the launderette', no matter what name appeared on the shop-front.

---○---

He was finding the most elemental human functions difficult to perform in the swaying, lurching blackness of his Pullman roomette. Air conditioning made the roomette almost cold . . .

Denison Hatch *The Stork*

---○---

For a word-buff, Wilde's negative reaction to -*ette* words is especially difficult to understand because many of them are so interesting. In the short story quoted above, for example, John Updike also uses the word **silhouette**. This is an eponym, derived from the name of Etienne de Silhouette (1708–67), French Minister of Finance for a few months in

VARIATIONS ON A THEME — NAMES FOR LAUNDERETTES

Clothesline	Launderland	Spring Clean
Coin-a-Matic	Launderlux	Suds-a-Mat
Coin Laundry	Laundermat	Tub-o-Suds
Coin-op Laundry	Launderneat	Washateria
Do-ur-own Laundry	Launderteria	Wash-a-way
EZ Wash	Laundertorium	Wash-n-dry
Hand Laundry	Laundrateria	Wash-o-mat
Helpy Selfy Laundry	Laundricoin	Wishee-Washee
Launderbrite	Laundrometer	Wonder Wash
Laundercentre	Laun-Dry	Washing Well
Launderelle	Lorna Drette	Washeteria
Launder-it	Posh Wash	

1759. He introduced reforms which were extremely unpopular and, as Cecil Hunt expresses it in his *Dictionary of Word Makers*, 'his name became a byword for anything plain and cheap. It was *à la Silhouette*'.

Various tales are told to account for the use of silhouette to mean a shadow-picture. Most commentators say that it was an insulting comment on Silhouette himself, who was no more than a fleeting shadow on the public scene, or was a man of no substance. Others have said that he practised the art of shadowgraphy and had a collection of examples at his château, but there seems to be no evidence to support this.

As for the name Silhouette, which is derived from a place name, the *-ette* is almost certainly a corrupt spelling which has nothing to do with smallness. There are many place names in France which begin with Si-, Ci- or Sci-, usually derived from Roman personal names, but the original meaning of Silhouette is unclear.

Finally, there is the most curious of all the words of this type — **omelette** (often **omelet** in the US). Think for a moment of its possible origin. Could it have been a small (or feminine) *omel*, whatever that might be? Was there a famous chef called Omelette who invented the dish? The answer is no in both cases, and it is necessary instead to launch into philological technicalities to arrive at the truth. The story of the word goes like this: whoever first made an omelette wanted to comment on its thin, flat shape. There was a word in Old French *lamelle*, derived from Latin *lamella*, itself a diminutive of *lamina* 'thin plate'. The original Latin word has given us **laminate**, **lamination**, etc.

---○---

'Altogether a sceptic.'
'Lor!' said Kipps, *'not a Natheist!'*

H.G. Wells *Kipps*

---○---

With the French definite article added, *lamelle* became *la lamelle*. This was then misinterpreted by later generations as *l'alamelle*, as if the noun was *alamelle*. The same process (metanalysis — 'wrong division') produced **ammunition** from *la munition*; in English it gave a **newt** from an **ewt**, a **nickname** from an **ekename**. (In reverse this process led to an **orange**, an **apron** from the earlier a *norange*, a *napron*.) The next stage in French brought the word *alamette* into being as a doublet

Teaser: In how many different ways can 'ough' be pronounced in English words?

(Answer page 231) **??**

of *alamelle*, *-ette* and *-elle* having precisely the same meaning.

Alamette subsequently proved to be the more popular form, and another common linguistic process known as metathesis then came into play. Metathesis describes the interchange of sounds or letters within a word, as when Old English *brid* became **bird**. By this process *alamette* became *amalette*. The change to initial *o-* was then due either to the influence of French *oeuf* **egg**, or to another dialectal French derivative of Latin *ovum*. The *o-* was, as it were, the final delicate ingredient in the recipe for the philologist's omelette.

ONOMANCY

Onomancy refers to divination by means of personal names. The belief that a name contains clues as to the character and future of the person that bears it is an ancient one. A Roman saying was *nomen est omen* 'a name is an omen', and generals would try to see that their men went into battle with soldiers named Victor or Vincent in the front ranks. This is taking note of obvious meaning: more complex ways of interpreting names involve the use of anagrams or alphabet mysticism, where each letter is thought to have a significance. Numerology can also be used, transposing each letter into a number and drawing conclusions from their total.

Onomancy is a curious word because its form suggests 'divination by donkeys' rather than 'divination by names'. In its full form the word should be **onomatomancy**, based on Greek *onoma* 'name'. The elided version relates it to a word like **onology** 'foolish talking, braying' from Greek *onos* 'ass'.

While few people today consciously practise onomancy, it could be argued that a belief in name magic of one kind or another is still widespread. Babies are often named after someone who is admired in the belief that the qualities of that person will thus be transferred to the child. Parents also talk about giving a 'strong' name to a boy or a 'pretty' name to a girl, and once again there is an underlying assumption that the name itself will influence the name-bearer. As a 'science' of divination, however, onomancy is relatively little known, though books on numerology are still published. Those wishing to put alphabet mysticism to the test at party-game level could do so by consulting *The Guinness Book of Names*. For most people, however, divination of the future means astrology, crystal-gazing, palmistry and the use of playing cards or tea leaves.

Not from the stars do I my judgement pluck,
And yet methinks I have astronomy;
But not to tell of good or evil luck
Of plagues, of dearths, or seasons' quality;
Nor can I fortune to brief minutes tell,
Pointing to each his thunder, rain and wind,
Or say with princes if it shall go well
By oft predict that I in heaven find;
But from thine eyes my knowledge I derive,
And, constant stars, in them I read such art
As truth and beauty shall together strive,
If from thy self to store thou wouldst convert.
Or else of thee this I prognosticate:
Thy end is truth's and beauty's doom and date.

William Shakespeare Sonnet 14

Shakespeare refers to what we now call **astrology** — for him it is always astronomy — in several of his plays. In *Sonnet* 14 his statement that he 'has astronomy' seems to mean that he has studied the subject in some depth. **Astromancy**, incidentally, would have been a better word for 'astrology', and was sometimes used in the past.

Sideromancy also occurs with the same meaning, though this can also refer to divination by the use of straws burnt with red hot irons.

Necromancy 'communicating with the dead in order to foretell the future' is often mentioned in 17th-century

WORDS REFERRING TO DIVINATION BY VARIOUS MEANS

Aeromancy — air or winds; forecasting by weather
Alectoromancy/alectryomancy — cock and grains of corn
Aleuromancy — meal or flour
Alphitomancy — barley
Ambulomancy — walking
Anthracomancy — burning coals
Arithmancy — numbers
Armomancy — shoulders of animals
Astragalomancy — dice
Astromancy — stars
Austromancy — winds
Axinomancy — axe head
Belomancy — arrows
Bibliomancy — opening a book (e.g. Bible) randomly
Botanomancy — plants
Capnomancy — smoke
Cartomancy — playing cards
Catoptromancy — mirrors
Cephalomancy — the head
Ceraunomancy — thunder
Ceromancy — melted wax in water
Cheiromancy/chiromancy — palmistry
Cleidomancy — keys
Coscinomancy — sieve on end of shears
Crystallomancy — crystal
Cubomancy — dice
Dactyliomancy — finger ring
Empyromancy — burning of objects of sacrificial fire
Enoptromancy — mirror
Gastromancy — sounds of the stomach
Geomancy — handful of earth thrown on to ground
Graptomancy — handwriting
Gyromancy — walking in a circle until dizzy
Haematomancy — blood
Halomancy — salt
Hieromancy — sacrificial remains
Hippomancy — horses and neighing
Hydromancy — water

Ichnomancy — footprints
Lampadomancy — flame of a torch
Lecanomancy — water in a basin
Lithomancy — stones
Logomancy — words
Lychnomancy — lamps
Margaritomancy — pearls
Meteoromancy — meteors
Metopomancy — facial features
Molybdomancy — molten lead
Myomancy — mice
Necromancy — communication with the dead
Nomancy — letters of words
Oenomancy — wine
Omphalomancy — knots in umbilical cord
Oneiromancy — dreams
Onychomancy — fingernails
Oomancy — eggs
Ophiomancy — snakes
Ornithomancy — flight of birds
Osteomancy — bones
Pedimancy — feet
Pegomancy — fountains of water
Pessomancy — pebbles
Phyllomancy — leaves
Pyromancy — fire
Rhabdomancy — rods (dowsing)
Rhapsodomancy — verses
Scatomancy — excrement
Schematomancy — personal appearance
Scyphomancy — cup
Selenomancy — moon
Spodomancy — ashes of a fire
Stichomancy — lines of poetry
Stignomancy — carving on a tree
Sycomancy — figs or fig leaves
Tephromancy — ashes of a sacrifice
Theriomancy — movements of wild animals
Tyromancy — coagulating cheese
Xylomancy — twigs, rods, wood
Zoomancy — animals

literature. It still has its adherents among those who attend seances, as perhaps do many of the other ways of prediction listed on page 137. The words all have the suffix -mancy, ultimately from Greek mantis 'prophet, diviner'. The latter word occurs again in the name of the insect which appears to be at its devotions, the **praying mantis**.

These words demonstrate as a group how desperate humans have always been to gain information about the future. We are rather more scientific about the matter today with our weather and business forecasts, but in other respects nothing has changed. The huge number of people who consult their 'stars' in the daily newspapers and would not be averse to having their palms read by a **chiromancer** are no nearer learning the truth about what will happen than were the ancient Greeks. The gamblers using their latest systems must still rely on chance. Almost the only thing certain about the future is that man will continue to be obsessed with it.

OUT

And one or two sad, separate wives, without
A fruit to bloom upon their withering bough,
Begg'd to bring up the little girl, and 'out',
For that's the phrase that settles all things now,
Meaning a virgin's first blush at a rout,
And all her points as thoroughbred to show:
And I assure you, that like virgin honey
Tastes their first season (mostly if they have money).

Lord Byron Don Juan

ORGAN

She touched his organ, and from that bright epoch, even it, the old companion of his happiest hours, incapable as he had thought of elevation, began a new and deified existence.

Charles Dickens Martin Chuzzlewit

Fritz Spiegl draws attention in *The Joy of Words* to the passage quoted above, remarking that 'surely Dickens cannot have been so innocent' as to be unaware of its potentially indecent interpretation. All one can reply to that is 'of course he could have been that innocent'. When Dickens wrote those words in 1843, professional biologists had only recently begun to refer to **sexual organs**. There is no reason to think that the phrase was in general use. As for **organ** itself, no record of it as a euphemism or slang term for penis exists until well into the 20th century.

As it happens, organ was much used in Dickens's time as a term in phrenology, the fashionable 'mental science' of the day. For the phrenologists, or craniologists as they were sometimes dubbed from their habit of feeling people's heads, an individual's mental powers consisted of separate faculties, each of which had its organ and location in the brain. The size of each organ was thought to indicate how well the faculty concerned was developed. Thomas Hood laughed at the subject in his *Craniology*, which begins:

'Tis strange how like a very dunce,
Man — with his bumps upon his sconce
Has lived so long, and yet no knowledge he
Has had till lately, of Phrenology —
A science that by simple dint of

Head-combing, he should find a hint
   of
When scratching o'er those little
   poll-hills,
The faculties throw up like mole-
   hills.

Dickens several times in his novels refers to phrenology, invariably in a jokey way. Earlier in *Martin Chuzzlewit*, for instance, Mr Pecksniff's daughters examine him after a door has blown shut in his face and knocked him down. Dickens says that his wounds 'were not very serious in their nature, being limited to what the eldest Miss Pecksniff called "the knobbly parts" of her parent's anatomy, such as his knees and elbows, and to the development of an entirely new organ, unknown to phrenologists, on the back of his head'. In other words, he had an extra bump there.

He now had an opportunity of observing that as to the phrenological formation of the backs of their heads, the Professing Philanthropists were uncommonly like the Pugilists. In the development of all those organs which constitute, or attend, a propensity to 'pitch into' your fellow-creatures, the Philanthropists were remarkably favoured.

Charles Dickens The Mystery of Edwin Drood

Dickens might play with the word organ, then, in its phrenological sense, but when he wrote about Mary Graham and Tom Pinch he fell into a trap which no author can avoid. It was impossible for Dickens to know what new, or secondary, meaning a word might have in a

OUTRIGHT

When I was a boy, our old farm workers had an unusual name for people who come round the villages from the town shops, stores and warehouses taking orders for goods – they called them 'Outrights'. Perhaps this was a variation on the word 'Out-rider', but anyway they were travellers or 'representatives' as we would call them today.

Fred Archer Under the Parish Lantern

hundred years' time. His character, Tom Pinch, loves playing the organ, as we learn early in the novel when he visits his friend, assistant to the cathedral organist. In the later scene with Mary, with whom Tom has fallen deeply in love, she lays her hand on Tom's harpsichord because she is standing beside him, singing while he plays.

Dickens says that Tom 'sat like one entranced', and anyone reading the passage cannot help feeling that the author himself was rather carried away with the scene he was creating. It is absurd to suggest that at such a moment Dickens would deliberately have written a sentence with a ribald undertone, even if organ at the time had had the meaning we can now read into it. If ever there was an innocent author in that respect, it was Charles Dickens.

FOR
RELIEF

PALTER-GHOST

<hr>

I do not imagine that you are familiar with the word 'palter-ghost', which is a private word of my own.

Jane Duncan *My Friends the Miss Boyds*

<hr>

Jane Duncan's **palter-ghost** is clearly based on **poltergeist** 'hobgoblin', a word we have taken into English from German. The *Polter* in the German original refers to 'noise, uproar', so a poltergeist is a spirit that announces its presence by making a great deal of noise.

Jane Duncan explains her version of the word as the coincidental occurrence of a word or topic once it has been raised. An expression which had no special significance suddenly seems to appear on all sides. As an example she mentions a doctor telling a patient one morning that she has 'housemaid's knee'. An article on that complaint will appear by magic in the weekly magazine that the patient reads. It will be the subject of a conversation overheard on the bus. When the radio or television is switched on, housemaid's knee will be the topic of discussion. All that has happened is that the patient's perception has been sharpened in a particular area. Something that would previously have blended into the background is now in focus. When such things happen, however, it seems to the person concerned like a remarkable series of coincidences.

<hr>

MACBETH:

*And be these juggling fiends no more believ'd
That palter with us in a double sense,
That keep the word of promise to our ear,
And break it to our hope!*

William Shakespeare *Macbeth*

<hr>

The palter of Jane Duncan's word is a verb which is now little used. Originally it meant to 'talk indistinctly'; later senses were to 'equivocate' and to 'haggle'. With her interesting 'palter-ghost', Jane Duncan seems to have imagined a spirit that delights in verbal trickery, haunting its victims with a word or phrase.

<hr>

PANTOMIME

<hr>

Mr Jackson smiled, and applying his left thumb to the tip of his nose, worked a visionary coffee-mill with his right hand, thereby performing a very graceful piece of pantomime (then much in vogue, but now, unhappily, almost obsolete) which was familiarly denominated 'taking a grinder'.

Charles Dickens *The Pickwick Papers*

<hr>

Dickens uses **pantomime** in its correct sense of 'all mime' in the passage quoted above. He is describing what was at one time a Cockney's reply to anyone who doubted his good faith. 'Pantomime' in its very English, Christmas entertainment sense has come a long way from its Italian original, *pantomima*. That in its turn was preceded by the **mime** (Greek *mimos*, Latin *mimus*) of the ancients, simple farce in which jesters **mimicked** different types of people. This kind of mime was always characterised by ludicrous exaggeration: the word now mainly makes us think of its wordless character.

As Dickens hints, we are likely to resort to mime occasionally to support the words we use. Some of our deliberate body language is conventionally polite, as when a man stands to acknowledge a woman's entrance, stands aside to let her pass in front of him, opens a door for her, and so on. When men wore hats, the raising of the hat was another polite mimic gesture.

'There was speech in their dumbness, language in their very gesture.'

William Shakespeare *The Winter's Tale*

One of the most frequent gestures used during a normal conversation is a nod or shake of the head. We know exactly what Dickens means when he describes, in *The Pickwick Papers*, 'a shake of the head which expressed a more decided negative than the most copious language could have conveyed'. The significance of the head-shake, however, is culture-bound, a fact which is soon brought home to us if we travel to a country like Sri Lanka where it happens to indicate agreement rather than disagreement.

Travelling can also make us aware that simple mime constitutes an effective international language. Most of the world's waiters, for instance, seem to understand that a customer who catches their eye and pretends to scribble something on a pad would like to be presented with the bill. Thomas Hood long ago gave further examples, inevitably in verse form, of such wordless communication. Part of his poem 'French and English' describes how he made up for his lack of French:

Signs I had to make
For every little notion,
Limbs all going like
A telegraph in motion,
For wine I reel'd about,
To show my meaning fully,
And made a pair of horns,
To ask for 'beef and bully'.

'Moo!' I cried for milk;
I got my sweet things snugger,
When I kissed Jeanette,
'Twas understood for sugar.
If I wanted bread,
My jaws I set a-going,
And asked for new-laid eggs,
By clapping hands and crowing!

If I wish'd a ride,
I'll tell you how I got it;
On my stick astride
I made believe to trot it.

'If you preach long and solemn, mister, I'll put me tongue out.'

Mary Webb *Gone To Earth*

Thomas Hood's antics may seem extreme, but most of us are called upon at times to interpret some kind of primitive mime. As motorists we interpret the conventional signals of a policeman on traffic duty, or perhaps respond to the thumb that is waved by a hitch-hiker. Some motorists also use mime to communicate personal messages to other drivers. The tapping of a forehead with a finger perhaps says: 'You drive like a madman.' Two fingers raised in a V sign return an answer along the lines of: 'Your stupid opinion is of no interest to me,' or a shaken fist says: 'Get out of your car and say that to my face and I'll knock your head off.'

The childish nature of such insulting gestures serves as a reminder that the language of mime begins in the playground. Children soon learn that there are situations where words can be supported by gestures. When necessary they stick their tongues out at one another, or put their thumbs on their noses and twiddle their fingers. Some express contempt by holding their noses and pulling an imaginary lavatory chain. Adults sometimes playfully recall their childhood by using such gestures, or they may allude to them. 'Wasn't the making of the guy a thumb-to-nose gesture on Mad's part?' asks a character in Daphne du Maurier's *Rule Britannia*.

PATRIOTISM

—○—

*Watching the newsreels had become every expatri-
ate Briton's patriotic duty.*

J.G. Ballard Empire of the Sun

—○—

The sentence quoted above is unusual.
Novelists do not often bring into such
close context words which are so closely
linked etymologically. Both **expatriate**
and **patriotic** are ultimately connected
with 'father', through Greek *patêr*, Latin
pater. The Latin word led directly to
paternal, **paternity** and the like. *Pater*
had developed in Latin to *patria* 'fatherland', which in turn led to the idea of
being banished from one's own country, *ex-patriare*. Modern expatriates, of
course, are usually living abroad by
choice. Latin *re-patriare* gave us **repatriate**
'return to one's own country'. The latter
word also lies behind **repair**, in a
sentence like: 'He repaired to the pub.'

Patriot, patriotic, etc., are from the
Greek word rather than the Latin, but are
clearly based on the same notion of
fatherland. **Patriotism** did not impress
Dr Johnson, who defined it as the 'last
refuge of a scoundrel'.

—○—

*She was tired of the whole theological vocabulary
of suffrage: 'economic independence of women',
'equal rights', 'equal pay for equal work', 'matri-
archy'. Like such senile words as 'idealism',
'virtue', 'patriotism', they had ceased to mean
anything.*

Sinclair Lewis Ann Vickers

—○—

English has a corresponding group of
words which derive from Greek *mêtêr*,
Latin *mater* 'mother'. **Maternity**, **mater-
nal**, **matron** and the like are from Latin;

PALIMPSEST

'Palimpsest,' says one of them to
Miss Russell, 'could you give us
the meaning?'
Great scott! My heart sank for her,
what a word! How could anyone
possibly? Miss Russell rolling her
head with the blow, can she, for
64 dollars? 'Palimpsest, yes, let us
see, it means a surface on which
things have been
written over other things.'
Knowledge! The blackboard with
its thousand messages, my heart
inscribed over and over with the
names of girls: palimpsests!

Barry Oakley
A Salute to the Great McCarthy

metropolis, **metropolitan** are from
Greek. Less obvious Latin derivatives
include **matrix**, **matriculate** and possibly **madrigal**. For the early Romans a
matrix was a 'female animal used for
breeding'. In later Latin the word came
to mean 'womb', which allowed the
more general sense of 'place or medium
in which something is developed'. The
English meaning of 'mould in which
something is cast or shaped' was a
natural development.

It is less easy to explain how *matricula*
in Latin, a diminutive of *matrix*, came to
mean a 'register of persons belonging to
a particular order or society'. The most
reasonable guess supposes that the names
were written on a parchment made of
uterine membrane. Many students would
explain **matriculation** as 'passing a
university entrance examination', but in
theory their names have been entered on
the university's register.

As for the origin of **madrigal**, this is
much disputed. *The Oxford English Dictionary* appears to favour a derivation from

an Italian word meaning 'herd'. The connection is then explained in terms of a madrigal once being a 'pastoral song'. Professor Weekley linked madrigal and *mater* and suggested that it was a song in the 'mother tongue'. In *Nouveau Dictionnaire Etymologique du Français*, Jacqueline Picoche says that Italian *madrigale* represents Latin *matricale* 'associated with the womb', and that the word described a 'primitive' piece of music because it was sung without accompaniment.

───────○───────

A royal husband in all save the ring —
Which, being the damn'dest part of matrimony,
Seem'd taking out the sting to leave the honey.

Lord Byron Don Juan

───────○───────

Some of these 'father' and 'mother' words, like **paternity** and maternity, form logical pairs, but **patrimony** and **matrimony** do not. Patrimony is property inherited from one's father: matrimony should therefore refer to property inherited from one's mother. Instead it describes the rite of **marriage**, which itself was regarded by the Romans as 'legalised motherhood'.

PEASANT

───────○───────

'But, madam, the peasants are rapacious. . . .'
To that Sophie would not listen. Like many people there were some words about which she was sentimental; one of these was 'peasant'. 'Peasants are simple and honest and kindly and quiet,' she said. 'They don't want what they don't possess. They have the wisdom to stay simple. They don't want to change. Primitive and beautiful. How picturesque they are!' said Sophie admiringly.
'And dirty,' said Teresa. It was true. They were very dirty.

Rumer Godden Kingfishers Catch Fire

───────○───────

Peasant may not be a very curious word, but Rumer Godden makes it an interesting one in the above quotation. She is speaking about the peasants in Kashmir, but illustrates more importantly the way a word can have a personal meaning which no dictionary is able to record. The novel, as it happens, shows in more general terms the problems that can be caused by such subjective interpretations.

There can be few people who do not fall into this trap where some words are concerned, allowing sentimentality or subjectivity to colour meaning. The difficulty is to know which items in one's own vocabulary are tinged in this way. Subjective interpretation is acceptable if we are aware of it and can be objective when necessary. As part of our own thinking it probably does little harm.

───────○───────

'Thought language can be entirely different from the language spoken aloud between two people — the words can have different meanings, different connotations, significances entirely personal to the mind that is using them.'

Jane Duncan My Friends the Miss Boyds

───────○───────

It is when two people try to use their different 'thought languages', as Jane Duncan calls them, for normal communication that problems arise. A man and a woman, perhaps, or an adult and child, believe that they have understood one another and later find to their frustration that they have not. Some of the key words used between them meant different things to each. Rumer Godden, in the extract from Kingfishers Catch Fire, demonstrates in passing a technique for dealing with such a situation. When there is any chance of a misunderstanding it is necessary to define one's terms.

Lewis Carroll left it to Humpty Dumpty to make the point in Through the Looking-

Glass. In a well-known exchange Humpty says to Alice: 'There's glory for you!' 'I don't know what you mean by "glory",' Alice tells him. The conversation continues: 'I meant, "there's a nice knock-down argument for you"!' 'But "glory" doesn't mean "a nice knock-down argument",' Alice objected. 'When I use a word,' Humpty Dumpty said in rather a scornful tone, 'it means just what I choose it to mean, — neither more nor less.' Carroll exaggerated for humorous effect but, as he well knew, the Humpty Dumpty syndrome that he described was more than an imaginative squib. Amongst politicians, for example, it is found in epidemic proportions.

PECULIAR

———————◯———————

Mr Weller's knowledge of London was extensive and peculiar.

Charles Dickens The Pickwick Papers

———————◯———————

The etymology of **peculiar** is unexpected, some might even say peculiar. The story begins with Latin *pecu*, which began by meaning 'cattle', then came to mean 'riches, money'. From this came *peculium*, which had the original meaning 'property allowed by a father to his son or by a master to a slave as his own private property'. Later the idea of private property seems to have led to the meaning 'standing apart from others' and, eventually, to the modern idea of a peculiarity, something 'strange, eccentric'.

Pecu also led to *pecunia* 'money' and a number of related words, including **pecuniary** 'to do with money', **impecunious** 'having little or no money', **peculate** 'embezzle money', originally to steal someone's *peculium*.

The Jews were at one time known as the **Peculiar People**. This was not an insult, merely a use of peculiar in its earlier sense. Deuteronomy 14.2 in the Authorised Version reads: 'The Lord hath chosen thee to be a peculiar people unto himself, above all the nations that are upon the earth.' The Revised Standard Version has: 'The Lord has chosen you to be a people for his own possess-

ion, out of all the peoples that are on the face of the earth.'

PERIOD

───────○───────

'You're really a beautiful cheerleader. But then you're beautiful period.'

John Updike *A Sense of Shelter*

───────○───────

Period is used in America far more than in Britain to mean the 'full stop', the punctuation mark that brings a sentence to a close. That meaning can then be extended in an interesting way, as in the sentence quoted above. It becomes a shorthand way of saying: 'That's an end to it, nothing else needs to be said, discussion over.' In this sense, period is likely to be a loan-translation, caused by someone thinking in Italian, say, and directly translating a native idiom into English.

───────○───────

He went to a hospital for observation but they found nothing worse than what they called a sensitive colon, which is I suppose an apt enough ailment for a man as meticulous about punctuation as he was.

Peter de Vries *Comfort Me with Apples*

───────○───────

Punctuation in more general terms is not a popular topic. The word itself is an artificial construction which describes an artificial practice. The rules and conventions governing the use of punctuation marks are meant to help someone who is silently reading in his understanding of written language. They are not, as is commonly said, meant to indicate where somebody reading that language aloud should pause for breath.

Readers are best able to make decisions about such matters for themselves. Readers, in fact, should hardly be aware of punctuation: it is the writer who must think about it.

───────○───────

May I beg of you to pay particular attention to the brackets which enclose certain paragraphs? I want my 'asides', you see, to whisper loud to you.

Oliver Wendell Holmes
The Autocrat of the Breakfast Table

───────○───────

The use of punctuation marks obviously confuses many people. Notices displayed in public, for example, frequently have an apostrophe in the wrong position — 'Ladie's night' instead of 'Ladies' night' — or have an apostrophe where none is needed — 'Parking for Disabled Driver's only'. It is as if punctuation is now thought to be pointless.

That last sentence constitutes an etymological pun, since punctuation is ultimately from Latin *punctum* 'point'. It belongs to a word family which includes **compunction**, **expunge**, **punctual**, **puncture** and **point** itself. **Poignant** also belongs here, describing as it does something that metaphorically pricks the emotions or senses.

───────○───────

Showing all her command of oral italics, ditto inverted commas, black-letter and illuminated capitals, she said . . .

Kingsley Amis *Girl 20*

───────○───────

Akin to punctuation marks are **diacritics**, signs which are used when writing to indicate a letter's sound. These are imported into English attached to foreign words and make life difficult for those who are not familiar with the languages concerned. A French word like *café*, for instance, has an acute accent on the final letter. *Tête-à-tête* shows the two other French accents, the circumflex (^) and the grave (`). All three accents give information about the way the vowels concerned are to be pronounced. French also makes use of the cedilla beneath the letter c in a word like façade. Once again the diacritic concerns pronunciation, showing that an s rather than a k sound should be used.

German makes use of the umlaut, as in the ü of the name München (Munich). This indicates a long sound which does not exist in English, one which the American Forces Network decided some years ago not to attempt. They ran a highly entertaining radio show called 'Luncheon in München' where the two words were made to rhyme. Spanish has the tilde, usually over an n, which has the effect of converting the n to ny. Señor is a well-known word in which it occurs.

───────────○───────────

'. . . made its new panels reëcho with a loud, free knock.'

Nathaniel Hawthorne
The House of the Seven Gables

───────────○───────────

Diacritics which are more rarely used in English include the diaeresis, macron and breve. The first of these is sometimes seen in names like Noël and Zoë. Its function is to point out that the second letter should be pronounced individually, not combined with the first to make a digraph as in a word like toe. Many British parents in recent years have preferred to use spellings like **Zoey**, **Zowey** to make the point. The

Teaser: A 'Presbyterian' is perhaps the most religious church goer. Why?
(Answer page 231) **??**

macron (ˉ) is used in special circumstances when it is necessary to indicate a long or stressed vowel. The short or unstressed vowel can be shown by the breve (˘).

Punctuation marks and diacritics, then, are little extras that help language compensate for all the information that is lost when words are written rather than spoken. They constitute a written paralanguage. Occasionally this language is imaginatively translated into visual or oral form. In recent years, for example, some academic lecturers have taken to holding up both hands with two fingers extended on each to show that what they are now saying is within quotation marks. The 'period' example with which this discussion began also demonstrated how to verbalise a punctuation mark. For many years Victor Borge has been entertaining audiences by punctuating spoken sentences with sounds that replace the marks. Wit and imagination can make even 'punctuation' an interesting subject.

─────────────────────────

PESSIMISM

───────────○───────────

I'm Smith of Stoke, aged sixty-odd
I've lived without a dame
From youth-time on; and would to God
My dad had done the same.

Thomas Hardy Epitaph on a Pessimist

───────────○───────────

Optimism came before **pessimism**, the former word being coined by Jesuits (as French optimisme) in 1737. They were referring to the theory of the German philosopher Leibnitz that this is 'the best of all possible worlds'. Leibnitz himself had used the Latin word optimum 'the best', on which optimism is clearly based. The word was taken up and made widely known by Voltaire for his famous satire *Candide*, which had the subtitle *l'optimisme*.

———————◯———————

The optimist proclaims that we live in the best of all possible worlds; and the pessimist fears this is true.

James Branch Cabell The Silver Stallion

———————◯———————

The word pessimism seems to have been invented at the end of the 18th century by Coleridge, who based it on Latin *pessimus* 'worst'. The most curious aspect of optimism and pessimism is that the words came into being so late. Both describe basic personality traits that are recognisable on all sides, and both are now used with great frequency. It is difficult to see how our ancestors managed to survive for so long without them.

PETTICOAT

———————◯———————

'Petticoat influence' is a great reproach,
Which even those who obey would fain be
    thought
To fly from, as from hungry pikes a roach;
But since beneath it upon earth we are brought,
By various joltings of life's hackney coach,
I for one venerate a petticoat —
A garment of a mystical sublimity,
No matter whether russet, silk, or dimity.

Much I respect, and much have I adored,
In my young days, that chaste and goodly veil,
Which holds a treasure, like a miser's hoard,
And more attracts by all it doth conceal —
A golden scabbard on a Damasque sword,
A loving letter with a mystic seal,
A cure for grief — for what can ever rankle
Before a petticoat and peeping ankle?

Lord Byron Don Juan

———————◯———————

A **petticoat** is now only an article of female clothing worn under a skirt or dress, but as the word hints, it was formerly something quite different. It began life as a 'small coat' worn by men beneath a doublet. In other words, it was a kind of **waistcoat**. When first worn by women in the 15th century it was presumably still in the form of a coat, but a century later the word had taken on its modern sense. It is now so closely associated with women that 'petticoat' can be used as that word's synonym in phrases like **petticoat goverment** and Byron's **petticoat influence**.

PINAFORE

———————◯———————

She is still pretty, but not so elegant as when she wore frocks and pin-a-fores.

Mary Russell Mitford Our Village

———————◯———————

There is something reassuring about words like **pinafore** (which in the 18th century was a washable cloth 'pinned before' a child's clothes or a woman's dress for protection). They seem to be natural, to have arisen in the course of normal speech rather than dredged from dictionaries and languages of the past. In that respect 'pinafore' is like **cutthroat**, **dugout**, **dust-up**, **go-getter**, **has-been**, **lah-di-dah**, **makeshift**, **shuteye**, **stay-at-home**. **Home-made** best describes them, since it is also in itself a good example of such words. It also shows how well they can survive, since it has been in regular use since the 17th century.

PLEASURE IMPLACABLE

Latin *placere* 'to please'. An implacable person 'cannot be pleased'.

PITCHER

—◯—

All thumbs and butter fingers, the pitcher thumped the pitcher down.

Bernard Malamud The Natural

—◯—

The curious sentence quoted above is about a baseball **pitcher** who thumps a pitcher of water on to a table. The two pitchers are homonyms — words which have the same spelling and pronunciation but different meanings. The baseball player **pitches** the ball; the pitcher of water looks back to a Latin *picarium*, also found as *bicarium*. The latter word led to **beaker**, which is also a container of liquid.

As with the two kinds of pitcher, homonyms usually have very different origins. Whereas they would normally have ended up as words differentiated from one another in sound, spelling and meaning, a series of linguistic accidents over many centuries makes them resemble one another to the eye and ear. Word buffs ought to be able to think — without recourse to a dictionary — of at least two very different meanings for the following typical homonyms: **bark**, **burden**, **count**, **down**, **flag**, **found**, **gin**, **hamper**, **jar**, **kit**, **lawn**, **main**, **moor**, **nap**, **ounce**, **punch**, **quarry**, **race**, **smack**, **wax**. To that short list they could add the word **buff** itself.

Needless to say, there are also words which have the same spelling, but differ in pronunciation and meaning. We say that an athlete is in the **lead** and that lead is a heavy metal. Oarsmen go for a **row** while two people who are arguing have a row. People who **live** in a city may go to a live concert. Those who **frequent** a particular pub are frequent visitors to it. Homographs, then, are words which one cannot be sure to pronounce cor-

CHAOS

Extract from a long, anonymous poem which comments on the fact that English words which have similar spellings can be pronounced in very different ways, or words spelled in different ways can have similar pronunciations. (See page 151.)

But be careful how you speak
Say gush, bush, steak, streak, break,
  bleak
Previous, precious, fuchsia, via
Recipe, pipe, studding-sail, choir;
Woven, oven, how and low,
Script, receipt, shoe, poem, toe.
Hear me say, devoid of trickery,
Daughter, laughter and Terpsichore,
Typhoid, measles, topsails, aisles,
Exiles, similes, reviles,
Wholly, holly, signal, signing,
Same, examining, but mining,
Scholar, vicar and cigar,
Solar, mica, war and far.
From desire desirable — admirable from
  admire;
Lumber, plumber, bier but brier,
Topham, brougham, renown but known,
Knowledge, done, lone, gone, none,
  tone,
One anemone, Balmoral,
Kitchen, lichen, laundry, laurel.
This phonetic labyrinth
Gives moss, gross, brook, brooch, ninth,
  plinth,
Billet does not end like ballet,
Bouquet, wallet, mallet, chalet,
Blood and flood are not like food,
Nor is mould like should and would,
Banquet is not nearly parquet,
Which exactly rhymes with khaki.

[There are over 200 more lines in similar style]

rectly if they are out of context. **Desert** and words like it are not one word but two, with different pronunciations and meanings: 'Nomads live in the desert'; 'Do not desert me.'

There are also international homographs. If the word **pain** is written on a sheet of paper, an English-speaker sees a word which he pronounces to rhyme with *pane* and which has to do with suffering. A Frenchman sees a word which he pronounces very nasally to sound something like *pan*. To him the word means 'bread'.

His death, which happen'd in his berth,
At forty-odd befell:
They went and told the sexton, and
The sexton toll'd the bell.

Thomas Hood *Faithless Sally Brown*

A SELECT LIST OF ENGLISH HOMOPHONES

Adds, adze	Chord, cord, cored	Grate, great	Loot, lute
Ail, ale	Cite, sight, site	Grill, grille	Made, maid
Air, ere, heir	Cleek, clique	Grisly, grizzly	Mail, male
Aisle, I'll, isle	Climb, clime	Groan, grown	Maize, maze
Allowed, aloud	Coarse, course	Guessed, guest	Mane, main
Altar, alter	Council, counsel	Guise, guys	Manner, manor
Aye, eye, I	Coward, cowered	Hail, hale	Marshal, martial
Bail, bale	Crews, cruise	Hair, hare	Mean, mien
Band, banned	Cue, queue	Hall, haul	Meat, meet, mete
Bard, barred	Cygnet, signet	Heal, heel, he'll	Medal, meddle
Bare, bear	Cymbal, symbol	Heard, herd	Metal, mettle
Baron, barren	Days, daze	Higher, hire	Mews, muse
Based, baste	Dew, due	Him, hymn	Might, mite
Bask, Basque	Die, dye	Hoar, whore	Mince, mints
Beau, bow	Discreet, discrete	Hoard, horde,	Mind, mined
Berth, birth	Doe, dough	whored	Miner, minor
Bell, belle	Done, dun	Hoarse, horse	Minks, minx
Berry, bury	Draft, draught	Hoes, hose	Missed, mist
Bier, beer	Ducked, duct	Hole, whole	Moan, mown
Billed, build	Earn, erne, urn	Idle, idol	Mode, mowed
Boar, bore	Ewe, yew, you	Innocence, innocents	Moose, mousse
Bolder, boulder	Fain, feign	Jam, jamb	Morning, mourning
Border, boarder	Faint, feint	Key, quay	Muscle, mussel
Born, borne, bourn	Fair, fare	Knave, nave	Mustard, mustered
Bough, bow	Faze, phase	Knead, need	Naval, navel
Boy, buoy	Feat, feet	Knight, night	Net, nett
Brake, break	Find, fined	Knot, not	None, nun
Bread, bred	Flair, flare	Know, no	Oar, or, ore
Brewed, brood	Flea, flee	Knows, nose	Ode, owed
Brews, bruise	Flew, flu, flue	Lam, lamb	One, won
Bridal, bridle	Flo, floe, flow	Lapse, laps	Paced, paste
Buy, by, bye	Flour, flower	Lays, laze	Packed, pact
Caret, carrot	For, fore, four	Leaf, lief	Pail, pale
Cause, caws	Foul, fowl	Leak, leek	Pair, pare, pear
Ceiling, sealing	Frees, freeze, frieze	Lessen, lesson	Passed, past
Cellar, seller	Gamble, gambol	Liar, lier, lyre	Patience, patients
Cents, scents, sense	Gate, gait	Limb, limn	Peace, piece
Chased, chaste	Gild, guild	Links, lynx	Peak, peek, pique
Choir, quire	Gnu, knew, new	Load, lowed	Peal, peel
Choler, collar	Gorilla, guerilla	Loan, lone	Pearl, purl
			Pedal, peddle
			Peer, pier
			Place, plaice

A third group of words are homophones — they have the same sound, but different spellings and meanings. If English were a logical language, then each of its sounds would be represented by a single letter or combination of letters. Its illogicality is in fact extraordinary. Widely different spellings can be used to represent a single sound: **aye**, **buy**, **eye**, **I**,

right, **rite**. The same spelling can call for widely different pronunciations. *Ough* is a well-known example, but there are many more. Consider the *ea*, for example, in words like **bead**, **beard**, **bread**, **create**, **great**, **theatre**, **theatrical**.

There once were some people named Sioux
Who spent all their time making shioux
Which they coloured in various hioux;
Don't think that they made them to ioux
Oh! no, they just sold them for bioux.

Anon, quoted in *Faber Book of Comic Verse*

As with the homographs, it is possible to have international homophones. Oscar Wilde reportedly told Cottsford Dick, a journalist: 'You and I ought to call ourselves the agriculturists.' 'Why?' 'Because, while I *mot*, you reap.' The pun is on French *mot* 'word' and English *mow*.

Rhyming dictionaries provide full lists of homophones. A brief indication of their range is given on page 150.

PITY

'One does not love people for what they are worth,'
she said gently. 'One loves them for themselves.'
What did she mean? When she said the word
love, did she mean pity?

Daphne du Maurier *Hungry Hill*

Pity belongs to a family of words that began with Latin *pius* 'pure'. **Pious** 'devout' obviously derives from the same word. In Latin a pious person was one who was dutiful to the gods and his parents, who demonstrated **piety** (Latin *pietas*). The feeling of compassion that we now call 'pity' developed from

Plain, plane	Sole, soul
Plum, plumb	Some, sum
Pole, poll	Son, sun
Pore, pour	Staid, stayed
Pray, prey	Stair, stare
Praise, prays, preys	Stake, steak
Pride, pried	Steal, steel
Principal, principle	Straight, strait
Profit, prophet	Succour, sucker
Psalter, salter	Suede, swayed
Quarts, quartz	Suite, sweet
Rack, wrack	Tacks, tax
Rain, reign, rein	Tail, tale
Rap, wrap	Taught, taut
Rapped, rapt, wrapped	Tea, tee
Read, reed	Team, teem
Receipt, reseat	Teas, tease, tees
Rest, wrest	Their, there, they're
Review, revue	Threw, through
Rheum, room	Thyme, time
Rhyme, rime	Tide, tied
Right, rite, wright, write	To, too, two
	Toad, toed, towed
Ring, wring	Tracked, tract
Road, rode, rowed	Troop, troupe
Roes, rose, rows	Trussed, trust
Root, route	Vail, vale, veil
Rough, ruff	Vain, vane, vein
Rung, wrung	Wade, weighed
Sail, sale	Wain, wane
Scene, seen	Waist, waste
Seam, seem	Wait, weight
Seas, sees, seize	Waive, wave
Serf, surf	Way, weigh
Serge, surge	Weak, week
Set, sett	Wear, where
Shake, sheik	Weave, we've
Sign, sine	We'd, weed
Slay, sleigh	Weld, welled
Sleight, slight	Whet, wet
Soar, sore	Wood, would
Soared, sword	Yoke, yolk

> ### PRAY
>
> 'Oh why, pray?' Emma knew that the word 'pray' following upon a question often elicited information, if spoken severely.
>
> **Daphne du Maurier** Rule Britannia

'piety'. **Expiation** is another word in this group, based on the idea of purging oneself from sin by doing pious deeds. **Pittance** also belongs here, since its earliest sense was a sum of money established by a pious bequest.

VIOLA:

I pity you.

OLIVIA:

That's a degree to love.

VIOLA:

No, not a grize; for 'tis a vulgar proof
That very oft we pity enemies.

William Shakespeare Twelfth Night

The passage quoted above discusses 'pity', but is of interest to the etymologist for its mention of **degree** and **grize**. Degree is from French degré, the gré being based on Latin gradus 'step'. Shakespeare's 'grize' represents an early form of grés, the plural of gré, used in English to mean either 'a flight of steps' or — as in Twelfth Night — a single step. The etymological complications parallel those of Shakespeare's plot. Viola pities Olivia because she has fallen in love with 'Cesario', who is really Viola dressed as a man. Fortunately, Viola has a twin-brother Sebastian to whom Olivia's love can later be transferred and who reciprocates her feelings.

POLY-PHLOESBOEAN

Two men are walking by the polyphloesboean ocean . . .

Oliver Wendell Holmes
The Autocrat of the Breakfast Table

Polyphloesboean was something of a 19th-century literary joke. The original Greek word, which means 'much roaring', is a favourite of Homer, who always uses it to describe the sea. *Blackwood's Magazine* seems to have begun the fashion of using the English word humorously in the 1820s. The word was applied to 'boisterous, loud-roaring' critics and was adapted for use in reviews: 'What hammering of epithets! what helpless polyphloisboioism!' (Variations in spelling are common.) Thackeray joined in the fun in his *Irish Sketch Book*: 'The line of shore washed by the **poluphloisboiotic**, nay, the **poluphloisboiatatotic** sea.'

PROVOCATE

'You told me never to use words like that except in ex-extreme provocation, and Francis provocated me enough to knock his block off.'

Harper Lee *To Kill A Mockingbird*

The child speaker quoted above is unaware that **provoke** is the verb associated with **provocation**, but makes a logical deduction that there is a verb **provocate**.

She is applying the principle of what is known as back-formation. This is the process that led, for example, to the verbs **burgle** from **burglar**, **beg** from **beggar**, **edit** from **editor**, **sculpt** from **sculptor**, **baby-sit** from **baby-sitter**, **audit** from **auditor**.

New back-formations are sometimes brought into being for humorous purposes. Thus, a **butler** is said to **buttle**, or somebody who is not **disgruntled** is said to be **gruntled**. G.K. Chesterton talked about a **grocer** who **groces**. These are recognised as jokes, but many words which have been formed in this way have come into general use. Purists sometimes object to them. The editors of *The Right Word at the Right Time*, for instance, say: 'Many careful speakers disapprove of such coinages as to *liaise* (from *liason*), to *self-destruct* (from *self-destruction*), and to *enthuse* (from *enthusiasm*). Enthuse at least should be avoided in formal speech and writing.' This seems to be an astonishingly prescriptive statement in a book which is otherwise admirably descriptive of the English language and its use.

PUBLICITY

Publicity also is a thoroughly typical euphemism or evasive term. Publicity does not mean revealing public life in the interests of public spirit. It means merely flattering private enterprises in the interests of private persons. It means paying compliments in public; but not offering criticisms in public. All this advertisement may have something to do with the freedom of trade; but it has nothing to do with the freedom of truth. Publicity must be praise and praise must to some extent be euphemism.

G.K. Chesterton *On Evil Euphemisms*

The early Latin word *poplus*, later *populus*, is responsible for our **people**, **populace**, **popular**, **populate** and the like. *Poplus* would normally have led to the adjectival *poplicus*, but under the influence of *pubes* 'adult men' it became *publicus*. From this derives **public**, **publican**, **publication**, **publish** and the word that Chesterton takes to task in the passage quoted above, **publicity**. This has been in regular use since the end of the 18th century, though its earliest meaning was merely 'open to public knowledge'. It was the opposite of **secrecy**, as a 19th-century writer pointed out when he said that 'the only guarantee of public honour is publicity, for the only protection rogues have is secrecy'.

As Chesterton says, 'publicity' no longer means making all the facts public. There has been an even greater change of meaning in the phrase **public school**, which in Britain now refers to a private school. This has been the case since the 19th century. Earlier, such schools were under public management and were for the use of the local or national public.

'Publish' is a curiosity in that, being derived from French *publier*, it should have become *publy*. 'Publy' was in fact the form of the word known to Caxton in the 15th century. The -ish ending is due to the influence of **distinguish**, **astonish**, **vanquish**, etc. Publish technically means 'to make known to the public', a sense still retained when marriage banns are published in a church.

FOR
THE BUS

QUARTER

His taxes are in arrear, quarter-day passes by, another quarter-day arrives; he can procure no more quarter for himself, and is summoned by —the parish.

Charles Dickens Sketches by Boz 'Our Parish'

Dickens was certainly aware from personal experience that **quarter-days** were dreaded by those who had debts to pay but no means to pay them. In 'Making

QUARANTINE

Few are aware that **quarantine** simply signifies a period of forty days; the word, though common enough at one time, being now only known to us through the acts of preventing the introduction of foreign diseases. There can be no reasonable doubt that this precise term is deduced from the period of Lent, which is in itself a commemoration of the forty days' fast of Christ in the wilderness. The period of forty days is, we need scarcely say, of frequent occurrence in Scripture. Moses was forty days on the mount; the diluvial rain fell upon the earth for forty days; and the same period elapsed from the time the tops of the mountains were seen till Noah opened the window of the ark.

William Chambers
The Book of Days

a Night of It', another sketch written while he was young, he made a further comment on the subject: 'The quarter-day arrived at last — we say at last, because quarter-days are as eccentric as comets, moving wonderfully quick when you have a good deal to pay, and marvellously slow when you have a little to receive.'

In England and Ireland the four traditional quarter-days were Lady Day (25 March), Midsummer Day (24 June), Michaelmas (29 September) and Christmas Day. In Scotland they were Candlemas Day (2 February), Whit Sunday (fixed as 15 May), Lammas Day (1 August) and Martinmas (11 November). **Quarter** in this sense is clearly from Latin *quartus* 'four'.

Dickens was not alone in ironically linking the expressions 'to give/receive quarter' to quarter-day. An anonymous poet is quoted in William Hone's The Every-Day Book:

Relentless, undelaying quarter-day!
Cold, though in summer, cheerless,
    though in spring,
In winter, bleak; in autumn,
    withering —
No quarter dost thou give, not for one
    day.

Here the word quarter has obviously come a long way from its original meaning, rather to the bemusement of scholars. In the 17th century a soldier who was at the mercy of his enemy and about to be killed would 'cry for quarter'. An early etymologist explained this by saying that the Dutch and Spanish had reached an agreement whereby a soldier who was spared would pay a ransom of one quarter of his pay.

Later philologists could not accept

> **Teaser:** *In which English-speaking country might you find a 'qar'?*
>
> *(Answer page 231)* **??**

this explanation, reasonable though it seems. They wondered whether the soldier was asking to be provided with **quarters**, a place to stay. This sense in turn presumably derives from a phrase like 'the military quarter', the location where the army is staying. It seems doubtful that a soldier in battle would grant such a request unless it was in his financial interest, which merely strengthens the early explanation. Early figurative use of the expression also supports the financial theory. By 1726 Daniel Defoe was writing, in *The Complete English Tradesman*, that 'the tradesman can expect no quarter from his creditors'. The statement remains as true today as it was then.

QUESTIONNAIRE

―――――――○―――――――

Tony Lumpkin: *Ask me no questions, and I'll tell you no fibs.*

Oliver Goldsmith She Stoops to Conquer

―――――――○―――――――

Questionnaire was adopted in English at the beginning of the 20th century. It is difficult to see why it was not normalized as 'questionary'. The -ary ending is as well established in English as the -aire in French, both being based on Latin -arius 'connected with'. We feel no need in English to use the French forms of words like adversary, antiquary, dictionary, elementary, library, literary, necessary, notary, ordinary, secondary, seminary, temporary, veterinary, so why

questionnaire? It is not as if we are making use of both forms, as is the case, say, with **legionary** and **legionnaire**.

The Frenchified form of questionnaire led to the early pronunciation *kestionnaire*. This is still sometimes heard, and is perhaps acceptable if the speaker was introduced to the word in such a way at least 70 years ago. Younger speakers who use this pronunciation, one suspects, are attempting an absurd one-upmanship for questionable (*kestionable?*) reasons.

QUIDDITY

―――――――○―――――――

Their own essential quiddity shines out in them.

J.I.M. Stewart A Use of Riches

―――――――○―――――――

Quiddity looks as if it should have something to do with tobacco or money. There may in fact be an etymological connection with **quid** in its sense of 'a pound sterling'; the tobacco **quid** is a

QUITE

'Mr Lanark, you're a complete bully.'
'That sparkling analysis of my hidden ego doesn't answer my question.'
'Quite!'
Then Lanark really was furious, for he knew where Aaron had stolen his *Quite*, which is the vitriol-in-the-face of conversation, from the recipe of a gentleman in the country.

Sinclair Lewis The God-Seeker

Shakespeare's Quick Words

VALENTINE:
Dumb jewels often in their silent kind
More than quick words do move a
woman's mind.

The Two Gentlemen of Verona

different word. The latter is easy to explain, since the American who chews a quid of tobacco (it is not a British habit) is chewing the **cud**. The two forms are variants of the same Old English word.

———————○———————

SUFFOLK:
Lady, wherefore talk you so?
MARGARET:
I cry you mercy, 'tis but quid for quo.

William Shakespeare Henry VI Part One

———————○———————

Quid in its British slang sense is more of a mystery. Because it resembles Latin quid 'something' it has been suggested that it

began as a youthful joke, a classroom translation of 'the wherewithal'. The joke could also have been based specifically on quid pro quo 'one thing in exchange for another'. The coin — the quid — was given in exchange for the item needed.

A connection with **liquid** also looks tempting, especially since **liquidate** in the 18th century could mean 'pay off a debt'. Liquid applied to assets that can quickly be converted into cash looks even more promising, but the word has only been used in that sense since the 19th century. Quid itself was already a term for a sovereign 200 years earlier.

If the Latin translation is the true explanation, then quiddity is certainly linked to it. The latter word refers to the real nature of something, whatever it is that makes a thing what it is. **Quality** and **quantity** express analogous ideas. In the passage quoted above quiddity is used of objects such as a bowl of fruit and a wall in a painting. The artist is said to have captured their essential nature.

QUOTATION

A book that furnishes no quotations is, me judice, no book — it is a plaything.

Thomas Love Peacock Crotchet Castle

R

FOR
MO

RAPIDITY

———○———

Rapidity is a word which is nicely suited to its meaning. Saying the word aloud illustrates in itself what the word is meant to convey. This effect is accidental: the word is certainly not onomatopoeic. It is obviously based on **rapid**, which derives from Latin *rapere* 'to seize, carry off, snatch'. It thus shares a common ancestry with **rape** 'violate a person'.

———○———

There is a pleasure in the pathless woods,
There is a rapture on the lonely shore,
There is society, where none intrudes,
By the deep sea, and music in its war . . .
        Lord Byron *Childe Harold*

———○———

The same Latin word leads indirectly to **ravish**, which in 18th-century novels also tends to mean 'rape a woman'. In those same novels, however, it is possible for someone to speak of being 'ravished with delight', where the meaning is 'filled with ecstasy, transported by the strength of one's feelings'. A person in such a state is **rapt**, or in a state of **rapture**, to use yet other words from the same Latin source. These senses were made possible by early versions of the Bible, where 'to be ravished' was equated with being 'carried off to heaven'.

Other words in this group derive either from the idea of violent speed or from forceful seizure. A **ravine** 'deep narrow gorge' is formed by the impetu-

Teaser: What is likely to be the smallest 'room' in the house?
??
(Answer page 231)

ous and forceful flow of water. To **ravage** 'plunder and destroy' is something done by **rapacious** people, who seize for themselves whatever they can lay hands on.

———————————

REBOUND

———○———

Jill had married him. There had been an element of rebound to it — an ugly word.

        J.I.M. Stewart *A Use of Riches*

———○———

Is **rebound** really 'an ugly word', as J.I.M. Stewart claims in the passage quoted above? The author presumably dislikes the meaning of the word in the context of human relationships, as used in the phrase **on the rebound**. What is described by that idiom may be disturbing, but the metaphor itself is extremely effective. It manages in just three words to suggest the state of mind of someone who is affected by the emotional shock of loss or rejection, likely to make judgements about a new partner unwisely and too hastily.

Proverbial sayings such as 'Marry in haste, repent at leisure' partly refer to the rebound phenomenon, but 'on the rebound' itself is a modern phrase, traced only to the 1920s. It had nevertheless been anticipated far earlier. Shakespeare uses rebound on only one occasion throughout his works, and applies it to intense emotional reaction in a way that could not possibly be called ugly. In *Antony and Cleopatra*, Dolabella is witness to Cleopatra's agony at the loss of Antony. Her anguish is such that he himself is deeply affected. 'I do feel, / By the rebound of yours, a grief that smites / My very heart at root.' 'On the rebound' may now be almost a cliché, but those to whom it applies are experiencing —

if only to a limited extent — the appalling sorrow of Cleopatra.

REFEREE

———————◯———————

'I've been a callin' to you half a dozen times,' said Sam, 'but you didn't hear me.'

'No, Sammy,' replied Mr Weller, again looking thoughtfully at the fire. 'I was in a referee, Sammy.'

Charles Dickens *The Pickwick Papers*

———————◯———————

Mr Weller obviously does not quite find the word he is looking for when he says he is **'in a referee'**. It would sound as if he were raving, but he clearly meant **'in a reverie'**, or daydream. As it happens, to **rave** may well derive from the same source as French *rêverie* and *rêver* 'to dream'. The etymologies of these words are obscure, but the fact that the earliest meaning of *rêver* was 'wander about' strengthens the possibility that it derives, *via* a postulated Old French *esver* and a Latin word of the type *exvagus*, from Latin *vagari* 'wander'. This would immediately connect it with **extravagant**, **extravaganza**, **vagabond**, **vagrant**, **vague**, the first two words having a basic meaning of 'wander beyond bounds'.

But the word that Mr Weller accidentally used is interesting in itself, one of a growing number, especially in American English, ending in -ee. The oldest English words of this type owe their origin to Anglo-French legal language. In French the -é ending of a verb is roughly the equivalent of English -ed, indicating the past participle of a verb. Instead of being translated into their normal English form, many French words were adapted slightly, the -é being simplified to -ee. The -ee words could then be seen either as passive equivalents of

agent nouns (**trainee/trainer**), or as direct objects of the verb on which they were based (trainee/**train**). Native English-speakers, needless to say, have never required such grammatical explanations. They have no difficulty deciphering referee as someone to be referred to, **interviewee** as someone to be interviewed, and so on.

———————◯———————

. . . before the arrival of his eleven-o'clock tutee.

Mary McCarthy *The Groves of Academe*

———————◯———————

Well established -ee words of the type described above include **absentee, addressee, amputee, appellee, appointee, devotee, deportee, detainee, draftee, employee, escapee, evacuee, examinee, guarantee, internee, legatee, lessee, licensee, mortgagee, nominee, parolee, patentee, payee, trustee**. These would be acceptable in all English-speaking countries. American sources can be found for **assignee, consignee, dedicatee, designee, donee, drawee, endorsee, enlistee, enrollee, evictee, expellee, franchisee, giftee, grantee, honoree, inductee, muggee, pawnee, permittee, pledgee, presentee, retiree, returnee, selectee, transferee, tutee, vendee**. Some of these might have more difficulty winning acceptance by British speakers of English, though all are of transparent meaning. Occasionally a word of this type is an intentional joke, as must surely be the case with **babysittee**.

Committee seems to stand out from this group because it applies to a group of people rather than one. That was not always the case: when the word first came into English from French in the 15th century it meant an individual, someone to whom a particular charge or trust had been committed. It was not until the 17th century that the word took on its modern meaning. **Divorcee**

is also rather different. This was a late borrowing from French where the -*ee* is grammatically feminine. A divorced man is properly a *divorcé*, his ex-wife a *divorcée*, though the accents are often omitted in English. **Fiancé** and **fiancée**, ultimately from Latin *fides* 'faith', are a similar pair.

───────○───────

Perhaps she was most valued by them as the possessor of a ready ear for confidences and for what they called 'repartee' — a light, bantering form of conversation then much in fashion.

Flora Thompson Candleford Green

───────○───────

There are other English words which were borrowed from French in their feminine past participle form. Examples include **repartee** 'started back, returned', **refugee** 'one who has fled', **mêlée** 'mixed', **levee** 'originally a reception held by the king on his "rising" from bed', **purée** 'squeezed out', **negligée** 'neglected', **fricassee** 'fried' and 'broken'. From French nouns rather than verbs came **entrée**, which is thought of as the 'entrance' to the main part of the meal, **soirée**, 'an evening of music and conversation at a private house', **toupee**, from *toupet* 'top-knot', **degree**, which adapts French *degré* in the same sense.

───────○───────

'What's that Portuguee bastard gonna poison us with today?'

Peter Benchley The Island

───────○───────

Other words in -*ee* derive from a fascinating range of sources. In traditional sailors' language, for instance, **Chinee** and **Portuguee** were used to denote an individual Chinese or Portuguese person. Those who invented the false singulars were probably illiterate. When they heard the words Chinese and Portuguese they thought they were plurals.

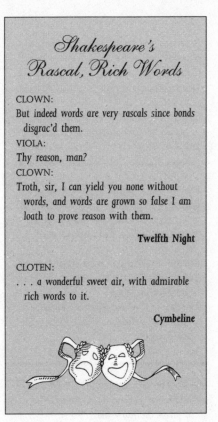

Shakespeare's Rascal, Rich Words

CLOWN:
But indeed words are very rascals since bonds disgrac'd them.
VIOLA:
Thy reason, man?
CLOWN:
Troth, sir, I can yield you none without words, and words are grown so false I am loath to prove reason with them.

Twelfth Night

CLOTEN:
. . . a wonderful sweet air, with admirable rich words to it.

Cymbeline

Marquee is a similar word. It is a corruption of *marquise* 'marchioness', and was originally a tent suitable for such a noble lady. **Yankee** may belong here if, as some claim, the word derives from the Dutch name *Jan Kes* (John Cornelius). Though it does not have the -*ee* ending, **cherry** is a member of this group. It is from the French dialect word *cherise*, a form of *cerise* 'cherry'. English-speakers took it to be a plural and invented 'cherry'.

───────○───────

Normally he was opposed to puttees and lipstick.

William Golding Free Fall

───────○───────

Beyond the groups described above, there are -*ee* words which need to be considered individually. They include:

Banshee — Irish 'fairy woman'

Cherokee — form of native American Indian word

Chimpanzee — form of an African word

Coffee — from a Turkish/Arabic word which means 'the drink'

Jubilee — Hebrew 'ram', a reference to the ram's horn used as a trumpet

Puttee — Hindi 'band, bandage'

Rupee — ultimately from a Sanskrit word meaning 'wrought silver'

Settee — a fanciful variation of 'settle'

Suttee — Hindi/Urdu 'faithful wife'

Tepee — a form of the native Sioux or Dakota word

Three — Old English, a cousin to similar words in most Germanic languages.

'She'll have all manner of grandees for her godfathers and godmothers. I wonder what those grand people are really like.'

Anthony Trollope
The Small House at Allington

Words where the ending has been added in an arbitrary way include **bargee**, **bootee**, **goatee**, **grandee**, **siree**, **whoopee**. Finally, there are some mystery words which etymologists are unable to explain. They include **jamboree**, **spree** and the very ordinary word **toffee**, which was earlier **taffy**. Perhaps at some stage in their history they have been subjected to the Mr Weller treatment, passing through the sudden and violent change of meaning and form which can turn a reverie into a referee.

> **RIPARIAN   ARRIVE**
>
> *Latin ripa 'river bank'. Arrive is ultimately ad-ripare 'to land'.*

REMUNERATION

'Might I be excused,' said Mr Dorrit, 'if I inquired what remune-'

'Why indeed,' returned Mrs General, stopping the word, 'it is a subject on which I prefer to avoid entering.'

Charles Dickens *Little Dorrit*

In the passage above Mrs General is being over-delicate about mentioning the subject of her **remuneration**, even though she is being interviewed for a job. She goes on to suggest that Mr Dorrit might inquire of her present employers 'what amount they have been accustomed, at quarterly intervals, to pay to my credit at my bankers'. She pretends not to know how much this is, but thinks that it would be a good idea if he were to increase it by one third.

'Remuneration' is from Latin munus, muneris 'gift', seen again in a word like **munificence**. In English it is a pompous word for 'pay' that was already a joke in Shakespeare's time. In *Love's Labour's Lost* Armado says to Costard: 'There is remuneration.' Costard looks to see what he has been given and says: 'Remuneration! O, that's the Latin word for three farthings. Three farthings — remuneration. Why, it is a fairer name than French crown. I will never buy and sell out of this word.'

Those people who think it rather vulgar to talk about money are likely to use other euphemistic expressions. In *Gideon Planish* Sinclair Lewis remarks: 'The "emolument" (a word used among the loftier teachers and the more amateur editors, and meaning "wages", just as the wages of lecturers are called the "honorarium") would be $4200 a year.'

RICH

It's the same the whole world over,
It's the poor wot gets the blame,
It's the rich wot gets the pleasure,
Ain't it all a blooming shame.

Anon First World War Song

Sociologist E. Digby Baltzell, of the University of Pennsylvania, discovered some years ago that members of the upper-classes happily describe someone as **rich**. Middle-class speakers tend to use the more genteel expression **wealthy**. People who are very rich indeed are sometimes called **filthy rich**, a phrase no doubt inspired by **filthy lucre**. Cole Porter was in the habit of distinguishing between the rich and the rich-rich.

RICOCHET

The shot buried itself in the soft sand. We had no ricochet to fear.

Robert Louis Stevenson Treasure Island

Ricochet is a mysterious word which first appeared in French in the phrase fable de ricochet, referring to an interminable series of questions and answers, an endless refrain. It had possibly begun as Latin recalcare 'retread', passing through obscure dialectal forms to emerge as ricochet. French folk-etymology has long preferred to link the word with a fable about a red cockerel.

The word was taken over by the military and used of 'bouncing' a projectile, such as a cannonball, along a surface. It was also applied in English to the children's game of duck and drake, in which a flat stone is skipped along the surface of water. Needless to say, it remains a far more deadly word in the military context of ricocheting bullets.

RIGMAROLE

Don't any of you feel you have got to stay, if he decides to tell me some long rigmarole.

Anthony Powell Casanova's Chinese Restaurant

Rigmarole now usually refers to a long and complicated series of actions that have to be gone through in order to achieve a particular end. Anthony Powell uses the word above in an earlier meaning, a series of pointless or misleading statements.

Alfonso paused a minute — then begun
Some strange excuses for his late proceeding:
He would not justify what he had done,
To say the best, it was extreme ill-breeding;
But there were ample reasons for it, none
Of which he specified in his pleading:
His speech was a fine sample, on the whole,
Of rhetoric, which the learn'd call 'rigmarole'.

Lord Byron Don Juan

The word is a spoken corruption of **ragman roll**, which is recorded in literature only until the beginning of the

17th century. 'Ragman roll' was originally the title of a 13th-century statute of Edward I. The king appointed justices to hear complaints about injustices suffered in the previous 25 years. It is not clear why the statute received this name. In Edward's time 'ragman' was one of the names given to the devil. **Ragamuffin**, recently revived for a musical style, was used in a similar way. It was only in the 16th century that 'ragman' described someone who collected rags.

To begin with the old rigmarole of childhood. In a country there was a shire, and in that shire there was a town, and in that town there was a house, and in that house there was a room, and in that room there was a bed, and in that bed there lay a little girl . . .

Elizabeth Gaskell *Wives and Daughters*

In the 14th century, 'ragman roll' also became the name of a game which was used for a kind of fortune-telling. The 'roll' had strings attached to the words written on it: a player would draw a string to discover something about his character. Presumably there was once again a reference to the devil making a judgement.

ROSEMARY

OPHELIA:

There's rosemary, that's for remembrance; pray you, love, remember. And there is pansies, that's for thoughts.

William Shakespeare *Hamlet*

Rosemary is a curious word because the plant concerned is not a rose and has nothing to do with Mary. It is an alteration of Latin *ros marinus* 'sea-dew', a name said to have come about because the shrub originally grew near the sea. By the 16th century rosemary was being used emblematically at weddings and funerals to signify 'fidelity in love'. The **pansies** that Ophelia mentions were certainly linked with 'thoughts', since **pansy** is an English form of French *pensée* 'thought' in the sense of 'souvenir'.

It was a difficult problem in the language of flowers because she was a recent widow. A red rose, symbol of flaming fashion, might offend her mourning. Yellow roses, which in another language were the flowers of good fortune, were an expression of jealousy in the common vocabulary. He had heard of the black roses of Turkey, which were perhaps the most appropriate, but he had not been able to obtain any for acclimatisation in his patio. After much thought he risked a white rose, which he liked less than the others because it was insipid and mute: it did not say anything.

Gabriel Garcia Marquez
Love in the Time of Cholera

Most people are dimly aware of this 'language of flowers', but could probably say little more than that red roses declare one's love. In *Vanity Fair* Joseph Sedley presents a nosegay to the scheming Rebecca, but is foolish enough to do it publicly. 'Do they talk the language of flowers at Boggley Wallah, Sedley?' says George Osborne, laughing heartily. Dickens also laughs at the idea obliquely in *Nicholas Nickleby*. Mrs Nickleby's mad neighbour has been throwing cucumbers and marrows over the garden wall. She chooses to interpret this as a declaration of love, though her son says: 'You know there is no language of vegetables which converts a cucumber into a formal declaration of attachment.'

FOR
YOU

SACRIFICE

I sacrificed my all for his love.

Tobias Smollett *The Adventures of Peregrine Pickle*

The woman who makes the statement quoted above refers elsewhere to leaving a man in the morning 'after the sacrifice I had made'. This is the 'love's full sacrifice' which Shakespeare's Cressida refers to when she says of Pandarus:

'Words, vows, gifts, tears, and love's
    full sacrifice,
He offers in another's enterprise.'

Sacrifice primarily refers to a **sacred** act, originally the killing of an animal as an act of homage. The animal itself was the sacrifice or victim and the word became associated with brutal butchery rather than an act of worship. The conventional use of sacrifice in a sexual sense, which continued for centuries, is an interesting reflection of former attitudes, but the word must have frightened countless women with its implications.

SAID

There exist in English what can be called verbal substitutes. They are not the same as synonyms, as examples will quickly make clear. Whereas synonyms are words of the same or very similar meaning, such as **street** and **road**, verbal substitutes are words that can occupy the same position in a particular context, performing a similar role, though the meaning of one of the terms may appear to be considerably stretched. Thus there are many who live in a road that is actually

identified officially as a **close**, **drive**, **mount**, **ride**, **rise**, **row**, **terrace**, **walk**, etc. (The present author's *Guinness Book of Names* lists about 180 such words.)

They explored every corner of the town. It was a place of pleasant sounding old names, richly English, and romantic. The names of the streets fascinated Christopher: Green End; Lombard Street; Baileygate; Golden Hill; The Tything; Market Row; Vine Court; Barbican; Angel Alley.

Warwick Deeping *Sorrell and Son*

These substitutes tend to be restricted to the written language: in ordinary speech the terms which have the general meanings are preferred. It is curious, however, that a person who refers unthinkingly to 'the street where we live' might not be very pleased if 'street' were part of its official name. Estate-developers have discovered in the past that houses sell more easily if they are in **avenues**, **crescents**, **dales** and the like.

A popular candidate for substitution in the written language is **say**, especially in its past tense form **said**. In the average novel there is a great deal of direct speech which needs to be accompanied by a formula which means 'he/she said'. Novelists vary 'said' partly to avoid boring repetition of a word, but mainly to provide some indication of how something was said. If the novelist does the job well, the average reader will not notice the substitution that is taking place. The words that are used merely help the supposedly spoken words to be heard in the reader's mind in a particular way. It is helpful to know that an utterance was **barked**, say, or **croaked**, **gasped**, **screamed**, **shouted**, **trilled**, **wailed**, **whispered**.

Once again, while these substitutes serve a useful purpose in written language, they tend not to be used in speech. A person who is recounting what someone else said can reproduce as necessary the tone of voice, stress and other features that were originally present. Where demonstration is possible, verbal description is unnecessary.

Novelists vary greatly in their use of 'said' substitutes, though Nigel Denis probably reflects average usage in a novel of normal length. In *Cards of Identity* he uses 'said' itself, plus 56 substitutes which include the eight quoted above. Fifty-six may seem a large number, but the range of words available is much greater. The list of such words on p. 180 comprises 'said' substitutes that were noted while reading about 80 novels, but attentive word-buffs would be able to add to their number. They would no doubt also suggest other key-words that are especially likely to be subjected to substitute treatment.

SALAAM

———O———

All the boatmen grew to know Sophie and the children, and salaamed, with their paddles across their knees, as they passed.

Rumer Godden *Kingfishers Catch Fire*

———O———

Salaam is the ceremonial Muslim greeting, accompanied by the placing of the right palm on the forehead and a bow. The word is Arabic, the equivalent of Hebrew *shalom* 'peace'. In the West the formal utterance of 'Peace be with you' tends to be restricted to church services. It is certainly sanctioned by the Bible: Judges 6.23 has — 'the Lord said to him, "Peace be to you; do not fear, you shall not die." Then Gideon built an altar there to the Lord, and called it, The Lord is peace. To this day it still stands at Ophrah.'

The Hebrew word appears in the

Teaser: What is curious about the word 'smiles'? ??
(Answer. page 231)

Bible in a number of forms, especially as proper names. **Solomon** means 'the peaceful', for instance, and **Salome** is 'peace'. The Salome named in the Old Testament is one of the women who follow and serve Jesus. The infamous Salome, who asked for the head of John the Baptist on a platter as a reward for her dancing, is referred to in Mark and Matthew only as 'the daughter of Herodias'. Her name is known from historical sources. But for the dance scene and its tragic consequences, Salome would probably have been widely used as a first name in all Christian countries. It has a pleasant meaning and sound, though it does come uncomfortably close to **salami**. The latter has nothing to do with 'peace', incidentally. The name refers to the 'salted' nature of the sausage.

Shallum is another biblical name based on Hebrew **shalom**, borne by no less than 15 different men. It has very rarely been used as a first name in English-speaking countries. Far older is **Shalem**, the name of an early God. It was he who gave his name to **Jerusalem** 'foundation of Shalem'.

SAW

———O———

'I like to hit the nail on the head with a saw.'

Peter de Vries *Comfort Me with Apples*

———O———

The joke in the quotation above is made possible by the two very different meanings of **saw**. As a synonym for 'proverb, wise saying, maxim' the word is connected with **say** and **saga**. In this meaning the word is little used in modern times. Young readers who come to Jaques's famous 'All the world's a stage' speech in *As You Like It* probably wonder why the justice is said to be 'full of wise saws and modern instances'.

The cutting instrument takes its name from a Germanic word meaning to 'cut'. There is a distant link with Latin *secare* 'cut (in two)' and thus with **bisect**, **dissect**, **insect** — which has a **sectional** body — **intersect**, **scythe**, **secateurs**, **section**, **segment**, **sickle**, **vivisection**.

'Saw' is also the highly irregular past tense form of see, though in some dialects 'I seed him' was once a regular form. In Thomas Hardy's *Far from the Madding Crowd* the farmhands regularise other verbs, saying things like: 'I knowed that old place'; 'She fleed at him like a cat'; 'It will be throwed away'. All this is quite logical, causes no misunderstanding and hints at the way the language could usefully be reformed.

SCHMUCK

'You big romantic *schmuck!*'

Erich Segal *Oliver's Story*

In the quotation above, **schmuck** is a 'covert endearment'. When two people know each other well enough, terms which are insulting in form can be accepted without rancour, provided they are spoken in the right tone of voice. A similar example occurs in *The Exhibitionist*, by Henry Sutton, where a woman addresses a man as 'you big horny **bastard**'. The novelist refers to this coyly as a 'thrilling vulgarity'; the man to whom it is addressed takes it as a compliment.

British speakers of English are gradually becoming aware of schmuck, or **shmuck** as many writers prefer. They would think of it as an American term, and have probably guessed from the contexts in which they hear it used in American films, or come across it in books by American authors, that it expresses contempt. It is, in fact, a Yiddish obscenity, referring to the penis. To call someone a schmuck is much the same as calling him a **prick**. Neither word would be used lightly by a sensitive speaker, especially in the presence of women or children.

The Yiddish expression began as a slang use of German *Schmuck* 'ornament, decoration, trimmings'. Although it is now fairly widely used, along with other taboo words, Jewish Americans are still aware of its force. Some would therefore make use of the euphemistic form **schmo** or **shmo** when speaking about a **jerk**, **dope** or **boob**.

'It *was his duty,*' Isidore said.
'Duty, *shmuty,*' Susan retorted.

Frederic Raphael *The Limits of Love*

The effect of Yiddish on English was explored in the late 1960s by Leo Rosten in his well-known book *The Joys of Yiddish*. Rosten pointed out that many insulting words besides schmuck in that language begin with the letters sh- or sch-. Those letters can therefore be used as prefixes to create what might be called 'nonce neologisms', words which are brought into being for the need of the moment but which have no permanent existence. Their purpose is to make fun of a word that has just been used. If somebody mentions the mayor, the response might be: 'Mayor, shmayor, it's his wife who does everything.' A non-Yiddish equivalent might be 'Mayor, my foot!' or 'Mayor, fiddlesticks!'

Many years ago the *Dallas Morning News* printed the sentence: 'There has been some confusion as to whom is and whom is not a reservist.' *The New Yorker* felt that some comment was needed on this absurd misuse of 'whom' for 'who'. Its headline was: 'Oh, confusion schmooshun!' More recently (February 1993), Howard Jacobson has published his survey of Jewish life. His attitude to his ethnic origins are summed up in the title of his work, *Roots Schmoots*.

SERVANT

Clear your mind of cant. You may talk as other people do: you may say to a man, 'Sir, I am your most humble servant.' You are not his most humble servant.

James Boswell *Life of Samuel Johnson*

Dr Johnson refers in the above passage to a conventional formula which was much used in the 18th century. Sheridan made fun of it in *The School for Scandal*, where gentlemen frequently bow to one

SEND-OFF

Jack Pertwee was getting married in the morning and the Kingsmarkham and District Darts Club were in the Dragon to give him what George Carter called a send-off.
'I don't like the sound of that, George,' said Jack. 'I'm getting married, not buried.'

Ruth Rendell *The Best Man to Die*

another with a great flourish while saying things like 'Your most obedient humble servant', 'Your ever grateful and perpetual humble servant'. **Servant** was so common in these expressions that it was often unnecessary to say it. Thus, in the same play, Snake bids farewell by saying: 'Mr Surface, your most obedient.' Surface replies: 'Sir, your very devoted.' In a similar exchange other speakers say: 'Your very obedient' and 'Sir, your most obsequious'.

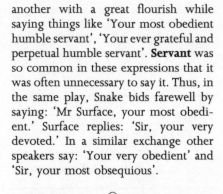

'A large farm?'

'No, not large. About a hundred.' (In speaking of farms the word 'acres' is omitted by the natives, by analogy to such old expressions as 'a stag of ten'.)

Thomas Hardy *Far From The Madding Crowd*

This phenomenon of omitted words in frequently used phrases occurs elsewhere. In colloquial London speech 'you haven't an earthly chance' becomes 'you haven't an **earthly**'; 'I haven't the foggiest idea' becomes 'I haven't the **foggiest**'. Rhyming slang expressions are frequently abbreviated, as in 'use your **loaf**', for 'use your loaf of bread' (head). Ad hoc omissions may occur in informal situations: 'Got any money?' 'Not a red.' (Sinclair Lewis, *Ann Vickers*); 'You can keep a stiff upper today, if I can.' (James Purdy, *Eustace Chisholm and the Works*).

To return to 'servant', social changes have almost caused the word to disappear in its domestic sense. The word has unpleasant associations with **servitude** and **servility** and is often avoided. Even **civil servants** must sometimes regret that description of their role. It is sometimes said that they are not always 'civil', but that word was merely meant to indicate that they were not concerned with military or church matters. The 'polite' meaning of 'civil' came about because of the artificial social behaviour of city-dwellers — exemplified by the use of 'your humble servant' and the like — as opposed to the rougher ways of countrymen.

HAMLET:
. . . this fell sergeant Death
Is strict in his arrest . . .

William Shakespeare Hamlet

Another kind of servant who is not always polite is the army **sergeant**. 'Servant' and 'sergeant' are doublets, both deriving ultimately from the present participle servientem of Latin servire 'serve', but it would be a brave soldier who would point this out to the man concerned. Other words from the same source or from servus 'slave' include **conserve, deserve, observe, preserve, reserve, reservoir, serf, serve, service, subserve**.

SEX-APPEAL

'Sex-appeal — it was important. Looking back from maturer years to her brief, happy engagement, she had seen that the common contemporary phrase explained it. He had had 'sex-appeal' for her. And no-one else had had it afterwards — until Matt Costello turned up.

Kate O'Brien Pray for the Wanderer

D.H. Lawrence was not fond of the word **sex-appeal**, though he was certainly interested in what it described. He commented fully on the subject in a rather sloppily written essay called Sex Versus Loveliness. After asking: 'Why is a woman lovely, if ever, in her twenties?' he continued: 'It is the time when sex rises softly to her face, as a rose to the top of the bush. First and foremost, sex appeal is the appeal of beauty.'

Lawrence was then at pains to define his terms: 'Beauty is an experience, nothing else. It is not a fixed pattern or an arrangement of features. . . . The plainest person can look beautiful, can be beautiful. It only needs the fire of sex to rise delicately to change an ugly face to a lovely one. That is really sex appeal: the communicating of a sense of beauty. . . . Handsome and good-looking women are the women with good features and the right hair. But a lovely woman is an experience. It is a question of communicated fire, of sex-appeal in our poor, dilapidated modern phraseology.'

'He was an intensely self-absorbed young man . . . yet he was attractive to women; the group admitted that he had S.A., the way some homely men teachers and clergymen had, and there was something about him, a dynamic verve . . .'

Mary McCarthy The Group

What Lawrence preferred to call 'communicated fire' has at other times been known by such terms as **allure, attraction, chemistry, fascination, oomph, personal magnetism**. The silent screen actress Clara Bow was said to have **it**. She appeared in a film with that title in 1928 and became known as 'the It girl'. Perhaps 'it' was the best general term for this mysterious quality which writers and poets have often tried to define. The word does at least suggest something indefinite. 'Sex-appeal', as D.H. Lawrence said, is a poor substitute, and gets its come-uppance when it crosses the English Channel. A French-speaker hears it as sex à piles, 'sex by batteries'.

SIZZLE

When you see a steak sizzling on a platter, when you hear it sizzling, your mouth waters. You want it — it's sold. So, in my lexicon, the sizzle stands for salability. It's the sizzle — and not the cow — that sells the steak, although the cow, of course, is mighty important.

Elmer Wheeler Word Magic

Books about the persuasive use of language were popular at one time. A typical example — *Word Magic* by Elmer Wheeler — was first published in 1939 and quickly went through several reprints. Wheeler offered readers his **sizzlegrams**, which were his suggestions for dealing verbally with typical situations. The **sizzle** is explained in the passage quoted above: the *-gram* of 'sizzlegram' came from **telegram**. In Wheeler's view a salesman's first ten words were as important as the next ten thousand. His advice, therefore, was to 'find the sizzle in whatever you are trying to get across; then express the sizzle in a telegraphic statement'.

From a transistor in the kitchen came the sound of Rimsky-Korsakov's Scheherazade, instead of the modish chat of disc-jockeys. Here was one young lady who didn't prefer the sizzle to the steak.

Guy Bellamy The Secret Lemonade Drinker

All this has long been familiar to the salesman, along with Wheeler's other basic points — such as asking which of two products a customer wants, not if he wants one of them, and thinking 'not so much about what you want to say as what the other person wants to hear'.

Wheeler went a step further and applied the principles of selling to daily life, on the basis that we all need to sell ourselves to others, including our families.

Whatever worldly expressions he might use in sub rosa conversations with the less sanctified theological students, in public he never so much as said 'doggone', and he had on tap, for immediate and skilled use, a number of such phrases as 'Brother, I am willing to help you find religion', 'My whole life is a testimonial to my faith'.

Sinclair Lewis Elmer Gantry

A writer who was highly aware of persuasive linguistic techniques was Sinclair Lewis, winner of the Nobel Prize for Literature in 1930. In Elmer Gantry, a novel which appeared a year after the publication of Elmer Wheeler's book, he demonstrated sizzlegram use in an unusual context. His hero trains to be a Baptist minister and acquires 'an elegant vocabulary'. It includes 'eighteen synonyms for sin, half of them very long and impressive, and the others very short and explosive and minatory —

SHIBBOLETH

'The party' for the Communist Party, 'Soviet' as an adjective for Russian, 'Fascists' as a collective term to include National-Socialists, 'The Daily' for the Daily Worker, 'social democrats' to describe members of the Labour Party — all those were shibboleths, and meant, if one had ever listened to the dialect of intellectual communism, that those who used them were not far from the party line.

C.P. Snow The New Men

minatory being one of his own best words, constantly useful in terrifying the as yet imaginary horde of sinners gathered before him.'

Elmer Gantry later becomes involved with professional evangelists and learns far more about what Lewis calls 'the trade terms of evangelism'. The use of words is discussed in a long conversation between two highly successful preachers, one of whom remarks, for instance, during a discussion of fund-raising techniques: 'If the appeal for the free-will offering is made strong enough, we usually have pretty fair results.' The other replies: 'I don't like the term "free-will offering", or "thank-offering". It's been used so much by merely second-rate evangelists, who, and I grieve to say there are such people, put their own gain before the service of the Kingdom, that it's got a commercial sound. In making my own appeal for contributions, I use "love-offering".'

Elmer Wheeler would have been proud of this, though Lewis was of course merely demonstrating appalling hypocrisy. His novels indicate clearly enough what he thought of 'sizzlegrams', wherever they surfaced. They are still with us, having reached almost an art form in the hands of skilled advertising copy-writers. Some would say that they are an insult to our intelligence, but how many of us could truthfully claim that we have never been sizzled?

SMILE

---○---

Harris proposed that we should go out and have a smile.

Jerome K. Jerome Three Men in a Boat

---○---

Jerome K. Jerome uses **smile** (above) in its 19th-century slang sense of 'drink',

especially a drink of whisky. Presumably the idea was that an alcoholic beverage brought a smile to the face, though a century earlier it was possible to speak of wine or beer that 'smiled' in the glass if it sparkled.

'Smile' first appeared in English in the 14th century. There are similar words in such languages as Danish, Norwegian and Swedish and it is thought that all derive from the same Germanic source. The facial gesture that the word describes ranges from a whole-hearted exhibition of pleasure to a sarcastic expression of scorn. In between is the enigma of Mona Lisa with her **smilet**, as Shakespeare might have called it.

---○---

What a pleasant influence lies in mutual smiles! We love the lips which welcome us without words.

Samuel Lover Handy Andy

---○---

We seem to have lost this diminutive form of the word, which was in use by the end of the 16th century. It is not one of Shakespeare's many inventions, though it occurs in King Lear in a fine description of Cordelia:

GENTLEMAN:
You have seen
Sunshine and rain at once: her smiles
   and tears
Were like a better way. Those happy
   smilets
That play'd on her ripe lip seem'd
   not to know
What guests were in her eyes, which
   parted thence
As pearls from diamonds dropp'd.

It is difficult to find a literary equivalent of the Mona Lisa smile, a single description, that is, which captures the imagination and stays in the mind. Shakespeare refers to a wide range of smiles, from those practised by the ridiculous Malvolio in Twelfth Night to

Quite suddenly, with an effort as though a gust of wind had swept aside a mass of dead leaves, uncovering the fresh verdure below, her whole face relaxed into a smile of disarming sweetness.

John Cowper Powys *Wolf Solent*

'the daggers in men's smiles' of Donalbain in *Macbeth*. Novelists make passing comments on the smiles exchanged by their characters or tell us, as does Jane Austen in *Pride and Prejudice*, that Mr Darcy acknowledges Miss Bennet to be pretty, 'but she smiles too much'. George Meredith, in *Evan Harrington*, has a lady who exclaims: 'There's no music in his smile. Oh! you should see a Portuguese nobleman smile. O mio Deus! honeyed, my dears! But Evan has it not. None of you English have.'

The best novelists, remarkably, have the power to smile at their readers through the printed word. Dickens does it constantly, with his witticisms and jokes, though he can also frown when he speaks of social injustice. George Washington Harris, too, is a master of the art. There is surely a broad grin on his face, for instance, when he has Sut describe the devastating smile of Sicily Burns, a mountain girl in *Blown Up With Soda*. Sut naturally turns to an alcoholic simile. He thus takes us full circle by linking 'smile' once again with 'whisky', though not in the Jerome K. Jerome sense: 'An' sich a smile! why, when hit struck yu far an' squar hit felt jis' like a big ho'n ove onrectified ole Munongahaley, arter yu'd been sober fur a month, a tendin ove a ten hoss prayer-meetin twist a day, an' mos' ove the nites. Three ove her smiles when she wer a tryin ove hersef, taken keerfully ten minutes apart, wud make the gran' captin ove a temprunce s'iety so durn'd drunk, he wudn't no his britches frum a par ove bellowses, ur a pledge frum a warter-pot.'

SNEEZE

Not to be sneezed at.

George Colman, the Younger *The Heir-at-Law*

Sneeze is decidedly more curious than the apparently similar **sniff**, **sniffle**, **snivel**, **snuff**, **snuffle**, **snore**, **snort** and dialectal **snork**, all of which are onomatopoeic, or imitative of the sounds to which they refer. Until the 14th century 'sneeze' was spelt **fnese**, which became **neeze** in northern English dialects. The *Oxford English Dictionary* thinks that the fn- was misread as sn-, something which could have happened far more easily when the long s character (ʃ) was used. Sn- was also a more usual beginning of a word than fn-. No doubt *fnese* itself, centuries before, had imitated the sound of a sneeze.

A sneeze also attracts a different response from those who hear it. The other noises merely irritate; a sneeze we are likely to greet with 'bless you'. This custom of saluting a sneeze is very ancient, and was explained by Aristotle as an honourable acknowledgement of the head, the seat of good sense and genius. The two other offensive eruptions of air, said Aristotle, were never met with a benediction. Isaac Disraeli reports this comment in his essay 'On the Custom of Saluting After Sneezing', adding that it is 'considerable nonsense'.

Another difference lies in the fact that

Her mother sniffily told him that she was to be found on the roof.

Sinclair Lewis *Martin Arrowsmith*

people do not sneeze deliberately in order to make a comment on something, whereas disapproval can be shown with a sniff or a snort. Dickens has fun with snorting in *Our Mutual Friend*, when he describes the 'widowed female of a Medusa sort' — Mrs Lammle's aunt: 'Medusa, besides unmistakably glaring petrifaction at the fascinating Tippins, follows every lively remark made by that dear creature with an audible snort; which may be referable to a cold in the head, but may also be referable to indignation and contempt. And this snort being regular in its reproduction, at length comes to be expected by the company, who make embarrassing pauses when it is falling due, and by waiting for it, render it more emphatic when it comes.'

On deck beneath the awning,
I dozing lay and yawning;
It was the grey of dawning,
Ere yet the sun arose;
And above the funnel's roaring
And the fitful wind's deploring,
I heard the cabin snoring
With universal nose.

William Thackeray The White Squall

In *Hard Times* Dickens also plays with 'snore', which is simply a snorting sound that occurs during sleep. Mrs Sparsit says of of Bitzer: 'I cannot say that I have heard him precisely snore, and therefore must not make that statement. But on winter evenings, when he has fallen asleep at his table, I have heard him, what I should prefer to describe as partially choke. I have heard him on such occasions produce sounds of a nature similar to what may sometimes be heard in Dutch clocks.' 'Well!' says the exasperated Bounderby, 'while he was snoring, or choking, or Dutch-clocking, or something-or-other — being

asleep — some fellows got to young Tom's safe, forced it and abstracted the contents.'

In *Tom Sawyer Abroad*, Mark Twain makes the profound comment: 'There ain't no way to find out why a snorer can't hear himself snore.'

SOMNAMBULISM

This had been turned into a popular song about 1950, and had recently enjoyed a fresh lease of life, or somnambulism, as that sadly different thing from a popular song, a pop song.

Kingsley Amis Girl 20

Somnambulism, the word that Kingsley Amis uses to condemn pop music in the passage quoted above, is based on Latin *somnus* 'sleep' and *ambulare* 'walk'. It therefore refers to walking in one's sleep. *Somnus* appears again in words like **somniferous** 'inducing sleep', **somniloquy** 'talking in one's sleep', **somnolence** 'drowsiness', **somnolent** 'causing drowsiness', **insomnia** 'inability to sleep'. *Ambulare* gives us words like **amble** and *perambulate*, but is also responsible for **ambulance**. This seems decidedly more curious, since the whole point about an ambulance is that a patient does not have to walk to the hospital.

It was the French who first talked of an *hôpital ambulant*, a 'walking hospital', at the beginning of the 19th century. These were something like field hospitals, wagons with beds and medical equipment which could be brought close to battle-lines. When first used in English, ambulance referred to such a

> ### SOUND
>
> Sound asleep! Sound? It is no name for it. I couldn't hear it thunder at such a time.
>
> **Mark Twain**
> *Carnival of Crime in Connecticut*

hospital cart, but the latter was soon being used to convey wounded soldiers to a more permanent hospital. Modern ambulances still perform both functions, being miniature mobile hospitals as well as conveyances.

SOPHOMORE

'I was a sophomore. No more.' She laughed. 'Sopholess, I guess.'

Garson Kanin *Moviola*

Sophomore is now only used by American speakers of English to describe a second-year student at a high school or college. The word for some reason seems to attract jokes. Garson Kanin's version is quoted above; others have turned it into Sophy Moore. The editors of Webster's *New Collegiate Dictionary* seem to think that the word was a joke to begin with, since they derive it from Greek *sophos* 'wise' and *moros* 'foolish'. The *Oxford English Dictionary* sees it more as based on **sophism**, so that the word would mean something like 'one who argues falsely'.

Webster's explanation is obviously more attractive, hinting at someone who is a mixture of wisdom and foolishness. The *soph-* part of the word occurs again in **philosopher**, someone who loves wisdom. *Moros* leads irregularly to **moron**, **moronic**. Perhaps a philosopher would say that we are all sophomores by Webster's definition.

SOUL

LYSANDER:
Stay, gentle Helena, hear my excuse;
My love, my life, my soul, fair Helena.

William Shakespeare
A Midsummer Night's Dream

Soul is a word of powerful significance, whether used in its secular or religious sense. The English word is from a common Germanic source which Friedrich Kluge, in his *Etymologisches Wörterbuch*, links with the word **sea**. This perhaps makes more immediate sense in German, where 'soul' is *Seele* and 'sea' *See*. Kluge suggests that our Germanic ancestors regarded the sea as the place where our souls resided before birth and after death.

In a non-religious context, the soul has long been associated with our emotions and feelings rather than thoughts. Poets have therefore frequently described the experience of love in terms of one soul meeting another. To address someone as **my soul** was once a passionate endearment, but it had considerably weakened by the 19th century. Mary Webb demonstrates in *Gone to Earth* that this was also the case in its dialectal usage: '"Tell us more, Hazel!" pleaded Edward. "What for do you want to hear, my soul?" Edward flushed at the caressing phrase, and Mrs Marston looked as indignant as was possible to her physiognomy, until she realised that it was a mere form of speech.'

What though we never silence broke,
Our eyes a sweeter language spoke;
The tongue in flattering falsehood deals,
And tells a tale it never feels:
Deceit the guilty lips impart,
And hush the mandates of the heart;
But soul's interpreters, the eyes,
Spurn such restraint, and scorn disguise.

Lord Byron To a Beautiful Quaker

Our subject in this book is words and language, but it is worth mentioning that souls are often said to have their own, wordless way of communicating with one another. Poets and writers tend to describe the 'language of the soul' in different ways. For Byron the eyes rather than the ears are the 'soul's interpreters' of a 'sweeter language' which, as he suggests in the above extract, is more direct and less capable of deceit than one which uses mere words. Mrs Aphra Behn had earlier referred to this same 'powerful' and wordless language in *Oroonoko*: 'Nor were his eyes silent, but answered hers again, as much as eyes could do, instructed by the most tender and most passionate heart that ever loved. And 'twas this powerful language alone that in an instant conveyed all the thoughts of their souls to each other.'

. . . the subject of love, upon which he expiated with great art and elocution, using not only the faculty of speech, but also the language of the eyes, in which he was a perfect connoisseur.

Tobias Smollett The Adventures of Peregrine Pickle

Emily Brontë would have supported the view that the soul's language is a visual one, though in *Wuthering Heights* she points out that love is not the only emotion with which it is concerned. She refers to what must be 'a look of hatred,

unless he has a perverse set of facial muscles that will not, like those of other people, interpret the language of his soul'. What the soul says, in other words, is interpreted in instinctive bodily reactions which are there to be interpreted by others in their turn.

For Thomas Hardy, in *Far from the Madding Crowd*, soul language is also wordless, though he does not mention what can be 'said' with the eyes: 'Silence has sometimes a remarkable power of showing itself as the disembodied soul of feeling wandering without its carcass, and it is then more impressive than speech. In the same way, to say a little is often to tell more than to say a great deal.'

There is no place like a bed for confidential disclosures between friends. Man and wife, they say, there open the very bottom of their souls to each other. . .

Herman Melville Moby Dick

On all sides, it would seem, this distrust of words exists when it comes to the communication of feelings, though George Eliot does allow 'unimposing words' into her version of this emotional language. In *Adam Bede* she says: 'Those slight words and looks and touches are part of the soul's language; and the finest language, I believe, is chiefly made up of unimposing words such as "light", "sound", "stars", "music" — words really not worth looking at, or hearing, in themselves, any more than "chips" or "sawdust"; it is only that they happen to be the signs of something unspeakably great and beautiful. I am of the opinion that love is a great and beautiful thing too; and if you agree with me, the smallest signs of it will not be chips and sawdust to you: they will rather be like those little words "light" and "music", stirring the long-winding fibres of your memory, and enriching your present with your most precious past.'

George Eliot's description of the soul's language is the fullest and probably the most accurate, including as it does 'slight words and looks and touches'. She is right to include the touches, which can say a great deal. It is not for nothing that Dickens writes in *Barnaby Rudge* that 'the eloquence of Joe's arm surpassed the most impassioned language, yet he said nothing'. He is referring to the arm which has 'crept round Dolly's waist'.

●

'Her silence was now as good as any speech. But as he did want more, she would, after her own way, reply to him. So there came upon his arm the slightest possible sense of pressure from those sweet fingers, and Harry Annesley was on a sudden carried up among azure-tinted clouds into the furthest heaven of happiness. After a moment he stood still, and passed his fingers through his hair and waved his head as a god might do. She had now made to him a solemn promise than which no words could be more binding.'

Anthony Trollope Mr Scarborough's Family

●

This soul language of 'slight words and looks and touches' is all very well, but it is naïve to think that unlike normal language, it is always truthful because it does not involve conscious thought. One has only to turn to Thackeray's anti-heroine, Becky Sharp, to see it being used deliberately and cynically. In *Vanity Fair*, when Becky is setting her cap at the ridiculous Joseph Sedley, she pretends to be revealing her feelings in spite of herself: 'She gave him ever so gentle a pressure with her little hand, and drew it back quite frightened, and looked first for one instant in his face, and then down at the carpet rods.' Thackeray adds, ironically: 'I am not prepared to say that Joe's heart did not thump at this little involuntary, timid, gentle motion

of regard on the part of the simple girl.'

●

Gently he lifted Mrs Pemberton's nearer hand, and stroked her fingers. 'There are so many things to do, and sometimes, I admit, I see more profit in a pretty woman's fingers than in the most sagacious discussion of the best-informed committee that ever sat.'

Mrs Pemberton looked at him shyly, and looked away again; and Mrs Nottingham, noisily turning the pages of her magazine, said sharply, 'Fingers don't argue, of course. If they can't acquiesce, they take themselves away.'

'You're under-rating them, my dear Elizabeth. Fingers are much more eloquent than that. They transmit the most delicate shades of meaning and emotion. They can be reluctant, or merely pretend to be reluctant, and let you know they are pretending. They can be simple and friendly, or as clever as a pianist, as clever as a diplomat in the old days of diplomacy. They can touch your heart with tenderness, or bargain like a Jew. They can say Yes, today; or Yes, tomorrow; or Yes, when it suits me. But you can't understand them, of course, unless you have learnt how to finger-read — and then you can understand them all.'

Eric Linklater The Faithful Ally

●

Becky is a clever actress, but in more normal circumstances the writers and poets have a point. There is little doubt that as a conversation becomes more truly emotional, the actual words used become less important. Information about feelings is mainly conveyed by such things as tone of voice and body language.

This can only apply, of course, when people are together. In *Peregrine Pickle*, Tobias Smollett has his hero write a love letter to Emilia, from whom he is temporarily separated, but the man who is acting as messenger ruins the sheet of paper. He decides not to report this, and instead asks a schoolmaster to write a replacement letter. Unfortunately, the schoolmaster is one who believes that

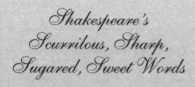

Shakespeare's Scurrilous, Sharp, Sugared, Sweet Words

CLOWN:
Let him approach singing.
PERDITA:
Forewarn him that he use no scurrilous words in's tunes.

The Winter's Tale

FORD:
[Of Falstaff] If he should intend this voyage toward my wife, I would turn her loose to him; and what he gets of her more than sharp words, let it lie on my head.

The Merry Wives of Windsor

LA PUCELLE:
By fair persuasions, mix'd with sugar'd words,
We will entice the Duke of Burgundy
To leave the Talbot and follow us.

Henry VI Part One

BEROWNE:
White-handed mistress, one sweet word with thee.
PRINCESS:
Honey, and milk, and sugar; there is three.

Love's Labour's Lost

written language should be as unlike its spoken version as possible. Though he himself begins his letter by using 'soul' as a term of address, he is not one to whom the word suggests George Eliot's 'unimposing words'. Emilia is decidedly irritated when she receives the following epistle:

'Divine Empress of my Soul, If the refulgent flames of your beauty had not evaporated the particles of my transported brain, and scorched my intellects into a cinder of stolidity, perhaps the resplendency of my passion might shine illustrious through the sable curtain of my ink, and in sublimity transcend the galaxy itself, though wafted on the pinions of a gray goose quill! But, ah! celestial enchantress! the necromancy of thy tyrannical charms hath fettered my faculties with adamantine chains, which, unless thy compassion shall melt, I must eternally remain in the Tartarean gulf of dismal despair. Vouchsafe, therefore, O thou brightest luminary of this terrestial sphere! to warm, as well as shine; and let the genial rays of thy benevolence melt the icy emanations of thy disdain, which hath frozen up the spirits of angelic pre-eminence. — Thy most egregious admirer and superlative slave, Peregrine Pickle.'

SPENDTHRIFT

Mr Potter and Mr Smithers had mutually agreed that, on the receipt of their quarter's salary, they would jointly, and in company, 'spend the evening' — an evident misnomer — the spending applying, as everybody knows, not to the evening itself, but to all the money the individual may chance to be possessed of, on the occasion to which reference is made. . .

Charles Dickens
Sketches by Boz 'Making a Night of it'

Dickens's joke (above) is possible because **spend** has been applied since the 14th century to time as well as money. The word is ultimately from Latin *pendere* 'weigh, hang', *dispendere* at first having the meaning 'weigh at the moment of distribution' then 'distribute'. **Dispense** is clearly from the same word. *Pendere* lies behind many other English words, including **append**, **compensate**, **depend**, **expend**, **impend**, **pending**, **pendulous**, **pendulum**, **pension**, **pensive**, **penthouse**, **perpendicular**, **recompense**, **suspend**.

Spendthrift seems to be a curious word, since **thrift** refers to careful, economical use of money, yet a spendthrift is someone who spends money wastefully and extravagantly. It is 'thrift' which has changed its sense. Originally a person who was **thrifty** was one who had **thrived** or been successful. Thrift was related to vigorous growth and prosperity. Later the accumulation of wealth seems to have been explained more in terms of spending one's money with great care. Spendthrift shows the earlier sense, and could be interpreted as a 'successful spender'.

SPIV

After the 1939-1945 war there were 'spivs', the offal-eaters who grew fat on the ugly by-products of war, such as food and clothing shortages, and 'dealing' in surplus stocks that the Government had for disposal.

Jane Duncan My Friends the Miss Boyds

As Jane Duncan suggests, **spivs** came into their own in Britain in the period immediately following World War Two. They were characterised by their flashy style of dress and lived by their wits. Webster's *New Collegiate Dictionary* is in no doubt that spiv was an alteration of **spiff**, which Partridge records in his *Dictionary of Historical Slang* in two main senses. A sentence like 'How spiff you look' meant 'how smartly dressed you are', with spiff as a noun meaning what

Partridge calls a **'swell'**. In the drapery trade, 'the spiff system' referred to the payment of spiff or spiffs as extra commission to an assistant who managed to sell off old stock. Both senses apply to the spiv.

'I don't like these slang words, Lily.'
'What slang words?'
'You know what you called Bernard's friend.'
'Oh, a swell. I fancy I do like slang. I think it's awfully jolly to talk about things being jolly. Only that I was afraid of your nerves I should have called him stunning. It's so slow, you know, to use nothing but words out of a dictionary.'

Anthony Trollope
The Small House at Allington

The word is now heard much less often, though Tony Thorne, in his *Dictionary of Contemporary Slang*, quotes examples of spoken usage in the 1980s. One would expect the word to be used only by middle-aged British speakers. 'Swell' in the meantime has survived in the USA far better than in Britain, though once again Thorne reports on recent British usage. Yuppies have apparently tried to revive the word as an acronym for a 'single woman earning lots of lolly', but this has not caught on widely. Its older meanings, presumably connected with the idea of 'swelling with importance', have been exemplified by American lyricists in lines like: 'We're a couple of swells, We stay in the best hotels.' Frank Sinatra has also been heard to declare: 'what a swell party this is'.

Use of slang is clearly one of the more noticeable aspects of the generation gap. Margaret Laurence makes the point well in *The Diviners*: '"He always thought I was kind of —" "What?" "Bourgeois. Square." "Square. I love your idiom, Ma. It's like an old dance tune from the forties." "Brat. You wait. Yours will be passé, too."'

VERBAL SUBSTITUTES

The following words have been extracted from a range of about 80 novels. Each word was a substitute for **said** after direct speech.

accepted
accused
acknowledged
added
addressed
adjured
admired
admitted
admonished
advised
affirmed
agreed
allowed
amended
amplified
announced
answered
anticipated
apologised
appealed
applauded
approved
argued
articulated
asked
assailed
assented
asserted
assured
attacked
attempted
averred
babbled
barked
bawled
bayed
beamed
began
begged
belched
bellowed
bemoaned
blazed
bleated
bluffed
blundered on
blurted out
blushed
blustered
boasted
boomed
bragged
brayed
breathed

bridled
broke in
broke off
broke out
brooded
brought forth
brought out
bubbled
burst out
cackled
cajoled
called
called out
came back with
came in with
came out with
carolled
cautioned
chafed
chaffed
chaffered
challenged
chanted
chastened
checked
cheered
chided
chimed
chipped in
chirped
choked
chortled
chorussed
chuckled
chuntered on
claimed
clamoured
clattered
click-clacked
clicked
coached
coaxed
comforted
commanded
commented
commiserated
complained
conceded
concluded
condescended
confessed
confided
confirmed
congratulated

considered
consoled
consulted
continued
contradicted
contributed
conversed
conveyed
cooed
corrected
coughed
counselled
countered
covered
crackled
cried
cried out
criticised
croaked
crooned
crowed
cursed
cut in
darted in
decided
declaimed
declared
delivered
demanded
demurred
denied
dictated
directed
dismissed
dissented
doubted
drawled
dreamed
droned
drooled
echoed
ejaculated
emended
encouraged
ended
enjoined
enquired
entreated
enunciated
essayed
evaded
exclaimed
excused
exhaled
exhorted
explained
exploded
expostulated
exulted

faltered
fenced
fibbed
finished
fired
flamed
flared
flashed
floundered
fluted
fluttered
followed up
formulated
frowned
fumbled
fumed
gabbled
gagged
gainsaid
gasped
gibbered
gibed
giggled
glared
gloated
gloomed
gobbled
gollopped
got in
got out
grated
greeted
grieved
grinned
gritted
groaned
groused
growled
grumbled
grunted
guessed
guffawed
gulped
gurgled
gushed
haggled
hailed
hallooed
harmonised
harrumphed
hazarded
hedged
hesitated
hissed
hollered
hooted
howled
hummed
humphed

hurried on
imitated
implored
indicated
inferred
informed
insinuated
insisted
instructed
interceded
interjected
interposed
interpreted
interrupted
intervened
intoned
introduced
invented
invited
jabbered
jeered
jerked out
joined in
joked
kept on
lamented
lashed
laughed
launched out
leched
leered
let out
lied
lisped
maintained
managed
mentioned
mimicked
moaned
mocked
mooed
morned
mouthed
mumbled
murmured
mused
muttered
nagged
narrated
nattered
neighed
nipped in
nodded
noted
objected
observed
offered
opened
ordered

owned
pacified
panted
paraphrased
parroted
parried
pealed
persisted
petitioned
piped
pleaded
plodded on
ploughed on
plunged on
pointed out
pondered
pounced
pouted
prattled
prayed
predicted
pressed
pressed on
probed
proceeded
proclaimed
prodded
produced
proferred
promised
prompted
pronounced
prophesied
proposed
protested
puffed
purred
pursued
put in
quavered
queried
questioned
quivered
quizzed
quoted
rallied
rambled on
ran on
ranted
rapped out
rasped
rattled
raved
read
read out
reasoned
rebuked
recalled
recited
recollected
reflected
reinforced

reiterated
rejoiced
rejoined
remarked
remembered
reminded
reminisced
remonstrated
repeated
replied
reported
reprimanded
reproached
reproved
requested
responded
restrained
resumed
retaliated
retorted
returned
revealed
riposted
roared
rumbled
ruminated
rushed on
sang
scoffed
scolded
scowled
screamed
seconded
shivered
shot back
shouted
shrieked
shrilled
shrugged
shuddered
sighed
simpered
slurped
smiled
smirked
snapped
snarled
sneered
snickered
sniffed
sniffled
sniggered
snorted
snubbed
snuffled
sobbed
soliloquised
soothed
sounded
spat
speculated
spluttered

sprayed
sputtered
squawked
squeaked
squealed
stalled
stammered
started up
stated
steamrollered on
stipulated
stormed
strained
stumbled on
stuttered
subsided
substituted
suggested
summed up
supplemented
supplied
swallowed
swept on
swore
taunted
teased
tempted
threatened
threw back
threw out
thundered
tittered
tossed out
translated
tried again
trilled
tutted
twanged
twittered
urged
uttered
ventured
volunteered
vouchsafed
vowed
wailed
warned
went on
wept
wheedled
whimpered
whined
whipped out
whispered
whistled
winked
wished
wondered
yattered on
yawned
yelled
yelped

When 'said' itself is used by a novelist, the way in which the words were spoken can be indicated by an adverb. The following have been used by writers as substitutes to fill the vacant position in a statement like: 'Good morning,' he said . . . .

abruptly	complacently
absently	confidentially
abstractedly	confusedly
accusingly	consolingly
acidly	contemptuously
acrimoniously	contentedly
admiringly	contritely
affably	conversationally
aggressively	convivially
agreeably	coolly
airily	coquettishly
amiably	cordially
angrily	courteously
animatedly	coyly
anxiously	crisply
apologetically	crossly
appealingly	cryptically
appreciatively	curiously
apprehensively	curtly
archly	cuttingly
authoritatively	decidedly
automatically	defensively
awkwardly	deferentially
belligerently	defiantly
benignly	deliberately
bitterly	delightedly
blandly	deprecatingly
blankly	derisively
bleakly	despairingly
bluntly	desperately
boastfully	determinedly
bravely	didactically
breathlessly	directly
breezily	disapprovingly
brightly	disgustedly
briskly	dismissively
brusquely	dispassionately
brutally	disrespectfully
calmly	distantly
candidly	distinctly
carefully	doggedly
carelessly	doubtfully
casually	drably
cattily	dramatically
cautiously	drawlingly
cheerfully	dreamily
chidingly	drearily
chirpily	drily
chummily	drowsily
clearly	drunkenly
cleverly	dubiously
coldly	dully
comfortably	eagerly
comfortingly	earnestly

easily	hesitantly	mysteriously	resentfully	sullenly
edgily	hoarsely	nakedly	resonantly	surprisingly
effortfully	hopefully	naturally	resoundingly	suspiciously
effusively	hopelessly	nervously	respectfully	sweetly
embarrassedly	horribly	nicely	restlessly	sympathetically
emphatically	hotly	nonchalantly	reverently	tactfully
encouragingly	huffily	noncommittally	rotundly	tartly
energetically	humbly	obediently	roughly	tearfully
enthusiastically	hurriedly	obligingly	roundly	tentatively
enviously	huskily	obstinately	ruefully	tersely
equably	icily	off-handedly	ruminatively	testily
evenly	illogically	ominously	ruthlessly	thickly
eventually	immediately	openly	sadly	thoughtfully
excitedly	impassively	over-rapidly	sagely	timidly
exclusively	impatiently	owlishly	sarcastically	tranquilly
expansively	impersonally	painfully	satirically	tremulously
explosively	imperturbably	passionately	savagely	trenchantly
expressionlessly	incredulously	pathetically	scornfully	triumphantly
facetiously	indifferently	patiently	secretively	truculently
faintly	indignantly	patronisingly	sensibly	truthfully
fairly	indirectly	peevishly	sententiously	uncertainly
feebly	inexorably	peremptorily	sentimentally	uncomfortably
feelingly	innocently	persuasively	seriously	unconcernedly
fervently	insistently	pertly	severely	unconvincingly
fiercely	instantly	petulantly	shakily	unctuously
finally	interminably	pitilessly	shamefacedly	understandingly
firmly	ironically	pityingly	sharply	uneasily
flatly	irrelevantly	placidly	shortly	unhappily
flippantly	irritably	plaintively	shrilly	unhesitatingly
fondly	jaggedly	platitudinously	shudderingly	unkindly
foolishly	jauntily	pleadingly	shyly	unwillingly
forcefully	jocularly	pleasantly	significantly	urbanely
frankly	jokingly	pointedly	silkily	urgently
frantically	judicially	politely	simply	vaguely
freshly	judiciously	pompously	sleepily	vehemently
fulsomely	kindheartedly	ponderously	slowly	venomously
furiously	kindly	precisely	slyly	viciously
fussily	knowingly	predictably	smoothly	victoriously
gaily	laconically	prickily	snappishly	vigorously
generously	lamely	primly	soberly	violently
genially	lazily	promptly	softly	virulently
gently	levelly	proudly	solemnly	vivaciously
gloomily	lightly	quaveringly	solicitously	warily
glumlygrandly	listlessly	quickly	sonorously	warmly
gratefully	loudly	quietly	soothingly	warningly
gravely	loyally	raggedly	sourly	wearily
grimly	madly	rapidly	spiritedly	wholeheartedly
gruffly	matter-of-factly	rashly	splenetically	wickedly
guardedly	meaningfully	raucously	steadily	wildly
half-audibly	mechanically	readily	sternly	winningly
happily	meditatively	reasonably	stiffly	wisely
harshly	mildly	reassuringly	stridently	wistfully
hastily	miserably	reflectively	strongly	witheringly
haughtily	modestly	regretfully	stubbornly	wittily
heartily	moodily	reluctantly	stuffily	wonderingly
heavily	morosely	reminiscently	sturdily	wryly
helpfully	mournfully	reproachfully	suavely	
helplessly	musingly	reprovingly	sulkily	

SQUAW

Sayward had nothing for the way squaws gave in to their men, waiting on them hand and foot, giving them the notion they were lords of creation.

Conrad Richter The Trees

Squaw is obviously an American Indian word, referring to an Indian woman or wife, but it is an unfortunate label for anyone to bear. The *squ-* is not a good beginning: there are not many words which begin that way in English but of those that do, most have unfortunate associations. Who would want to be linked phonetically to **squalid**, **squall**, **squander**, **squash**, **squat**, **squawk**, **squeak**, **squeal**, **squeamish**, **squelch**, **squint**, **squirm**, **squirt**?

As if that was not enough, American Indian squaws have earned a reputation for self-effacement and for making themselves voluntary domestic slaves. Squaw is therefore used disparagingly of any woman who acts in what is thought to be a squaw-like manner. A conversation in Anthony Powell's *Casanova's Chinese Restaurant* runs: "'If Hugh had wanted to marry a squaw, he could easily have found a squaw. They abound in musical circles. It is the answer for lots of artists." "Hugh has always been against squaws. Rightly, I think. In the long run, in my opinion, a squaw is even more of a nuisance than her antithesis — and often cooks worse too.'"

The young hero of Eric Linklater's *Magnus Merriman* tells an intimate friend: 'You've got a lovely caressing voice, a very good figure, a handsome chin, the most delicate and alluring of nostrils, a complexion almost as good as it used to be, really beautiful ears, and well-brushed hair.' All might have been well had he stopped at that point. The woman con-

> ## SUBMISSION
>
> Charles: On what submissive message art thou sent?
> Lucy: Submission, Dauphin! 'Tis a mere French word: We English warriors wot [know] not what it means.
>
> **William Shakespeare**
> Henry VI Part One

cerned leaves the room in a rage because he continues: 'but under all that there's a squat, square-faced, beady-eyed squaw with a baby at her breast and her bottom on the earth, and nothing in her heart but perpetual hunger and the will to survive. You're the eternal squaw.'

Not only a squaw, notice, but 'squat' and 'square-faced', words attracted as if by a magnet to that *squ-* sound, which a linguist might call a phonaestheme or a submorphemic differential. Squ-, in other words, has no distinct meaning or grammatical function, but that fact does a squaw no good at all.

STEPMOTHER

'Why do you call her your Mam?' Will asked. 'She's not, so why call her it?'

'But she's been my Mam, since they got married. What should I call her? Stepmother sounds nasty.'

Raymond Williams Border Country

The *step-* in **stepmother** and similar words has nothing to do with a kind of **step-ladder** relationship, one step down, as it were, from a blood relationship. Old English *steop*, which led to **stepbairn**, stepchild, originally meant 'orphan', as did both those words in their earliest meanings. Stepmother then came to mean 'one who becomes mother to an orphan'; stepson and stepdaughter became 'orphan who becomes a son/daughter by the marriage of a surviving parent'. The orphan meaning was then lost, putting the emphasis on a relationship brought about by the remarriage of a parent for whatever reason.

The *step-* prefix has been widely used beyond stepparents and stepchildren. It is possible to have a step-aunt or step-uncle, step-grandfather or step-grandmother. Step-mother-in-law has also been recorded, as well as stepbrother, stepsister, step-cousin, step-niece, step-nephew. By the 17th century stepmothers had acquired an unpleasant reputation, evidenced by such traditional children's stories as *Cinderella*, so words like step-devil 'stepmother' and steplord were also formed. The latter term referred to landlords who charged excessive rents and generally behaved in a nasty way. In

---

MISS PRUE:

Mother, Mother, Mother, look you here.

STEP-MOTHER:

Fie, miss, how you bawl — Besides, I have told you, you must not call me Mother.

MISS PRUE:

What must I call you then? Are you not my father's wife?

STEP-MOTHER:

Madam; you must say Madam. By my soul, I shall fancy myself old indeed, to have this great girl call me Mother.

William Congreve Love for Love

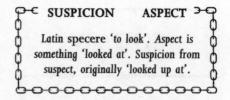

SUSPICION   ASPECT

Latin specere 'to look'. Aspect is something 'looked at'. Suspicion from suspect, originally 'looked up at'.

dialectal usage a **stepmother's blessing** was the ironic name for an **agnail**, a piece of torn skin at the root of a finger nail which causes soreness.

This background reputation of wickedness is hardly helpful to the modern stepmother, who is trying to cope with a difficult situation. Stepfathers also have their problems, but at least the word that describes them does not automatically suggest evil. Not that stepfathers escape scot free in literature. Dickens's portrayal of Edward Murdstone, who makes young David Copperfield's life such a misery, is blood-chilling. At one point David is driven to bite his stepfather and is locked up as a punishment. 'The length of those five days I can convey no idea of to anyone. They occupy the place of years in my remembrance.'

The problem of what to call a stepparent can cause real difficulties. Captain D. Bromley-Martin R.N., writing to *The Times* in July 1984, reported that his own family had had a family conference on the subject of how to address a step-grandmother. They had decided on **Steppie** and had duly adopted this term. This particular vocative might not appeal to others, but the family conference idea and use of a private word appears to be one worth copying. If a stepparent is addressed by his or her first name, the special relationship that exists is not acknowledged as it probably needs to be.

**FOR
TWO**

TALION

Not being an idealist, he was indifferent to the law of the talion.

Mary McCarthy *The Groves of Academe*

We are more familiar with the **talion** that Mary McCarthy speaks of in the form **retaliate**. In Roman law the *Lex talionis* was the principle of exacting retribution on an 'eye for eye, tooth for tooth' principle. It was also a law that made people think twice before they accused someone of a crime. If the accused was found not guilty, it was the accuser who received the appropriate punishment. To accuse someone of a crime that was punishable by death was therefore to put one's own life at risk.

The Latin word *talio* is from *talis* 'such, the like'. The earliest meaning of 'retaliate' was to 'repay in kind' in the broadest sense, so that if someone wished you good fortune, you could retaliate that wish. In Germany a speaker is still likely to reply *Gleichfalls* 'likewise, same to you' to someone who expresses the hope that he will enjoy his lunch. In modern English, of course, **retaliation**

TART

'The old French tart was telling me the whole system last night.' Lady Montdore was famous for picking up words she did not quite understand and giving them a meaning of her own. She clearly took the word tart to mean old girl, trout, body. Mrs Chaddesley Corbett was delighted.

Nancy Mitford *Love in a Cold Climate*

suggests only 'getting one's own back', avenging an injury, as when a footballer instinctively kicks a player who has fouled him. This is now frowned upon. Had the ancient Romans invented football, the *Lex talionis* might have become one of the rules of the game.

TARTAR

Who killed John Keats?
'I,' says the Quarterly,
So savage and Tartarly;
''Twas one of my feats.'

Lord Byron *John Keats*

Thomas Hood, in *A Tale of Temper*, remarks that 'cooks are generally Tartars'. In the poem he describes a particular woman who is not only a **Tartar** but a **shrew**, **Xantippe** and **Termagant**. Shrew refers to the insect-eating animal with a long sharp snout, commonly thought at one time to be venomous. Xantippe, or **Xanthippe**, was the wife of Socrates and a scold by reputation. For medieval Christians Termagant was the name of an imaginary god supposedly worshipped by Mohammedans. In the religious plays of the time he was always represented as violent and overbearing. Termagant was at first applied to a bullying person of either sex, but was later restricted to a quarrelsome woman.

The name Tartars describes the people who live in Central Asia, including the Mongols and Turks. The original ethnic name was **Tatar**, but this seems to have been altered deliberately to associate it with Greek **Tartarus** 'hell'. For this the reputation for savagery gained by the 13th-century leader Genghis (Jenghiz) Khan and his followers was no doubt responsible.

We allude to this reputation when we use **tartar sauce** to add a touch of 'fieriness', as John Ayto calls it in *The Glutton's Glossary*, to our fish. The chopped capers, onions and pickles that are added to the mayonnaise give the sauce its piquancy. **Steak tartare** is usually raw minced beef with an uncooked egg, though John Ayto says that in the authentic version horse meat replaces the beef.

In another of his poems Thomas Hood says that 'all children are tartars'. On this occasion he is back to his usual puns and does not mean that they are 'little savages'. He has redefined 'tartars' to mean 'those who are fond of tarts'.

TAXI

Every journalist has his idea of what the vehicle should be called. It has been described as the (1) taxi, (2) motor-cab, (3) taxi-cab, (4) taximeter-cab.

Daily Chronicle, March 1907

Taxi has become a truly international word, pronounced in roughly the same way throughout the world but sometimes spelt strangely. For a short time, at the beginning of the 20th century, it was usually referred to in print as the **taxy**, with a more normal English ending. 'Taxi' soon prevailed, an abbreviation of **taximeter**. Early forms of this device simply measured the distance that a passenger had travelled, but it was soon adjusted to calculate automatically the **tax** that was to be paid.

The taximeter was patented in Germany in 1890 and was called a *Taxameter*, though there had been an earlier German version called a *Taxanom*. The French changed 'taxameter' to 'taximètre' when

Teaser: What is curious about the name of the River 'Thames'? (Answer page 231)

taxis first appeared in Paris, and the English adapted the French term.

Tax itself is directly from Latin *taxare* 'censure, reckon, value', ultimately from Greek *taxai* 'to place'. In the Middle Ages the words tax and task were synonyms: even today 'take someone to task' is very similar in meaning to 'tax someone with something'. The words later went their separate ways, with tax taking on its special meaning of a 'compulsory contribution', but both belong to a larger word family which includes **syntax**, **tactics**, **taxidermy**, **taxonomy**.

*This was Don Juan's earliest scrape; but whether
I shall proceed with his adventures is
Dependent on the public altogether;
We'll see, however, what they say to this.
Their favour in an author's cap a feather,
And no great mischief's done by their caprice;
And if their approbation we experience,
Perhaps they'll have some more about a year hence.*

Lord Byron Don Juan

A taxi is often known as a **cab**, an abbreviation of **cabriolet**. In the 18th century this was the name of a light carriage drawn by one horse, so called because of its bounding motion. The springiness reminded people of the **capering** of a goat (Latin *capra*), what horsemen would call a **capriole**, a high leap made without advancing. *Capriolet* would in fact have been a more correct form of cabriolet, so we should perhaps be referring to taxis as 'caps' rather than cabs. It would also be etymologically satisfying if a taxi-driver was both **capricious** and a **Capricorn**. Both words, like Byron's **caprice** (above) have to do with the goat.

TEENY-WEENY

She liked to think that her care of me had been a little bit, a teeny bit, a teeny-weeny bit responsible for the things of beauty I was able to give the world.

William Golding Free Fall

There are a number of words in English which consist of two parts, each part closely linked in sound and sometimes in meaning to the other. Some, like **teeny-weeny**, are rhyme-words; others vary the vowel rather than the consonant, as in **fiddle-faddle**, **chit-chat**, but the structure of the component parts remains the same. Other words merely have parts which are alliterative or share an internal sound, as in **topsy-turvy**, **whipper-snapper**.

Such words form an interesting group, but etymologists often find them difficult to explain. For that matter, etymologists seem to find them difficult to name as a group, often using the absurd term **reduplicating**. The development of these words has often been illogical and whimsical, based on an unscientific sense of fun. Children, especially, are likely to exhibit a linguistic playfulness, creating strings of word noises that do not necessarily have much meaning. They play both with names — **Georgie-Porgie** — and words. One thinks of the little girl who wanted J.M. Barrie to be her **friendy-wendy**, thus suggesting to him the name Wendy for use in *Peter Pan*.

Children enjoy hearing these sound-words, as parents have long known. A baby's foot to a doting adult therefore becomes its **footsey**, and is soon its **tootsey-wootsey**, perhaps its 'teeny-weeny tootsey-wootsey'. **Teeny** is simply an emphatic form of **tiny**. The -weeny serves no serious linguistic purpose, unless the giving of aural pleasure can be counted as such.

'She's your tootsey-wootsey in the good old summer time.' (Quoting a popular song)

Sinclair Lewis Elmer Gantry

Once these curious words have been brought into being, they can be subjected to more normal linguistic processes, such as semantic change. Because baby talk, like the word **baby** itself, can be extended to an adult love-partner, **tootsey/tootsie** became an endearment, either in that form or as **toots**. Al Jolson made it famous with his 'Toot, toot, tootsie, goodbye'. Women now see the term as condescending. By an odd twist of fate it was left to Dustin Hoffmann, playing the part of a woman called Dorothy in the film *Tootsie*, to tell the men of the world that this form of address was now unacceptable.

Goody-goody is another item of child-talk which has changed its meaning, unless separate meanings arose independently. The word used to be the equivalent of French bon-bon 'sweet candy', but is now associated with the smug self-satisfaction exhibited by boring people.

Writing this skimble-skamble stuff in her cottage, she had agreed to cut the play here.

Virginia Woolf Between the Acts

Words of this type are as likely to become obsolete as any others. Virginia Woolf makes use of **skimble-skamble** in the passage quoted above, but the only modern speaker who would use such a word would be somebody steeped in Shakespeare's works. *Henry IV*, Part One has Hotspur complaining of the 'skimble-skamble stuff' to which Glendower subjects him. He means 'incoherent nonsense', but few people hearing the word today would make the connection with words like **scramble** and **shamble** and guess its meaning. In *Every Man in his Humour*, Ben Jonson likewise refers to making a husband a

'They say she's a rosy-cheeked, tisty-tosty little body enough.'

Thomas Hardy *The Withered Arm*

hoddy-doddy 'fool' or 'cuckold'. This obscure word has also disappeared.

Other terms may always have been

KNICK-KNACKERY

101 alliterative or rhyming words and phrases.

Airy-fairy
Argy-bargy
Arty-crafty
Arty-farty
Big-wig
Black-jack
Boogie-woogie
Brain drain
Busy-body
Cat-nap
Chiff-chaff
Chitter-chatter
Chock-a-block
Clap-trap
Clip-clop
Colly-wobbles
Creepy-crawly
Criss-cross
Dead-head
Dilly-dally
Ding-dong
Dribs and drabs
Eager-beaver
Eeny-meeny
Even-stevens
Fair and square
Fiddle-faddle
Flibberty-gibberty
Flim-flam
Flip-flop
Fuddy-duddy

Gew-gaw
Heebie-jeebies
Helter-skelter
Hi-fi
Higgle-haggle
Higgledy-piggledy
High and dry
Hip-hop
Hob-nob
Hobson-Jobson
Hodge-podge
Hoity-toity
Hotch-potch
Hot-shot
Hugger-mugger
Humdrum
Hurdy-gurdy
Hurry-scurry
Itsy-bitsy
Jeepers-creepers
Jiggery-pokery
Jingle-jangle
Knick-knack
Know-how
Kow-tow
Lovey-dovey
Might and main
Mish-mash
Namby-pamby
Nig nog
Nit-wit
No go
Now or never
Okey-dokey
Palsy-walsy

Part and parcel
Pell-mell
Pit-a-pat
Pot-shot
Rack and ruin
Rag-bag
Rag-tag
Raggle-taggle
Rat-tat
Riff-raff
Ring-a-ding
Rough and ready
Safe and sound
Shilly-shally
Silly-billy
Sin-bin
Sing-song
Slip slop
Spick and span
Teasy-weasy
Tell-tale
Tick-tock
Tic-tac
Tip-top
Tit for tat
Tittle-tattle
Walkie-talkie
Wear and tear
Wheeler-dealer
Whim-wham
Whipper-snapper
Wiggle-waggle
Willy-nilly
Wishy-washy
Zigzag

dialectal. Hardy's **tisty-tosty**, as he uses it in the above quotation, appears to mean 'pleasantly plump'. The woman concerned is perhaps like Dylan Thomas's Polly Garter, well-rounded in all parts, with 'a roly-poly bum' as Captain Cat expresses it. **Roly-poly** shows a formation typical of many words of this type, being clearly based on 'roll' but converted to an affectionate diminutive. In the same story, incidentally, Hardy refers to 'some **harum-scarum** young woman'. This presumably has to do with 'haring about' in a wild and reckless way.

I always felt there had been some hanky-panky.

Maie Casey *An Australian Story*

With a word like **hanky-panky**, recorded only from the mid-19th century, one regrets the lack of information about its origin. There may be a link with **hocus-pocus**, through **hokey-pokey**. How did such a useful word, one which perfectly suggests the behaviour it refers to, come into being? Since no solid evidence exists, there is a certain amount of scope for ingenious guesswork. For the -turvy of **topsy-turvy**, for example, which is equally mysterious, somebody proposed a corruption of 't'other way'. Unfortunately, it is easier for scholars to show that this cannot have been its origin than it is for them to give the true explanation.

A few words that now belong to this curious group have been adapted from their original foreign forms to make them suitable. **Mumbo-jumbo** 'meaningless ritual' is a corruption of some African word, originally applied to a kind of bogey man. **Pow-wow** is an Anglicised form of an American Indian term for a group discussion. Occasionally, English retains a word or expression that was already of this type in the

original language. **Bric-à-brac** 'things of no great value collected by chance', is an example.

Some verbal bric-à-brac on this theme is collected on page 189. The list is not exhaustive, as word-collectors will quickly realise. It is meant to be a collection of tit-bits which invites expansion.

TELEVISION

She gets three magazines a week and can hardly get through them for watching telly. 'Telly.' I don't like that word somehow. It always reminds me of fat ignorant pigs swilling stout and cackling like hens at the sort of jokes they put on them coloured seaside postcards: all about fat bellies and chamber pots and that sort of thing.

Stan Barstow *A Kind of Loving*

What Stan Barstow is implicitly saying in the passage quoted above is that he does not like the kind of people who habitually say **telly**. Others have disliked the word **television** itself, on the grounds that it mixes Greek and Latin elements. The saying that 'no good will come of this device' because of that mixing is usually attributed to C.P. Scott.

Greek *tele* 'far off' should have been followed by another Greek word. Had **telescope** not already existed in a different sense (the -scope from Greek *scopeo* 'look at'), that might well have become the word for 'television'. Rather than an unsatisfactory all-Greek alternative — perhaps something like **telorama** or **teleorama**, based on *horama* 'view' from *horeo* 'to see' — the hybrid television was rightly preferred. The -vision is ultimately from Latin *videre* 'to see'. **Telephone** is a purer formation, *phone* being the Greek word for 'voice' or 'sound'.

Another school of thought says that words like television and telephone are bad because they are clearly 'un-English'. The Germanic tradition, runs the argument, requires the formation of new words from native elements. German Fernsehen 'television' and Fernsprecher 'telephone', respectively 'far-seeing' and 'far-speaker', demonstrate what should be done. Against this it can be said that English does indeed use native compounds like **far-seeing**, as the existence of that word proves. There are also advantages to using Greek and Latin to create international words, common to many languages. German itself has for that reason tended to abandon Fernsprecher in favour of Telephon.

Why should people go out and pay money to see bad films when they can stay at home and see bad television for nothing?

Samuel Goldwyn

Anyone who tries to insist on etymological purity in the formation of new words is obviously fighting a losing battle. Tele- is now freely used to form words where no thought is given to linguistic compatibility, although the meaning is usually apparent. The prefix indicates the use of either the telephone or a television set in words like **telebanking**, **telebetting**, **telebroking**, **teleconference**, **telemarketing**,

telemeeting, teleordering, telepundit, teleshopping, telethon, televangelist.

Another modern tele- word is **telespud**, which describes the kind of person Stan Barstow had in mind. It is a synonym for **couch potato**, which in turn is a pleasant joke. The full story of the expression is told in The Oxford Dictionary of New Words. Basically, **potato** was suggested by **tuber**, someone who watched the **boob tube**, or telly.

THUNDERSTRUCK

Trunnion was thunderstruck at this piece of intelligence.

Tobias Smollett The Adventures of Peregrine Pickle

We talk curiously about being **thunderstruck** when we feel as if we have been struck not by thunder but by lightning. The ancients believed that when lightning struck a tree or building, the damage was caused by a **thunderbolt**, a kind of dart discharged by a god. In Old Norse mythology the god concerned was **Thor**, his name being derived from the Norse word for 'thunder'. This same god is remembered in German Donnerstag, and **Thursday**.

Thunder is interesting to the etymologist because it provides an example of epenthesis, the intrusion of an extra sound or letter in a word. In Old English 'thunder' was thunor, more clearly related to modern German Donner. The sound of the d gradually intruded itself until pronunciation of the word altered permanently.

The Times newspaper was known as the **Thunderer** in the 19th century, the nickname having been applied at first to Edward Sterling. He was writing for the newspaper 1830–40. As for **thunder**

and lightning, the phrase has been applied figuratively at various times to combinations of contrasting things. In the 18th and 19th centuries flashy articles of clothing were described in this way, especially if they were of strongly contrasting colours. In slang the phrase was also applied to 'gin and bitters' or 'treacle and clotted cream'.

TIME

—◦—

'He's of a roving nature, ma'am — from flower to flower — from sweet to sweet — but his is the butterfly time of life, and we must not be hard upon such trifling.'

Charles Dickens *Barnaby Rudge*

—◦—

Time is one of those complex words that is used in a wide variety of meanings and is seemingly capable of being defined anew by each generation. Our ancestors would have been bemused, for instance, by our **quality time** and **time-share**, as well as the broadcasters' **prime time** and **needle time**, yet such concepts are now commonplace. They are fairly recent additions to what is almost an 'alphabet of time'. It consists of phrases such as **appointed time**,

THEY

'They try to stop me enjoying what's good for me. But they won't manage it.'
They. It was an ominous word. One grows to dread the complications aroused by the mysterious 'They.'

Joanna Jones *Nurse Is A Neighbour*

borrowed time, **closing time**, **daylight-saving time**, **free time**, and many more.

Especially interesting, however, are the imaginative qualifications of time that the great writers suggest to us. Dickens gives us **butterfly time** in the quotation above, and we know exactly what he means. In passing he uses a word which is curious in itself, since the connection between a **butterfly** and **butter** is by no means clear. The Oxford English Dictionary cites a Dutch name for the insect which 'suggests that the insect was so called from the colour of its excrement', but others have suggested that the name may refer simply to the colour of common varieties of butterfly.

—◦—

She had often said to her sister, in the confidence of curling-time (ladies wore curls in those days) 'that the only man who could ever bring her to think of matrimony was Mr Gibson.'

Elizabeth Gaskell *Wives and Daughters*

—◦—

Elsewhere, in *David Copperfield*, Dickens is rather less successful with his individual definition of time. Steerforth is talking about 'evening' when he says: 'I detest this **mongrel time**, neither day nor night.' This sounds almost Shakespearean but is not: Shakespeare can nevertheless be relied on for a wide range of terms, ranging from **devouring time** and **witching time** to **golden**, **ripened** or **hasty-footed time**.

—◦—

'Even borrowed time gives out and I've been on it for more than I'm entitled to.'

Fannie Hurst *Anywoman*

—◦—

All writers agree on an aspect of time that the dictionary-makers are obliged to ignore: the nature of time changes according to individual circumstances. 'Time travels in divers paces with divers persons,' says Rosalind, in *As You Like It*, and expounds on the theme at some length. An inscription on the pendulum of the tower clock, in St Lawrence's Church, Bidborough, Kent, prefers to say that it varies according to a person's age:

When as a child I laughed and wept
— Time crept.
When as a youth I dreamed and talked — Time walked.
When I became a full-grown man — Time ran.
And later as I older grew — Time flew.
Soon I shall find when travelling on — Time gone.
Will Christ have saved my soul by then? — Amen.

Young Courtly: How can you manage to kill time?
Grace: I can't. Men talk of killing time, while time quietly kills them.

Dion L. Boucicault London Assurance

Others point out that our perception of time is subjective, no matter what our age. In *Under the Garden*, Graham Greene says: 'Time isn't measured by clocks. Time is fast or slow or it stops for a while altogether. One minute is different to every other minute. When you make love it's a pulse in a man's part which measures time and when you spill yourself there's no time at all. That's how time comes and goes, not by an alarm clock.' John Cowper Powys is more succinct in *Wolf Solent*: 'Time's like a telescope. It compresses itself or lengthens itself, according to our feelings.'

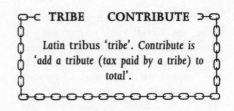

TRIBE   CONTRIBUTE

Latin *tribus* 'tribe'. Contribute is 'add a tribute (tax paid by a tribe) to total'.

TOWNIE

They were 'townies' and something apart. The word townie was the worst reproach that could be made. A townie dressed differently, spoke differently, lived differently, and knew nothing — that is, nothing that really mattered.

Geraint Goodwin The Heyday in the Blood

Townie in the above quotation is an interesting example of linguistic revenge. Traditionally, the townsman has laughed at the **bumpkin**, **chawbacon**, **clod-hopper**, **hayseed**, **hick**, **hillbilly**, **peasant**, **pot-walloper**, **rustic**, **yokel**. Townie at least shows that there is another view on the matter.

The -*ie* suffix seems to have acquired a meaning of 'person associated with' the preceding word. It allowed the formation of **roadie**, for example, as a shortening of 'road-manager', the person who handles equipment and makes practical arrangements when a group of rock-musicians are 'on the road'. **Foodie** also exists. Ian Murray, who runs *Word of Mouth*, a bookshop devoted to food and drink, was quoted in a *Times* article (January, 1993) as saying: 'Foodies — I hate the word but it's so appropriate — can be terribly boring to their friends because their conversation inevitably turns to food and drink.'

Junkie is another modern word; older examples include **bookie**, **cabbie**, **goalie**. Thomas Pyles identified such terms as 'clipped forms with hypocoristic suffix', thus relating them (through hypocoristic, based on Greek korê 'young girl') to childish pet names. That they are not always meant affectionately is shown by the contemptuous townie and junkie.

In his British *Writers of the Thirties*, Valentine Cunningham talks of **youthies**. He is referring to writers such as W.H. Auden, Louis MacNeice, Cecil Day Lewis, Christopher Isherwood and Graham Greene, who were all young during the period he is discussing. The term has little to commend it and has not come into general use.

Shakespeare's Third, Tricksy Words

FALSTAFF:

This same starv'd justice hath done nothing but prate to me of the wildness of his youth and the feats he had done about Turnbull Street; and every third word a lie.

Henry IV Part Two

LORENZO:

The fool hath planted in his memory
An army of good words; and I do know
A many fools that stand in better place,
Garnish'd like him, that for a tricksy word
Defy the matter.

The Merchant of Venice

TURNPIKE

It would necessitate her keeping to the turnpike road.

Thomas Hardy *The Withered Arm*

A turnpike was originally a revolving barrier, armed with pikes or spikes. In the 15th century it was used as a military defence, but by the 17th century the word was being applied to the barrier across a toll-road. In modern times turnpike is one of those interesting words which the British have abandoned but which survives in North America, usually applied to a toll expressway. It was not quite this that Byron had in mind when he wrote in Don Juan:

What a delightful thing's a turnpike road!
So smooth, so level, such a mode of shaving
The earth, as scarce the eagle in the broad
Air can accomplish, with his wide wings waving.

TWAT

They talked of his having a Cardinal's hat,
They'd send him as soon an old nun's twat.

Vanity of Vanities (1660)

The 19th-century English poet Robert Browning is known to have read the above couplet. He was unfamiliar with the word **twat** but guessed from the context that it referred to part of a nun's dress. He therefore used the word in that sense in his dramatic poem *Pippa Passes*, published in 1841.

Unfortunately, Browning had not taken into account the earthy quality of his source. His guess as to the meaning of twat was inaccurate, to say the least. Eric Partridge, in his *Dictionary of Historical Slang*, goes so far as to refer to Browning's 'hair-raising misapprehension — the world's worst literary "brick".' This is because twat is in fact an extremely vulgar reference to the vulva, the equivalent of another four-letter word that ends in -t. Browning and his publishers were protected by their innocence, as were various other poets who subsequently — on Browning's authority — used the word as he had used it.

The year's at the spring,
And day's at the morn;
Morning's at seven;
The hill-side's dew-pearled;
The lark's on the wing;
The snail's on the thorn;
God's in his heaven —
All's right with the world.

Robert Browning *Pippa Passes*

It would give a false impression of Browning to mention only this mistake. He was, after all, responsible for such lines as:

That's the wise thrush; he sings each
    song twice over
Lest you should think he never could
    recapture
The first fine careless rapture!

TUB

Tub — it has a strangely old-world sound in English nowadays; but in Yugoslavia, on the other hand, it is exceedingly up-to-date. Which leads us on to that very odd class of international English words that have never been good English at all. A Smoking, for example, a Dancing, a Five-o'clock — these have never existed except on the continent of Europe. As for High-Life, so popular a word in Athens, where it is spelt iota, gamma, lambda, iota, phi — that dates from a remote, mid-Victorian epoch in the history of our national culture.

Aldous Huxley *Those Barren Leaves*

It is also easy to forgive the slip, which occurred only because Browning constantly experimented with language. In his *Short History of English Words*, Bernard Groom remarks: 'Browning's vocabulary is vast, but it is the vocabulary of living passion, of philosophical analysis, rather than of pure poetry. New words occur in his verse, but many are such as the language has no need of, such as the strange *encolure* for the mane of a horse. If, however, he is the inventor of *artistry*, of which the first known instance occurs in *The Ring and the Book*, at least one good word stands to his credit.' Let him be remembered, then, for that contribution rather than the mistaken 'twat'.

FOR
ME

UMPTEENTH

I tell her for the umpteenth time that I haven't been in the place.

Stan Barstow A Kind of Loving

The Concise Oxford Dictionary describes **umpteen** and **umpteenth** as jocular formations referring to an indefinite number. Their original use had a more serious motive than this suggests. When the words first appeared during World War One, Morse code was in regular use. In signallers' slang, **iddy** and **umpty** were the words for the dots and dashes of the code.

This made it possible for umpty to be used in other contexts where a dash might be demanded by military censorship. In writing or speaking about his division or brigade, for instance, a soldier would substitute umpty for the relevant number. It was then quite natural for this numerical association of

UMBRELLARIAN

Except in a very few cases of hypocrisy joined to a powerful intellect, men, not by nature umbrellarians, have tried again and again to become so by art, and yet have failed — have expended their patrimony in the purchase of umbrella after umbrella, and yet have systematically lost them, and have finally, with contrite spirits and shrunken purses, given up their vain struggle, and relied on theft and borrowing for the remainder of their lives.

R.L. Stevenson Philosophy of Umbrellas

Teaser: What is curious about the word 'unhyphenated'?

(Answer page 232)

??

umpty to bring about the change to umpteen.

Umpteen and umpteenth have since firmly established themselves, especially in the phrases 'umpteen times' and 'for the umpteenth time'. English-speakers clearly felt the need for a word which referred to a fairly large, indefinite number.

UNDERTONES

'You're reminding me of all those Freudian bullshit artists who convinced the public that a woman who was raped must have gone out of her way to get it. Not that I want to give this thing sexual undertones.'

'Overtones.'

'Whatever.'

Judith Rossner Any Minute I Can Split

The speaker in the above passage did not need to be corrected. In this context, both **undertones** and **overtones** have the meaning of 'something suggested rather than stated'. This makes the words rather curious: **under** and **over** are usually very distinct opposites whether used as separate words or as prefixes. It is strange to find a pair of words where they act as if they are synonymous.

Pointed use of under-/over- pairs of words is fairly common. Road safety campaigners are keen to remind us that a careless **overtaker** is likely to end up with the **undertaker**. The once witty **underwhelmed** variant of **overwhelmed** has been repeated often enough to find a place in the dictionaries. What is surprising, perhaps, is that several of the words in this group do not have their potentially useful opposites. We do not tell a friend that he has **understayed** his welcome or say that an easy task has **undertaxed** us. We speak of workers on **overtime** but do not use **undertime** for those who leave early or work badly. Iris Murdoch talks of having **disenjoyed** an evening (see page 54); should she not also have been **underjoyed** at what had happened? We appear to be **underusing** our linguistic resources.

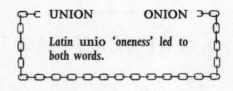

UNION   ONION

Latin **unio** 'oneness' led to both words.

insist') — that a sentence must never end in a preposition. Sidney Greenbaum and Janet Whitcut say in their *Longman Guide to English Usage* that it is sometimes quite natural for a sentence to do so, and that an alternative structure would be difficult to find. How else would you say: 'It wasn't worth arguing about'; 'The details have been attended to'; 'What are they like?'

The meaning of 'up' seems to need no

UP

---○---

'That's the kind of sentence up with which a sensitive Old Wellingtonian should not on any occasion be asked to put,' Colonel Savage said. 'But I presume you dislike Churchill.'

John Masters Bhowani Junction

---○---

John Masters clearly expected most of his readers to pick up the allusion in the above quotation. It was Sir Ernest Gowers, in *Plain Words*, who told us that Sir Winston Churchill wrote in the margin of a document: 'This is the sort of English up with which I will not put.' It was an ironic comment on a 'rule' which teachers of English used to insist on (or 'on which teachers used to

UNFORTUNATE

Henry Mulcahy, an 'unfortunate' personality in the lexicon of department heads.

Mary McCarthy The Groves of Academe

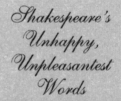

Shakespeare's Unhappy, Unpleasantest Words

[To Petruchio, who has announced that he wishes to marry Kate]
BAPTISTA:
Well mayst thou woo, and happy be thy speed!
But be thou arm'd for some unhappy words.

The Taming of the Shrew

[On hearing that Antonio's ventures have failed]
BASSANIO:
O sweet Portia,
Here are a few of the unpleasant'st words
That ever blotted paper!

The Merchant of Venice

explanation, yet there comes a point in *Bhowani Junction* where John Masters feels obliged to pause and define both **up** and **down**. The title of the novel hints at the reason for this, with its railway connotations: 'I ought to explain here that "down" means the direction going away from Bombay, and "up" means going to Bombay. Every railway has its own words, but that's what we use on the Delhi Deccan.' This usage did not begin with the railways. People have been talking of going up to a city, such as London, since the 15th century.

○

Life is chequer'd, a patchwork of smiles and of frowns;
We valued its ups, let us muse on its downs.

Frederick Locker-Lampson London Lyrics

○

In other contexts, up can become a decidedly curious word, especially when it is not a preposition. It is often very difficult to say what the word means. In *What A Word!* (1935) A.P. Herbert commented that up was being increasingly used as what he called an 'adverbial particle, verb-follower or tail-twister'. He cited the British use of **ring up** 'telephone'. What is the meaning of up in such an expression? Does it have any meaning at all?

A.P. Herbert continued: 'You do not wash your dirty plates; you wash them up, and then you clean up the sink. I suspect that you wind up your watch. Then perhaps you hurry up (you may even dress up) because you want to dash off with your wife to the pictures — or the pub. At the pub she will tell you to drink up because she is fed up. You may then fall out and come home done up.' Herbert accepted that in some of these instances the 'up' was necessary, giving the verb that preceded it a distinctive new meaning. To **dress up** is to do more than **dress**, just as to **drink up** is not just to **drink**. He was right, nevertheless, to remind us that as careful speakers and writers we should consider whether an adverbial particle is necessary.

UNKED

On Tuesday afternoon Molly returned home — to the home which was already strange, and what Warwickshire people would call 'unked' to her. New paint, new paper, new colours . . .

Elizabeth Gaskell
Wives and Daughters

FOR
VICTORY

VERBICIDE

Life and language are alike sacred. Homicide and verbicide — that is, violent treatment of a word with fatal results to its legitimate meaning, which is its life — are alike forbidden. Manslaughter, which is the meaning of the one, is the same as man's laughter, which is the end of the other.

Oliver Wendell Holmes
The Autocrat of the Breakfast Table

Verbicide in the above quotation is the author's playful invention, and ought strictly to refer to the 'killing' of a word rather than its 'violent treatment'. Even by Holmes's definition, verbicide was rather a strong term to use. He was merely referring to puns.

Holmes defines **homicide** as **manslaughter**, though the latter word has acquired the special legal sense of 'the unlawful killing of a human being without malice aforethought'. He no doubt had in mind the earlier and more general sense of manslaughter: 'the killing of a human being by a human being'. Most people in Britain would think of homicide as an American word for which

VAQUERO

'A vaquero is a Mexican cowboy,' he said crisply. 'Did you ever hear the word buckaroo? That's what the old Texas pioneers made of vaquero, they couldn't get the hang of the Spanish word vaquero. You see — vaca, cow. Vaquero — fellow who tends cows.'

Edna Ferber *Giant*

they themselves would use 'murder'.

We are familiar with *-cide* as a suffix which means '-killer'. It has been established by words like **suicide**, **insecticide**, **spermicide** and the like. An article in *The Observer* (14.2.93), headed 'Halt use of suspect **pesticide**,' reported on the worries of people living in Lincolnshire. A **fungicide** called benomyl was being circumstantially linked there to children born without eyes.

Infanticide is practised as extensively and as legally in England, as it is on the banks of the Ganges.

Benjamin Disraeli *Sybil* (1845)

The familiarity of the suffix has made it possible, as Oliver Wendell Holmes demonstrated, for authors to invent new terms of this type. Those who have done so often have some *ad-hoc* purpose which is not always serious. It is not really necessary, for example, in an article on bull-fighting, to refer to **tauricide**, but the readers will know what is meant. What the writer must avoid, in theory, is an ugly mix of languages, such as 'bullicide'. The base-word must be in its Latin form.

That rule having been made, it can sometimes be effectively broken. In an episode of the television series *Northern Exposure*, for example, an argument occurred between a man and woman about the morality of hunting. A reference at one point to **Bambicide** summed up in a single word what the woman thought of the matter. In her view, the man she was disagreeing with had a cloyingly sentimental view of animals. For him, hunting was the killing of cute Bambi-like creatures. To be strictly accurate, one should say 'Bambi-like creatures as depicted by Disney'. The original young deer that appears in the Felix Salten children's novel *Bambi* is decidedly more realistic.

KILLER WORDS	Fratricide (brother)	Perdricide (pheasant)
	Fungicide (fungus)	Pesticide (pest)
	Genocide (race, nation)	Prolicide (infant)
Some -*cide* words where	Germicide (germ)	Regicide (king)
the suffix means 'killer'.	Giganticide (giant)	Rodenticide (rodent)
	Homicide (human being)	Senicide (old man)
Acaricide (mite, tick)	Infanticide (infant)	Sororicide (sister)
Amicide (friend)	Insecticide (insect)	Spermicide (sperm)
Apicide (bee)	Macropicide (kangaroo)	Suicide (oneself)
Avicide (bird)	Mariticide (husband)	Taeniacide (tapeworm)
Bactericide (bacteria)	Matricide (mother)	Tauricide (bull)
Bovicide (ox)	Microbicide (microbe)	Tyrranicide (tyrant)
Canicide (dog)	Miticide (mite)	Uxoricide (wife)
Ceticide (whale)	Muricide (shell fish)	Vaticide (prophet)
Femicide (woman)	Parricide (parent)	Vermicide (worm)
Filicide (son or daughter)	Patricide (father)	Vulpicide (fox)

The word **decide**, which obviously has nothing to do with killing, looks as if it falls into this group by accident. It nevertheless stands beside the other words in its own right. The -*cide* of these words is ultimately from Latin *caedere* 'to cut, kill'. It is the 'cut' meaning that lies behind decide, which originally meant 'to cut off, cut the knot, reach a decision'.

VERMILION

———————————O———————————

Her complexion was a rich and mantling olive, and when watching the glow upon her cheeks I could almost swear that beneath the transparent medium there lurked the blushes of a faint vermilion.

Herman Melville *Typee*

———————————O———————————

There are certain words which are innately poetical: **vermilion** appears to be one of them. The word demands attention, and it is interesting to see where Melville, in the passage quoted above, places the word. Gerard Manley Hopkins uses it in a similar way, to bring his

poem on *The Windhover* to a triumphant conclusion. In an image of great beauty he describes the 'blue-bleak embers' which 'fall, gall themselves, and gash gold-vermilion'. Charlotte Brontë, as it happens, had earlier commented in *Villette* on a room, 'warm in its amber lamp light, and vermilion fire flush'.

———————————O———————————

Wilde derived an exquisite pleasure even from the sounds of syllables, and in conversation would dwell on such words as 'vermilion', 'narcissus', 'amber', 'crimson', pronouncing them as if tasting them.

Hesketh Pearson *The Life of Oscar Wilde*

———————————O———————————

John Keats uses the word in *Endymion*, where he talks of fish which are 'golden, or rainbow-sided, or purplish, vermilion-tail'd'. In the same poem occurs the mainly adjectival form of the word, **vermeil**, which Keats applies to 'daisies, vermeil rimm'd and white'. The entry for 'vermeil' in *The Oxford English Dictionary* specifies that it is 'chiefly poetical' and proves the point with quotations from Wordsworth, Gray, Moore, Tennyson and Milton. All these poets could have picked up the word from Edmund Spenser, who returns to it again and again in *The Faerie Queene* and then invents the unique form **vermily** as a synonym of 'vermilion'.

Etymology sometimes plays curious tricks, and the history of 'vermeil, vermilion' strips away much of the poetry. Both words are based on Latin *vermis* 'worm'. The diminutive *vermiculis* 'little worm' was applied first to the cochineal insect which yields a scarlet dye, then to the colour. Words from the same Latin source include **vermine**, the pasta **vermicelli** — literally 'little worms', **vermicide** 'medicine for killing intestinal worms', **vermiculated** 'worm-eaten', **vermicule** 'small worm, maggot or grub', **vermivorous** 'feeding on worms'.

Because of more etymological trickery, **vermouth** does not belong with this group, even though the word represents a French version of German *Wermuth* 'wormwood'. **Wormwood** has nothing to do with worms — the word is a corruption of Old English *wermod*, which appears to mean 'man-courage'. Professor Weekley suggested in his *Etymological Dictionary of Modern English* that the plant earned this name because it was in early use as an aphrodisiac. Vermouth, which is white wine flavoured with

> ### VEHICLE   WAGON
> Indo-European *wegh* '*carry*' is the ultimate origin of both words.

wormwood, is now usually drunk as an aperitif and is meant to stimulate an appetite other than carnal.

VICE

○

My uncle's lapses into insobriety had no vice about them, they were purely therapeutic.

Nancy Mitford *Love in a Cold Climate*

○

A few pages before the above passage occurs, Miss Mitford talks of the 'best-looking Viceroy we ever sent to India'. The title of a **Viceroy**, or for that matter, a **vice-captain**, **vice-chairman**, **vice-admiral**, **vice-chancellor**, **vice-president**, etc., clearly does not link with **vice** in its sense of 'evil conduct'. The prefix is from an oblique form of Latin *vix* 'change' and means 'in place of' or 'in succession to'. It will be noticed that, of the examples quoted above, 'Viceroy' differs from the others in that **roy** 'king' is not used independently in English. In Old French the prefix was often *vis-*, a form which survives in **viscount**. *Vice* itself is much used in the expression **vice versa** 'the other way round', where *versa* is from *vertere* 'turn'. We also have **vicissitude** 'change of circumstances'.

Latin *vix* also led to *vicarius* 'substitute', found in our words **vicar**, **vicarious**. The former was originally a priest who acted in place of a rector. We experience something vicariously in our imagination, having heard about it from the person to whom it really happened.

VARSITY

She tried once or twice to ascertain whether he came from Oxford or Cambridge, but she missed her timid opportunities. She tried to get him to make remarks about those places to see if he would say 'go up' to them instead of 'go down' — she knew that was how you told a 'Varsity' man. He used the word 'Varsity' — not university — in quite the proper way.

H.G. Wells *Miss Winchelsea's Heart*

Public schools are the nurseries of all vice and immorality.

Henry Fielding Joseph Andrews

Vice in its evil sense is from Latin vitium 'fault, defect'. It is linked with **vicious**, **vitiate** 'corrupt, debase, contaminate' and **vituperate** 'revile, abuse'.

The third kind of vice, the tool that is used to clamp objects, takes its name from the screw which tightens the jaws. Latin vitis literally means 'vine', but the metaphorical reference is to the spiral growth of the tendrils. Vice has been applied in English at different times to other kinds of 'spirals'; in the 14th century, for example, it meant a spiral or winding staircase. The tool was named at the beginning of the 16th century.

VOICE

LEAR:
Her voice was ever soft,
Gentle and low, an excellent thing in woman.

William Shakespeare King Lear

The word **voice** came into English from French, but looks back to Latin vox, vocis 'voice'. There is a whole family of connected English words, some taken directly from Latin, others borrowed from French. They include: **advocate**, **avocation**, **convocation**, **convoke**, **equivocate**, **evocation**, **evoke**, **irrevocable**, **provocation**, **provoke**, **revoke**, **vocabulary**, **vocalise**, **vocation**, **vocative**, **vociferation**, **vouch**, **voucher**, **vouchsafe**, **vowel**.

Her voice is pitched lower than ever. It has a husky note, now, which she has taken pains to develop. It involves the listener, willy-nilly, with the night she spent before — was it full of sex or tears, or both? What dreadful, fearful, marvellous things might that voice not speak of next?

Fay Weldon Down Among the Women

Language is primarily spoken rather than written, and a speaker's voice in itself can do far more than merely produce strings of sounds which are analysed by the hearer as words. It can affect the underlying message of whatever is said, especially by imparting an erotic quality to words which are otherwise innocent. This aspect of the voice is often mentioned by writers. Philip Roth, in The Counterlife, has: 'Maria speaks in the most mesmeric tones, and it's the voice that does the seducing, it's the voice that I have to caress me, the voice of the body I can't possess.'

When she spoke a peculiar melody struck the hearer's ears. Her voice was soft and low and sweet, and full at all times of harmonious words. . .

Anthony Trollope Mr Scarborough's Family

The seductive quality may lie in the accent identified with the voice. Imogen

---

VERB

'A Werb is a word as signifies to be, to do, or to suffer (which is the grammar, and enough, too, as ever I wos taught); and if there's a Werb alive, I'm it. For I'm always a-bein', sometimes a-doin', and continually a-sufferin'.'

Charles Dickens Martin Chuzzlewit

Winn, in *Coming to Terms*, says: 'His voice had a soft lilt that she found envelopingly sexy. "What is your accent?" she asked him. "My mother was Irish and my father was Italian. I think the accent is what is known as international".' Elizabeth Gaskell in *Wives and Daughters*, has: 'Her voice was so soft, her accent so pleasant, that it struck him as particularly agreeable after the broad country accent he was perpetually hearing.'

———————————○———————————

'And oh, the summer in his voice, then and always!'

Mary Webb Precious Bane

———————————○———————————

Dickens jokes on the subject of erotic voice quality as he does on everything else. His victim is Mrs Micawber in *David Copperfield*, who sings to the assembled company one evening in what David describes as 'a small, thin, flat voice, which I remember to have considered when I first knew her, the very table-beer of acoustics'. Mr Micawber fortunately does not share David's view. For him, Emma's voice is an important part of her appeal. It was when he first heard her sing, he says, that she 'attracted his attention in an extraordinary degree; he had resolved to win that woman or perish in the attempt'.

VULGAR

———————————○———————————

We none of us spoke of money, because that subject savoured of commerce and trade, and though some might be poor, we were all aristocratic. It was considered 'vulgar' (a tremendous word in Cranford) to give anything expensive, in the way of eatable or drinkable, at the evening entertainments. Wafer bread-and-butter and sponge-biscuits were all that the Honourable Mrs Jamieson gave, and she was

sister-in-law to the late Earl of Glenmire, although she did practise such 'elegant economy'. 'Elegant economy!' How naturally one falls back into the phraseology of Cranford! There, economy was always 'elegant', and money-spending always 'vulgar and ostentatious'; a sort of sour-grapeism which made us very peaceful and satisfied.

Elizabeth Gaskell Cranford

———————————○———————————

We know exactly what Elizabeth Gaskell means when she speaks of **vulgar** being a 'tremendous' word in Cranford. She uses **tremendous** in its original sense of something that causes 'trembling'. To the Cranford ladies who considered that they were socially far above the *vulgus*, the 'common crowd', it did indeed strike fear into their hearts to think that something they said or did might be

> ## VIRTUE
>
> Penny was a serious man, and he seriously believed that Kershawe had a natural virtue — in the older sense of the word — which an English upbringing, an English education, had regrettably obscured.
>
> **Eric Linklater** *The Faithful Ally*

called vulgar. The word was a deadly condemnation which instantly stripped away their good breeding.

Vulgar is used in modern times to mean little more than 'rude', and only snobs talk about vulgar people to mean those of a lower social class. The word might still be linked, however, with **ostentation**, the unnecessary flaunting of wealth and luxury. There is a link of a different kind with the word **divulge**, which is from the same Latin root as vulgar. To divulge something is to make it known to the common crowd, to publish it.

Mrs Gaskell also highlights the word **economy**, which is of Greek rather than Latin origin. It referred originally to 'house management' and is closely related to religious words such as **ecumenical** 'representing world-wide Christianity' and **diocese** 'district governed by a bishop', which are based on Greek *oikos* 'house'. A less obvious connection is **parish**, from French *paroisse*, Latin *parochia*; the *-ochia* is again from Greek *oikos*.

———○———

LAFEU:
O, will you eat
No grapes, my royal fox? Yes, but you will
My noble grapes, an if my royal fox
Could reach them.

William Shakespeare
All's Well that Ends Well

———○———

In passing Mrs Gaskell invents a word of her own, though it seems so natural that few would question it. **Sour-grapeism** as such is not recorded by the dictionaries, though **sour grapes** is recognised. Use of the expression is a tribute to Aesop, whose tale of the Fox and the Grapes so accurately hit upon an aspect of human behaviour. Pretending to dislike something helps to ease one's disappointment at not being able to obtain it.

Teaser: What is curious about the word 'vair'? (Answer page 232)

FOR
QUITS

WALLAH

'I'll see the medical wallahs.'

Ernest Hemingway *A Farewell to Arms*

Hemingway correctly reports on a long-standing item of military slang when he talks of **medical wallahs**. **Wallah** has come to mean 'man', sometimes 'man in charge', though strictly speaking it derives not from a word but a suffix. In that respect it is similar to **bus**, say, an abbreviation of Latin *omnibus* 'for all'. 'Wallah' represents Hindi *-wala*, which is tagged on to nouns much as *-er* is added to English nouns. Thus Hindi *nao-wala* is 'boater, (man) connected with boat, boatman'. *Dilli-wala* means 'connected with Delhi, an inhabitant of Delhi'.

'Nabobs don't mind what they spend on their toys. The only rub is they want a sure return — of course. They're box-wallahs.'

A box-wallah is a businessman, and Mother Morag felt sure that if she had not been there he would have said 'Bloody box-wallahs'.

Rumer Godden *The Dark Horse*

Anglo-Indians began to use the Hindi construction in English as early as the 18th century, adding wallah after a noun as if it meant 'man'. **Banghy wallah** became the term for a porter who carried loads with a *banghy*, or shoulder-yoke. A **punkah wallah** operated the *punkah*, or large swinging fan. **Lootie wallahs** were those chiefly concerned with looting captured cities, loot itself deriving from a Hindi word meaning 'plunder'. Europeans were known to the Indians as **topi wallahs** because they always wore *topis* or *topees*, the light-weight cork helmets. Members of the Indian Civil Service, admitted by a competitive system after 1856, soon became known as **competition wallahs**.

'The petrol wallah' they had christened me when I had arrived in September 1939.

John Welcome *Stop at Nothing*

The usage was revived by British soldiers in World War One, who picked up wallah and amended its meaning slightly to 'man or officer responsible for'. G. Subba Rao, in his *Indian Words in English*, mentions such terms as **Lewis gun wallah** and the more imaginative **Amen wallah** 'padre' as coming into use at that time. World War Two introduced the **signals wallah**, **sanitary wallah**, **rickshaw wallah**. Soldiers who managed to keep behind the front lines were known as **base wallahs**.

J.L. Hunt and A.G. Pringle in their *Service Slang* refer also to **ordnance wallahs** and **camouflage wallahs**. They add that 'wallah is used rather more by Officers than by other ranks in the Army'. That statement was written in 1943 and might now have to be amended. Wallah is now perhaps only used by old-age-pension wallahs.

WATERCOLOUR

There is a magnificent paragraph in Joyce Cary's *The Horse's Mouth* where the author plays with the word **watercolour**. Cary describes an art gallery in the following terms: 'Usual modern collection. Wilson Steer, water in watercolour; Matthew Smith, victim of the crime in slaughtercolour; Utrillo, whitewashed wall in mortarcolour; Matisse, odalisque in scortacolour; Picasso, spatchcock horse in tortacolour; Gilbert Spence, cocks and pigs in thoughtacolour; Stanley Spencer, cottage garden in hortacolour; Braque, half a bottle of half and half in portercolour; William Roberts, pipe dream in snortercolour; Wadsworth, rockses, blockses, and fishy boxes all done by self in nautacolour; Duncan Grant, landscape in strawtacolour; Francis Hodgkins, cows and wows and frows and sows in chortacolour; Rouault, perishing Saint in fortacolour; Epstein, Leah waiting for Jacob in squawtacolour.'

It was a spacious chamber (Oda is
The Turkish title), and ranged round the wall
Were couches, toilets — and much more than
*   this*
I might describe, as I have seen it all.
But it suffices — little was amiss;
'Twas on the whole a nobly furnish'd hall,
With all things ladies want, save one or two,
And even those were nearer than they knew.

Lord Byron Don Juan

Many of these nonce neologisms are both witty and etymologically sound, though a few are esoteric enough to need explanation. Matisse's 'odalisque in scortacolour', for example, is a reference first of all to a female slave or

WEEK-END

'I want to take her out into the jungle for the week-end. I want your approval.'
Pater sat down. He said, 'Oh, I see. For the week-end.' "Week-end" is a wicked word. "Three days" sounds much more virtuous.'

John Masters Bhowani Junction

concubine, especially one in the harem of the Sultan of Turkey. **Odalisque** is based on Turkish *odah*, a chamber or room in a harem. **Scortacolour** is a reference to Latin *scortari* 'to associate with prostitutes'. The rarely used English words **scortation**, a synonym of 'fornication', **scortator** 'one who associates with prostitutes' and **scortatory** 'pertaining to lewdness' are from the same source.

People of the intelligenzia liked to come and stay in the place and call in to hear Raymond talk about their contemporaries. No one could better serve you a spatchcocked contemporary than Raymond.

H.G. Wells The Bulpington of Blup

Cary's **spatchcock** is a mainly Irish word, an abbreviation of 'dispatch cock'. The reference is to a fowl which is split open and grilled. **Tortacolour** is from Latin *tortus* 'crooked, twisted', and recalls words such as **torture**. **Hortacolour** and **nautacolour** are similarly based on Latin *hortus* 'garden' and Greek *nautes* 'sailor,' from *naus* 'ship'. Greek *khora* 'region' gives us words like **chorography** 'the systematic description of a region or district' and is the basis of Cary's **chortacolour**. **Fortacolour** clearly links with **fortitude**, and the display of courage in times of great danger and distress. As with **forte**, **fortify**, **fortress**, fortitude is based on Latin *fortis* 'strong'.

Cary could perhaps have added Van Gogh in **vortacolour** (Latin *vortex* 'eddy') to his list, but his wordplay — or waterplay — was of the highest order.

In his *Selected Occasional Verses 1956–74*, George Walker has a poem *A, Ab, Absque* . . . which is based on a similar idea of varying a basic word. Mr Walker is in the Thomas Hood tradition, his versified witticisms being sparked off by phrases he has come across. In this instance the Minutes of A.E.I. Traction Division,

8 December 1964 were the source of: 'trouble due to the dezincification of tubes'. Mr Walker elaborated:

It's plain to the merest of glances
They don't make the most of their
    chances:
There's
The desinkification of ships,
The deslinkification of hips,
The dethinkification of scholars,
The dechinkification of dollars,
The destinkification of drains,
The delinkification of chains,
The deinkification of blots,
The dedrinkification of sots,
The dekinkification of hoses,
The depinkification of roses,
The declinkification of gaols,
The deminkification of frails,
The debrinkification of heights,
The deshrinkification of tights,
The dewinkification of glad-eyes,
The deblinkification of bad eyes —
And all they can manage, poor
    boobs,
Is 'dezincification of tubes'.

WHEREFORE

○

JULIET:
O Romeo, Romeo! wherefore art thou Romeo?

William Shakespeare Romeo and Juliet

○

The above line is frequently quoted in comedy sketches and the like, but script-writers seem to be convinced that it means 'where are you, Romeo?' **Wherefore** means 'for what reason?' In the phrase **whys and wherefores** the two words have exactly the same meaning.

Juliet's anguished question could be roughly modernised as 'why of all names are you called Romeo Montague?' Juliet herself is a Capulet, and their two families have long been bitter enemies. Juliet goes on with her famous lines:

What's in a name? That which we
    call a rose
By any other name would smell as
    sweet;
So Romeo would, were he not
    Romeo call'd,
Retain that dear perfection which he
    owes
Without that title. Romeo, doff thy
    name
And for thy name, which is no part
    of thee,
Take all myself.

Juliet knows quite well, however, that Romeo cannot 'doff' or put aside his name as easily as she suggests. He would still be a member of the Montague family. She should have been thinking instead of ways to reconcile the two families. The reconciliation does of course occur, but it is brought about only by the deaths of herself and Romeo.

WIFE

○

'...as I was saying to my wife.'
'Faith,' said Coggan, in a critical tone, 'the man hev learnt to say "my wife" in a wonderful naterel way, considering how very youthful he is in wedlock as yet.'
'I never heerd a skilful old married feller of twenty years' standing pipe "my wife" in a more used note than 'a did,' said Jacob Smallbury. 'It might have been a little more true to nater if't had been spoke a little chillier, but that wasn't to be expected just now.'
'That improvement will come wi' time,' said Jan.

Thomas Hardy Far from the Madding Crowd

○

In the quotation above, the farm-labour-ers are making fun of Gabriel Oak a few hours after his wedding to Bathsheba. Gabriel, as they say, refers easily to his **wife**; many men seem to be reluctant to do so. They will use a jokey substitute, such as **ball and chain**, **trouble and strife**, **'er indoors**, the latter made popular by the television series *Minder*, or refer to **the missus**, **my better half**, **my other half**, **the old lady**, **the old woman**. In former times a wife was **the little woman**, but few men would dare to use such an expression now.

'You know something, Hagar? There's men in Manawaka call their wives "Mother" all the time. That's one thing I have never done.'

It was true. He never did, not once. I was Hagar to him.

Margaret Laurence *The Stone Angel*

Some of the wife terms are also used for 'mother'. The two terms become almost synonymous in certain dialects. In Clifford Hanley's *The Taste of Too Much* the character who says: 'Aw, it's no me, it's the old wife' is referring to his own mother. Some older husbands might refer to their wives as **mother**, especially in front of their children. What is noticeable is that wife is now almost never used as a term of address, other than as a joke. The word was once common in that role, though genteel custom of the 19th century dictated that Mr Smith should address his wife in public, and often in private, as Mrs Smith.

In third person usage, to refer bluntly to 'your wife' seems to be considered impolite. Men who know one another well may resort to the humorous syno-

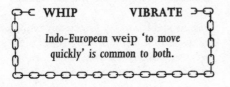

WHIP   **VIBRATE**

Indo-European weip 'to move quickly' is common to both.

WHOM

'Where did you go last night? Whom were you with?' Nobody he had ever met, Henry thought, could bring out a 'whom' with such assurance.

Jeremy Brooks *Henry's War*

nyms mentioned above. The vicar will qualify the word and ask: 'How is your good wife?' or 'How is your lady wife?' He may avoid it altogether and ask 'How is Mrs Smith?' Perhaps in modern times, when a live-in partner is not necessarily a wife, there is some point in his using the old formula: 'How is your good lady?' It would be **lady** rather than **woman**, of course, though the earliest meaning of wife, as it happens, was simply 'woman'. The earlier meaning has been retained in **fishwife** and **old wives' tales**.

WOE

The absolute refusal of his colleagues to enrich discussion was a matter of some woe to him. He used that word — woe — right there in Treece's office, and Treece supposed that it was the first time the word had been used there, in the ordinary passage of conversation, in forty years.

Malcolm Bradbury *Eating People is Wrong*

Malcolm Bradbury is clearly correct, in the above quotation, to imply that woe is now an archaic word. It rarely occurs in conversation, and English people no longer exclaim 'Woe is me!' 'Oy vay!' is possible, however, for a Jewish speaker. The Yiddish *vay* is a form of German *Weh* 'woe, pain'. Like woe itself, the German word was originally little more than a noise occasioned by grief. The French exclamation **ouais** appears to be related, but this is used to express surprise and is a variant of *oui* 'yes'.

It is curious that a vague human noise of distress ever developed into a proper word, as it did in both English and German. In English it led to expressions like 'Woe betide you', a linguistic fossil that might still occasionally be heard. It would probably be a fairly literary parent who would say: 'Woe betide you if you get home after eleven.' The child who nevertheless does so may later look **woeful** or even **woe-begone** — the latter being another verbal fossil which means 'beset by woe'. **Woefully**, in a phrase like 'woefully inadequate', has lost the force it once had.

PRINCE:
For never was a story of more woe
Than this of Juliet and her Romeo.

William Shakespeare Romeo and Juliet

It is still possible to use woe in literature without it seeming out of place. 'I've had scores of cables,' says someone in J.I.M. Stewart's *A Use of Riches*. 'They pour in all day prophesying woe.' In the literature of the past the word is firmly entrenched. Shakespeare uses it in most of his plays, but *Romeo and Juliet* is surely his most 'woeful' play. The words quoted above bring the play to an end, and could be interpreted almost literally. Earlier the Nurse, finding Juliet dead, has said in her grief:

> O woe! O woeful, woeful, woeful day!
> Most lamentable day, most woeful day
> That ever, ever, I did yet behold!
> O day! O day! O day! O hateful day!
> Never was seen so black a day as this.
> O woeful day, O woeful day!

WORD

I am omniverbivorous by nature and training. Passing by such words as are poisonous, I can swallow most others, and chew such as I cannot swallow.

Oliver Wendell Holmes
The Autocrat of the Breakfast Table

It is impossible to say how many words there are in the English language, partly because **word** is not easy to define. Are **is** and **was** separate words, for example,

---

Shakespeare's Wench-like, Wild and Whirling, Wise Words

GUIDERIUS:
Prithee, have done
And do not play in wench-like words with that
Which is so serious.

Cymbeline

HORATIO:
These are but wild and whirling words, my lord.

Hamlet

BENEDICK:
Old signior, walk aside with me; I have studied eight or nine wise words to speak to you.

Much Ado About Nothing

WINE

Wine, like bread and oil — 'God's three chief words' — is a thing of itself — a thing of earth and air and sun — one of the great natural things, such as the stars and flowers and the eyes of a dog.

William J. Locke *Jaffery*

or are they included in the verb **to be**? Is **box** meaning a container the same word as box meaning to fight with the fists? Is **drawing-room** one word or two? What does one do with phrasal verbs, where a particular meaning is created by two or more words operating in unison?

There are also historical problems. **Cavenard** ('villain') is known to have existed in Old English but is no longer used. Should it still be counted as an English word? There are many other difficulties related to slang, dialect, technical vocabularies, and the like. Figures are therefore almost meaningless, though the number of head-words in the original version of *The Oxford English Dictionary* has often led to the statement that English has a vocabulary of roughly half a million words.

Nor is it easy to say how many words the average person uses, or how many words constitute a good vocabulary. We know only that we understand far more words than we regularly use, and that it is possible to get by in most normal social situations with a vocabulary of only 2000 or 3000 words. A very large number of specialised words that exist can, after all, be glossed in simple terms, as when we say of a person that he 'doesn't like foreigners' instead of 'he is xenophobic'. It is not always appropriate in any case to use a learned term instead of a simpler phrase. A good communicator wants his audience to understand what he is saying: there is little point in impressing them with the size of his vocabulary if they have no idea what he is talking about. It is a skill in itself — one which is probably under-valued — to be able to explain complex matters in simple words.

Things had come to a pass with Helen that he could only describe in his own expressive idiom as 'words'.

H.G. Wells *Kipps*

A list of the most frequently used English words will naturally vary according to the corpus on which the word-count is based. Counts based on printed texts do not necessarily reflect what is happening in the millions of social conversations that are taking place at any one time. In any count, however, words such as *the* and *a*, which have a grammatical function rather than a specific meaning, will usually be in the top 20. Conversational English, according to counts based on recorded interviews, also makes intensive use of the following: **about; and; but; can; can't; come; could; did; didn't; do; don't; feel; felt; get; go; got; had; has; have; he; her; him; I; I'm; in; is; it; it's; just; know; like; make; me; mean; mind; my; of; said; say; see; she; that; them; they; think; this; to; want; was; we; what; would; you; your; you're. Guess** should probably be added if the speakers are American.

Computers now make it easy to be more precise about word-frequency in particular texts. Thus, according to the

Teaser: What is curious about the word 'wear'?
(Answer page 232) **??**

WUTHERING

Wuthering Heights is the name of Mr Heathcliff's dwelling. 'Wuthering' being a significant provincial adjective, descriptive of the atmospheric tumult to which its station is exposed in stormy weather. Pure, bracing ventilation they must have up there at all times, indeed.

Emily Brontë *Wuthering Heights*

Longman Mini-Concordancer computer program, the main body of this work as it leaves the word-processor consists of some 96 000 words, of which the ten most frequently used are: **the**; **a**; **of**; **to**; **in**; **and**; **is**; **it**; **that**; **as**; **was**.

These are not words which excite a great deal of interest to any but the devoted specialist, though pronouns, for example, deserve full-scale academic treatment in themselves. Nor is word, regrettably, a word that arouses much curiosity in itself. It occurs slightly disguised in several Germanic languages, and is ultimately linked with Latin *verbum*. Its most powerful meanings occur in phrases like **word of honour** and **the word of God**. In **have a word with** someone it looks inappropriately singular, though **have words with** someone has taken on the separate meaning of 'quarrel' with that person.

Now words had a meaning indeed, for they were flies cast on the waters of conversation to attract her smiles, her favour, and her interest.

Eric Linklater *Magnus Merriman*

In *Antony and Cleopatra* Shakespeare makes interesting use of 'word' as a verb. Cleopatra is speaking of Caesar when she says: 'He words me, girls, he words me, that I should not / Be noble to myself.' She means that he has been urging her with words. Special uses of word also occur in compounds such as **household word**, **watchword**, **byword**, **keyword**.

The keyword was marriage. Pyle believed in being involved.

Graham Greene *The Quiet American*

Watchword has come to mean a word or phrase which summarises a guiding principle, a slogan, though it was originally a password which had to be given to a sentry or watchman. 'Let forward be our watchword' says someone in *A God and His Gifts*, by Ivy Compton-Burnett. Byword has also changed its meaning from 'proverb' to 'notable example' of something. Geraint Goodwin, in *The Heyday in the Blood*, has: 'Its ham and egg teas were a byword among the townsfolk.' Keyword seems to hint at a password which will cause a key to unlock a gate, but the reference is to a word which is either the key to a cipher or a significant word used in indexing.

No research has been done on the subject, but instinct suggests which word is probably the most popular in English. It is likely to be the one that most of us wish to have when any kind of disagreement occurs — **the last word**.

FOR
BREAKFAST

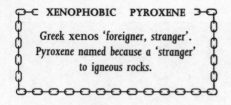

XENOPHOBIC PYROXENE

*Greek xenos 'foreigner, stranger'.
Pyroxene named because a 'stranger'
to igneous rocks.*

X-RAY

'*I'm pretty good at inventing phrases — you know,
the sort of words that suddenly make you jump,
almost as though you'd sat on a pin, they seem so
new and exciting even though they're about
something hypnopaedically obvious. . . . Words
can be like X-rays, if you use them properly —
they'll go through anything. You read and you're
pierced.*'

Aldous Huxley *Brave New World*

In 1895, when the German scientist
W.C. Röntgen discovered rays which
had mysterious qualities, he acknowledged their unknown nature by calling

X, Y, Z

What fat black letters to begin
with! 'A was an archer, and shot
at a frog.' Of course he was. He
was an apple-pie also, and there
he is! He was a good many things
in his time, was A, and so were
most of his friends, except X, who
had so little versatility that I
never knew him to get beyond
Xerxes or Xantippe—like Y, who
was always confined to a yacht or
a yew tree; and Z, condemned for
ever to be a zebra or a zany.

Charles Dickens *A Christmas Tree*

them *X-Strahlen*. The term was translated
into English as **x-rays**, though references to **Röntgen rays** also appeared for
a while in scientific papers. X-ray is
therefore one of that small group of
words whose origin can be precisely
pinpointed. We even know that it was
the 17th-century French philosopher,
René Descartes, who first used X as a
mathematical symbol for an unknown
quantity.

X-ray comes as a welcome relief to

XEROGRAPHY

Suppose a sheet of white paper is
electrically charged. The charge
would attract any fine particles of
carbon that might be present, and
the entire sheet would be covered
with a thin layer of carbon. Light,
impinging on the paper, would
cause it to lose the charge.
But suppose light shines through a
paper with print on it and strikes
the charged paper. Everywhere,
except where the print casts a
shadow, the charge is lost. Carbon
powder clings only to the shadow.
The paper is heated so that the
powder (which contains a resin to
make it stick) clings permanently.
The second paper is then a copy
of the first.
The process is called xerography,
from the Greek words meaning
dry-writing, since nothing wet is
used. By 1960 the American
inventor Chester Carlson had
made the method practical
enough for eventual use in almost
every office. The system most
familiar to the general public has
the trade name Xerox, from
xerography.

Isaac Asimov *Words of Science*

hospital patients who are bombarded with the technical terms of modern medicine. The function of x-rays is understood, and the word is easy to remember. Other medical terms are not so '**hypnopaedically** obvious', as Huxley might have chosen to call them. His word derives from two Greek elements and refers to something that is 'sleep-teachable', which can be 'learnt while asleep'. *Hypnos* 'sleep' is familiar in its derivatives **hypnosis**, **hypnotic** and the like. *Pais, paidos* 'boy, child' also form the basis in Greek of words to do with 'child-raising, education'. They lead to English words such as **paediatrics** 'medical treatment of children', **orthopaedics** 'correct education' and **paedagogue** — now usually **pedagogue** — 'teacher'. The latter is literally a 'child-leader' and once meant precisely that. The Greek word originally described the slave who accompanied an Athenian child to school.

Teaser: Why is 'Xmas' used as a spelling of Christmas?

(Answer page 232)

??

Shakespeare's X Word

[The only word in any of the Shakespeare plays that begins with X appears to be the name **Xantippe**, normally **Xanthippe**, the wife of Socrates. By reputation she was of a shrewish disposition, though her husband is said to have recognised her better qualities.]

PETRUCHIO:

Signior Hortensio, 'twixt such friends as we
Few words suffice; and therefore, if thou know
One rich enough to be Petruchio's wife,
As wealth is burden of my wooing dance,
Be she as foul as was Florentius' love,
As old as Sibyl, and as curst and shrewd
As Socrates' Xantippe or a worse —
She moves me not, or not removes, at least,
Affection's edge in me, were she as rough
As are the swelling Adriatic seas.
I come to wive it wealthily in Padua;
If wealthily, then happily in Padua.

The Taming of the Shrew

FOR
MISTRESS

YES-MAN

○

'Superiors are often heard to say that they don't want yes-men. This is a lie: they do. If the top man wants to win an argument, let him. But it's good strategy, just occasionally, to make him wait a few seconds for your "yes". Darryl Zanuck once snapped at an over-eager assistant: "Don't say yes until I've finished talking".'

William Davis Money Talks

○

Yes-man is a modern term for a **sycophant** or **toady**, a **please-man** as Shakespeare calls him. In *Love's Labour's Lost*, Berowne discovers that he and his companions have been declaring their love to the wrong women, who were hidden behind masks. The women have deliberately misled the men in order to have a good laugh at their expense. 'I see the trick,' Berowne declares. 'Some carry-tale, some please-man, some slight zany, / Some mumble-news, some trencher-knight, some Dick, / That smiles his cheek in years and knows the trick / To make my lady laugh when she's dispos'd, / Told our intents before.'

Shakespeare's **carry-tale** and **mumble-news** could be thought of as English forms of sycophant, which derives from a Greek word meaning 'informer', though it now means a flatterer. The Greek word literally translates as 'fig-shower', and is said to have alluded originally to someone who gave information about the illegal exportation of figs. Toadie, a synonym of sycophant, is an abbreviation of **toad-eater**. The ref-

erence is to the assistant of a quack doctor who would in former times pretend to eat poisonous toads. The doctor's patent medicine would then miraculously cure him, boosting sales amongst the incredulous.

○

'And the boys in the cricket eleven —'
   'Men,' interrupted the child firmly.
   'I beg your pardon.'
   'Men,' repeated the child. 'We are all men here [at Winchester public-school]. There are no boys.'
   Donald, by now quite dizzy, bowed and thanked the man for his trouble.
   'It was a pleasure,' replied the man, bowing courteously and removing his hat again and going on his way.
   Donald, hat in hand, turned and watched him, and was immensely relieved to see the man halt after going a few yards, and extract a huge and sticky piece of toffee from his trouser-pocket, and cram it into his mouth.

A.G. Macdonell England, Their England

○

The origin of yes-man is rather more obvious, but the word is interesting to the word-buff for at least three reasons. First there is **yes**, which at an earlier stage of its career was a specially emphatic form of **yea** or **ay**. It would have been used to reply positively to a negative statement or question, such as: 'You don't like my dress, do you?' A Frenchman in such circumstances would reply *si* rather than *oui*; a German would say *doch* 'yes indeed' rather than *ja*. In English the emphasis would now have to be expressed by saying 'Yes, I do'. The meaning of yes has thus been considerably weakened.

In passing it should be noted that phrasing ideas in a negative way can sometimes lead to great confusion when speaking to foreigners. They may interpret things in a different way. In Japanese, for example, when a wife says to her husband: 'You don't like my dress,

Teaser: How should 'ye', as in 'ye olde tea shoppe', be pronounced?
(*Answer page 232*) **??**

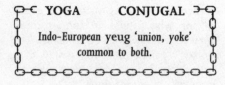

YOGA   CONJUGAL

Indo-European yeug 'union, yoke'
common to both.

do you?' she certainly does not want him to say 'yes'. She knows that if he does so, he means 'Yes, you are quite right — I don't like your dress.'

He was a woman's man, they said — supremely so — externally little else. To men he was not attractive; perhaps a little repulsive at times. Musician, dandy, and company-man in practice; veterinary surgeon in theory. Personally he was not ill-favoured, though rather un-English, his complexion being a rich olive, his rank hair dark and rather clammy — made still clammier by secret ointments, which, when he came fresh to a party, caused him to smell like 'boys'-love' steeped in lamp oil.

Thomas Hardy The Fiddler of the Reels

Another interesting point about yes-man is the way it refines the meaning of **man**. There are at least a thousand compound nouns in English which have -man as the second element, giving the general word a more specific meaning. Thomas Hardy gives two examples in the extract above, though we would now say **ladies' man** instead of **woman's man**. **Company-man** also suggests in modern times a man who shows loyalty to the company that employs him rather than a man who is fond of female company.

Of special interest to word-collectors are the compound -man words that do not actually refer to men. Had Hardy's novel been set in the north of England, he might have used such a word instead of **boy's love**. His reference is to southernwood, a bushy kind of wormwood, which has different names in different parts of the country. Elizabeth Gaskell mentions it in Ruth: 'While the kettle was boiling she came out to enjoy the flowers. She gathered a piece of southernwood, and stuffed it up her nose, by way of smelling it. "Whatten you call this in your country?" asked she. "Old-man," replied Ruth. "We call it here lad's love".'

Old-man as a plant name is a simple metaphor; **talisman** is far more curious, being a -man word only by accident. It derives ultimately from Greek telos 'end'. The meaning of 'an object which has the power to bring good luck' only came about after diminutive forms of telos had passed through several languages, changing their meaning along the way. Talisman is the word to drop into a conversation when items of useless knowledge are being bandied about. Is mans ever the plural form of 'man', for instance? Yes, if you're talking about talismans.

She was pale, round-shouldered, reticent, a fresh-man, the daughter of a commercial artist.

Mary McCarthy The Groves of Academe

A third interesting point about yes-man is hinted at in the above quotation. Mary McCarthy has no hesitation in referring to a female student as a **freshman**. Would a writer or speaker today amend this to **freshwoman** or **freshperson**? (British student slang avoids the problem with **fresher**.) In a similar way Alan Sillitoe, in Uncle Ernest, uses **spokesman** of a girl who is speaking on behalf of herself and her younger sister, though **spokeswoman** would have aroused no comment. The same author refers to a **forewoman** in The Fishing-Boat Picture.

Arguments have raged about **chairman/chairwoman/chairperson**, leading some speakers to employ **chair**. It is a pity that man has not retained the meaning it had in Old English, defined by *The Oxford English Dictionary* as 'a human being, irrespective of sex or age'. It was that meaning which allowed **woman**, originally 'wife man, female being' to come into existence. (Amateur etymologists have preferred to link 'woman' with the **woe** that Eve brought to mankind, or with a woman's wish to be **wooed**. The pronunciation of **women** has been linked to feminine **whims**.)

It is true that words ending in -*man* can be inappropriate and perhaps, occasion-

---

SOME OF SHAKESPEARE'S MEN

Almsman a man dependent on charitable donations

Apron man a mechanic, artisan

Artsman learned man, scholar

Backsword man a fencer, using a sword with only one cutting edge

Beadsman one paid to pray for others. The reference is to the rosary beads

Bellman night watchman who rang his bell every hour.

Book-man student, scholar

Chapman merchant, trader; buyer, customer, haggler

Churchman clergyman

Deathsman executioner

Footman walker, pedestrian; servant who ran before his master's carriage

Goodman husband; title of courtesy used before name of occupation; yeoman, cultivator of small estate

Hangman executioner; Cupid

Henchman squire, page of honour

Hoodman blindfolded player in the game of Blind Man's Buff, which was also known as hoodman-blind

Huntsman huntsman, also manager of hunt

Husbandman manager of a household, steward

Journeyman qualified workman employed by the day; used derogatively of one not master of his trade

Leman sweetheart; wife's lover

Liegeman vassal, owing allegiance to a superior

Markman marksman

Please-man sycophant, a servile flatterer, a yes-man

Seedsman sower of seed

Serving man servant

Shearman shearer of woollen cloth

Shipman sailor

Singing man church choirman

Slaughterman killer, slayer

Swordman swordsman, fighter

Three-man-song-man three-men songs, later known as freemen songs, were lively round songs in Elizabethan times

Trencherman hearty eater

Watchman sentry

Wealsman statesman

Woodman hunter

Workman skilled craftsman

Yeoman sheriff's officer; keeper of the wardrobe; small estate holder

---

SOME SLANGY MEN

From James Morton's *Low Speak: A Dictionary of Criminal and Sexual Slang*

Alias man (West Indian) criminal, worthless person

Backdoor man sodomite; married woman's lover

Bagman person who collects bribe money and delivers it to police

Battyman (West Indian) homosexual

Beastman (West Indian) policeman

Beesman (West Indian) policeman

Bullerman (West Indian) policeman

Candyman dealer in heroin

Fat Man the electric chair

Fireman Visiting free-spending visitor from out of town

Greyman (West Indian) a white man

Hatchet man hired killer

Honeyman man who cleans the cess pit

Iceman professional killer; bagman; jewel thief

Magsman petty thief, formerly a well dressed swindler

Meat salesman pimp

(continued on page 222)

ally, offensive. This applies also to words ending in **-master**, which is why British Rail changed **stationmaster** to **station manager**. Perhaps the process of linguistic adjustment should go even further. Sinclair Lewis has a teacher in *Ann Vickers* who is talking to a young woman student and is obviously aware of political correctness. He says: 'Your **confrères** — or **consoeurs**, if you prefer — seem to have as cheerful an antipathy to scholarship as the young gentlemen I have known in the

Outside man lookout who stays outside building
Peterman safe-breaker
Pocketman member of gang who holds proceeds of crime until shareout
Scragsman hangman
Sweetman pimp
Swordsman sexually active male; receiver of stolen property
Wheelman expert driver
Yeggman safe-breaker

SOME AUSTRALIAN MEN

From G.A. Wilkes A Dictionary of Australian Colloquialisms

Bagman a tramp who carries all his possessions with him, or a swagman on horseback. In the 1930s the term was applied to an unemployed man who travelled around looking for work. The *Bagman's Gazette* refers to graffiti left by bagmen.
Big man another term for the ruckman in Australian Rules football, usually powerfully built.
Big-note man a bookmaker or punter who handles or places very large bets.
Bushman a man who lives or travels in the Australian bush, the sparsely settled areas away from the towns. A **Piccadilly bushman** is a wealthy Australian. The **bushman's breakfast** is variously described: 'a drink of water and a good look around' seems to have been the original version, extended to 'a shave and a shit and a good look around'. The kookaburra, or laughing jackass, is sometimes called the **bushman's clock** because its laugh is heard at dawn and sunset.

Dogman a man who 'rode the hook' of a crane, giving directions to the crane-driver by hand signals.
Flying Pieman nickname of William Francis King, who died in 1874. He was known for such feats as walking 32 miles (51 km) in six hours, from Sydney to Parramatta and back.
Government man 19th-century term for a convict.
Knockabout man an unskilled odd-job man or station-hand, a rouseabout.
Man in white a referee or umpire.
Man on the land a farmer.
Man outside Hoyt's jokingly alluded to in various ways, often in the context of false self-importance. The reference is to the commissionaire who stood outside Hoyt's Theatre in Melbourne in the 1930s. His uniform was extravagantly elaborate.
Old man adjectivally used to mean of exceptional size, the reference being to an old man kangaroo, one which is fully grown. In modern use the old man is a slang term applied to the penis, a variant of the **old boy**, the **old fellow**.
Returned man a returned serviceman.
Standover man a petty criminal who uses or threatens physical violence to intimidate his victims.
Swagman a tramp or traveller who carries his essential belongings rolled in a blanket. Some writers distinguish between swagmen and travellers on the grounds that the latter are genuinely looking for work.
Wild white man, the nickname of William Buckley, a 19th-century convict who escaped and lived for 32 years with the natives.
Yarraman a horse (a 19th-century Aboriginal term, probably from its neighing).

University of Chicago.'

No general rule can be given that allows easy conversion of male words into neutral or feminine forms. **Salesperson** is somehow an acceptable alternative for **salesman**, just as **saleswoman** is a reasonable feminine form, but each word must be considered separately. **Yesperson**, for instance, manages to sound absurd, and **yes-woman** would suggest sluttishness rather than sycophancy.

YOUNG

He had just reached the time of life at which 'young' is ceasing to be the prefix of 'man' in speaking of one. He was at the brightest period of masculine growth, for his intellect and his emotions were clearly separated. In short, he was twenty-eight, and a bachelor.

Thomas Hardy *Far from the Madding Crowd*

The dictionary definition of **young** as something or someone that has 'not existed for very long' is all very well, but this is a word that we redefine subjectively as our age increases. People celebrating their 60th birthday may still

YOU

Who would succeed in the world
should be wise in the use of
his pronouns.
Utter the word *You* twenty times
where you once utter the *I.*

John Hay *Distichs*

Shakespeare's
Y-Clad Words

KING:
Her sight did ravish, but her grace in speech,
Her words y-clad [clothed] with wisdom's
majesty,
Makes me from wond'ring fall to weeping
joys,
Such is the fulness of my heart's content.

Henry VI Part Two

feel that 'young' could apply to them. It has much to do with their state of mind; whether, for instance, they feel that they have progressed only a short way along an interesting path that ought to continue indefinitely.

A young person is not necessary **juvenile**, in the derogatory sense we now often give that word. Juvenile, like **rejuvenate**, is from Latin *juvenis* 'young', which led to *juvenior* then **junior** as the comparative form. These words look very different from *young*, but traced back far enough, they eventually meet up in a postulated Indo-European *juwnkos*.

Junior is more widely used in North America than in Britain, and has rather different connotations. A male American may add the word after his name to indicate that he bears exactly the same name as his father. (American mothers more rarely impose this burden upon their daughters.) The practice is dying out, perhaps because psychiatrists have had much to say about the possible harmful effects on a boy who has to think of himself as his father's shadow.

Junior is also sometimes used in the US as a term of address, not just to a son. As an occasional first name, it can take the diminutive **June**. Young people in Britain would probably not respond well to the vocative, since they cease to be juniors when they leave junior school at the age of 11. American students, by contrast, will cheerfully attend the 'junior prom' when they are in their third year of high school.

FOR
EFFECT

ZENANA

The growth of the admirable Zenana missions has of late years made this word more familiar in England.

Sir Henry Yule and Arthur C. Burnell
Hobson-Jobson

———○———

The **Zenana** missions referred to in the above quotation occurred at the end of the 19th century. They involved missionary work by Christian women among native Indian women. In East India (and Iran) the zenana is the part of a house where the women are secluded. It thus corresponds to the **harem** or **seraglio** of the Arabic-speaking Moslem countries.

Of these three words, 'zenana' is the one most easily linked to English. Persian *zan* is related to Greek *gyne*, English **queen**, all having a basic sense of 'woman'. The Greek word is an element in **gynaecology** 'medical study of the female sex organs', **misogyny** 'a hatred of women', **gynarchy** 'form of government by a woman or women', **gyne-phobia** 'an abnormal fear of women'. English formerly used **quean** as well as queen. Both derived from the same word, but referred to women of very different social standing. A quean was little more than a prostitute, while queen had its modern sense. The two forms occur, with their different meanings, in Shakespeare's *All's Well that Ends Well*, but modern English

Teaser: Can you think of ten, ten-letter words with 'z' as, progressively, the first, second, third, etc., letter?

(Answer page 232) ⁇

```
╭─⊂ ZANY        JOHN ⊃─╮
│  Zany is from Zanni, Italian dialectal
│  form of Giovanni, 'John'.
╰──────────────────────╯
```

has done away with quean. Plenty of other words are available to describe a woman in disparaging terms.

———○———

We got messages on the walkie-talkies that sent me to houses where Moslem ladies, their men away, were entrenched in the zenanas and refusing to admit the Gurkhas.

John Masters Bhowani Junction

———○———

'Harem' is from an Arabic word that describes anything forbidden. In modern parlance, the harem is a kind of no-go area, as it were. 'Seraglio' has a more complicated history. It came into English from Italian *serraglio*, where its meaning was 'an enclosed area', but the word had come into being by a misunderstanding. Turkish *serai* 'palace' was wrongly associated with Latin *sera* 'lock', *serare* 'close with a key'.

Women's quarters do not normally form part of a western household, though harem is sometimes used jokingly. Dickens says of Mr Mould, the undertaker in *Martin Chuzzlewit* who has a wife and two daughters at home, that 'his harem, or, in other words, the common sitting room of Mrs Mould and family, was at the back'.

Public buildings usually have a **ladies' room** or **powder room**. ('Powder room' in former times had quite a different meaning: it was the room on a ship where the gunpowder was stored.) The vague resemblance between powder and **purdah** is accidental, the latter word referring in Urdu to the 'curtain' which is used to screen women from strangers. Substitution of the one word for the other is nevertheless tempting. John Masters makes the joke in the novel quoted above: 'A row of doorways opened off the platform into the various rooms, and a sign hung out over each door: First-Class Waiting Room; Second-Class Waiting Room; Third-Class Waiting Room; Ladies' Waiting Room — what we always called the Purdah Room.'

ZOO

The camel's hump is an ugly lump
Which well you may see at the Zoo
But uglier yet is the Hump we get
From having too little to do.

Rudyard Kipling How the Camel Got His Hump

When the London Zoological Society opened its gardens to the public in the 19th century, a learned word was soon transformed into something that a child could say and understand. A trip to the **Zoological Gardens** became a visit to

ZOO

'Toby Chuzzlewit, who was your grandfather?' To which he, with his last breath, no less distinctly, solemnly, and formally replied . . . 'The Lord No Zoo.' It may be said — it has been said, for human wickedness has no limits — that there is no lord of that name. Is it not manifest — that the Chuzzlewits were connected with some unknown and illustrious House?'

Charles Dickens Martin Chuzzlewit

the **zoo**. Zoo has the advantage of being the kind of word that satisfies a child, with its interesting sound and easy spelling. Perhaps the original Greek word *zoion* 'animal' also satisfied those children who used it. Ultimately *zoion* links with *zoe* 'life', a word which in recent years has become a popular first name in Britain. The name Zoe looks back to two Roman martyrs who bore it and hoped for 'life eternal'.

The city is not a concrete jungle, it is a human zoo.

Desmond Morris The Human Zoo

The inhabitants of the human zoo that Desmond Morris talks about make use of a partly zoological language. In English there are a large number of animal idioms of the **raining cats and dogs**, **hen-pecked** type. They are used to convey a general sense and do not necessarily bring the animal concerned to mind. Thus Joanna Jones, in Nurse is a Neighbour, is speaking of a dachshund bitch when she says that 'her ears drooped **sheepishly**'.

In the 17th century animal expressions were in frequent use as vocatives. Beaumont and Fletcher, in The Knight of the Burning Pestle, have a conversation between a husband and wife which runs: '"Husband, I prithee, sweet **lamb** . . ." "What is it, **mouse**?. . . . **Chicken**, I prithee heartily, contain thyself." "Ay, when Ralph comes, **cony**!"' This same husband also addresses his wife as **duck**, which might still be heard in modern times. Non-vocative use could also be dense. In As You Like It Rosalind says to Orlando: 'I will be more jealous of thee than a Barbary **cock-pigeon** over his **hen**, more clamorous than a **parrot** against rain, more new-fangled than an **ape**, more giddy in my desires than a **monkey**. . . . I will laugh like a **hyena**, and that when thou art inclin'd to sleep.'

'A dog! I'll teach him to come caterwauling about my doors. A goatish ram-faced rascal! Why, he's a perfect parish bull, as I hope to live!'

Tobias Smollett *The Adventures of Peregrine Pickle*

Zoological allusions occur less densely, but effectively, in a wide range of literary sources. In *Miss Mix*, his parody of Charlotte Brontë's *Jane Eyre*, Bret Harte writes: 'He stood with his back to the fire, which set off the herculean breadth of his shoulders. His face was dark and expressive; his under jaw squarely formed, and remarkably heavy. I was struck with his remarkable likeness to a Gorilla.' Elizabeth Gaskell, in *Wives and Daughters*, has: 'I'm capable of a great jerk, an effort, and then a relaxation — but steady, everyday goodness is beyond me. I must be a moral kangaroo!' The more usual reference to this animal occurs in John le Carré's *The Honourable Schoolboy*: 'Smiley was forced to hold a kangaroo court.'

Dickens put the literary lions of his day in their place by creating Mrs Leo Hunter in *The Pickwick Papers*. This lady's husband says of her that she dotes on poetry and 'has produced some delightful pieces herself', including her 'Ode to an Expiring Frog'. He quotes the opening verse:

Can I view thee panting, lying
On thy stomach without sighing
Can I unmoved see thee dying
  On a log,
  Expiring frog!'
Mr Pickwick's sole comment on this is 'Beautiful!'

'Us rich kids are always raised to think poor but I foxed 'em.'

Judith Rossner *Any Minute I Can Split*

Shakespeare's Zed Word

[The word beginning with z- most frequently used by Shakespeare is **zeal**. 'Let not my cold words here accuse my zeal,' spoken by Mowbray in *Richard II*, is typical of its use. Mowbray means that he is ready to fight with swords rather than words. The more interesting Shakespearean z- word is the letter 'z' itself converted into a word.]

CORNWALL:
Speak yet, how grew your quarrel?
OSWALD:
This ancient ruffian, sir, whose life I have
  spar'd at suit of his grey beard —
KENT:
Thou whoreson zed! thou unnecessary letter!
  My lord, if you will give me leave, I will
  tread this unbolted villain into mortar.

King Lear

A number of animal and bird words can also be used as verbs, though appearances can be deceptive. To **grouse** 'complain' is from army slang and seems to have no connection with the game-bird, even though it might be thought that the latter has plenty to complain about. Similarly, to **raven** was used by Ben Jonson and other 17th-century playwrights to mean 'devour voraciously', but the bird-name was from an entirely different source. To **carp** is from Latin *carpere* 'to pluck' rather than the fish: **cow** as a verb is from an Old Norse *kuga* 'to tyrannise', not from the animal (nor, oddly enough, from **coward**, which is another separate word).

Sometimes it was the verb which came first, as with the **duck**, named for its habit of ducking its head in the water. To **rabbit**, in its modern slang sense of 'chatter excessively', clearly does not derive directly from the animal. The reference is to a Cockney phrase 'rabbit and pork', rhyming on 'talk'. An indirect connection is also likely to account for **bitch** 'complain', since the word has long been applied to a shrewish woman.

Complications apart, there are still many references to characteristic animal behaviour in verbs applied to humans. We might **chicken out** of doing something, **winkle** a secret out of someone, be **rooked** by a con man, **ram** into something, **lark** about with a friend, **ape** someone we admire, **crane** our necks, **ferret** out some information, **hare** off to the pub, **rat** on a colleague, **fox** an opponent, **cock** an ear, **monkey** about with something, **beaver** away at our work, **snipe** at or **hound** someone. Some further examples of this zoogenic vocabulary are given below.

Badger   'If you want to badger me with any more of your infernal scruples, I won't hear them.' Wilkie Collins *The Woman In White*

Beetle   'Young Jim beetles off to bed.' Stan Barstow *A Kind of Loving*

Crab   'It was sheer ingratitude to crab at her present actions.' Frederic Raphael *The Limits of Love*. The same novel has: 'Mr Walker crabbed his chalky fingers over the snowstorm paperweight on his desk.'

Crow   'I'm not going to be crowed over by you.' Charles Dickens *Martin Chuzzlewit*

Dog   'The invisible police officer of the Fates, who has the constant surveillance of me, and secretly dogs me . . .' Herman Melville *Moby Dick*

Goose   'If I've guessed wrong and Jason has found out right, then we are goosed.' John Welcome *Stop at Nothing*

Hawk   'At length he hawked up, with incredible straining, the interjection "Ah!"' Tobias Smollett *The Adventures of Peregrine Pickle*

Horse   'Sam Hopkins horsed me — and I was flogged. . .' William Thackeray *The Fatal Boots* [This is the horse-whipped sense; 'horse around' is now 'play the fool'.]

Magpie   'He [a journalist] is supposed to read all the papers every day, to see what the opposition is up to, and to magpie good ideas.' Philip Howard *The Times*

Skylark   'He had been skylarking with me. . .' Herman Melville *Moby Dick*

Squirrel   'The latter was furtively squirreling together the family bankbooks.' Joseph Heller *Good as Gold*

Wolf   'The young men in the street outside who wait to wolve and whistle.' Dylan Thomas *Under Milk Wood* [More normal usage refers to wolfing one's food.]

Worm   'I am not so sure you won't worm it out of me.' Wilkie Collins *The Woman in White*

ENVOY

It was the custom in the past for an author to append an **envoy** to a long poem or a prose work. Envoy is an English form of the French phrase *en voie* 'on the way'. The author's parting words were meant to bid the work farewell and send it out into the world. 'Go, litel book, go litel myn tragedie' says Chaucer at the end of his *Troilus and Criseyde*, rather more modestly than is necessary given the quality of what has gone before.

Peter Muffet, who wrote *A Commentarie upon the Whole Booke of the Proverbs of Solomon* in 1596, had hopes that his book would generally set the world to rights. An edited version of his envoy reads:

Go forth, my book, into the world,
As far as sea doth flow:
Beyond the sea if winds thee drive,
The pith of wisdom show.
Touch no estate, no ill tongue fear,
With no contention mell:
Leave unsaluted no good man
Care for no fiend of hell.
Teach children parents to obey,
Bid servants please the Lord:
Will kinsmen to be kind to kin,
Move brethren to accord.
Tell suitors that an happy choice
Proceedeth from above;
Wish wives to be their husbands
    crowns,
Husbands their wives to love.
Commend the hand of diligence,
Commend the lip of truth:
Commend the gray head of old age,
Commend the strength of youth.
Dispraise dame pride, and chide
    fierce wrath,
Inveigh against foul sloth:
To wake, or rise, to go abroad,
To worke in winter loth.

There is much more besides, including an apology from the author for the quality of his verse. He tells us that he seldom makes use of it.

The following envoy is from *The Pragmatic Sanction*, printed in Paris, 1507, reprinted in *Book Verse* (1896), edited by W. Roberts. It sums up the wishes of the present author:

May this volume continue in motion,
And its pages be each day unfurl'd,
Till an ant has drunk up the ocean,
Or a tortoise has crawl'd round the
    world.

ENVOY

Go, little book, into the
largest world,
And blaze the chasteness of
thy maiden muse;
Regardless of all envy on
thee hurl'd,
By the unkindness that the
Readers use:
And those that envy thee by
scruple's letter,
Let them take pen in hand, and
make a better.

Sir John Harington
Philoparthen's Loving Folly (1628)

ANSWERS
TO
TEASERS

Teaser 'A' (page 18)
The six letters are in alphabetical order. **Biopsy** and **chintz** are similar words in that respect.

Teaser 'B' (page 29)
The only ten-letter word in English that begins and ends with a *b* appears to be **breadcrumb**. There are no such words which begin and end in *j, q, u, v, x* or *z*, but examples can be found for the other letters. For *o* one needs to turn to **octodecimo**, a size of book or page based on the Latin word for '18'. The rare word **wappenshaw** 'weapon-show, a volunteer rifle-meeting' serves for *w*. Sample words for the other letters are **aspidistra, acrophobia; concentric, cybernetic; determined, dreamworld; effeminate, everywhere; flameproof, fallingoff; Godfearing, gunrunning; hallelujah, horseflesh; illuminati, intermezzi; knickknack, kibbutznik; liturgical, logistical; mainstream, memorandum; navigation, nonfiction; pillowslip, penmanship; researcher, ringleader; scandalous, spectacles; torchlight, triumphant; yearningly, youthfully**.

Teaser 'C' (page 40)
A letter can be changed in each position to give the new words: **blinker, chinker, clanker, clicker, clinger, clinkar, clinked**. This is stretching things somewhat, since 'clinkar' is listed in The Oxford English Dictionary only as a recorded variant of 'clinker'. There may be a seven-letter word which yields seven undisputed words.

Teaser 'D' (page 52)
It contains a six-letter string — *d e f g h i* — though not in the correct order, in a word of only ten letters.

Teaser 'E' (page 63)
It can be represented in letter form: X L N C. A rather literal lover once wrote to his beloved: 'In X L N C U X L all others.'

Teaser 'F' (page 70)
In a song about Spring at the end of Love's Labour's Lost we are told:
The cuckoo then on every tree
Mocks married men, for thus sings
  he: 'Cuckoo;
Cuckoo, cuckoo' — O word of fear,
Unpleasing to a married ear.'
Cuckoo and **cuckold** derive from the same word. 'Cuckold' is the older form, applied to the husband of an unfaithful wife since the 13th century. The reference is to the cuckoo's habit of laying its eggs in the nests of other birds.

Teaser 'G' (page 72)
The word was humorously coined by the American Walter Kiernan as a feminine form of **boycott**. It therefore means a group of girls having nothing to do with one of their number. [For the origin of 'boycott' see page 77.]

Teaser 'H' (page 82)
Honorificabilitudinitatibus occurs in Love's Labour's Lost, where it is quoted as a typical long word. It is not as difficult to say or remember as one might think, though it helps to break it into parts: 'honorific — abilitud — initatibus'. It is medieval Latin, the ablative plural of honorificabilitudinatas, and means 'honourableness'.

Teaser 'I' (page 90)
Ideograph. All three words in the phrase have an ideographic form — £ & $. The £ is normally explained as the first letter of Latin librae 'pounds'. The early moneymen were mostly Italians so the first

letter of *lire* is another possibility. The **ampersand** sign & takes its name from the phrase 'and *per se* and', meaning '& by itself = and'. The dollar sign $ is thought by some to be a combination of the letters US. Some ideographs denote ideas rather than individual words, e.g. + can be spoken as **plus** or **added to**.

Teaser 'J' (page 94)
One day, since the word is a form of French *journée* 'day'. A **journeyman** was originally someone who was employed to do a day's work at a time. Other words of similar origin — from Latin *diurnalis*, ultimately from *dies* 'day', include **journal**, **journalist**, **diary**, **diurnal**, **adjourn**, **sojourn**.

Teaser 'K' (page 102)
The words are from the language of gambling. The full passage runs: 'Men talk of high and low dice, Fulhams and bristles, topping, knapping, slurring, stabbing, and a hundred ways of rooking besides; but broil me like a rasher of bacon, if I could ever learn the trick on 'em!' 'You have got the vocabulary perfect, sir, at the least,' said Nigel. 'Yes, by mine honour have I,' returned the Hector; 'they are phrases a gentleman learns about town.' **Fulhams** and **bristles** were loaded dice. **Topping**, **knapping**, **slurring** and **stabbing** were all ways of cheating (**rooking**) at dice.

Teaser 'L' (page 105)
It is the longest normal word with only two vowels, just as **strengths** is the longest normal word with only one vowel.

Teaser 'M' (page 114)
It appears to have no true rhyme, although an anonymous wit once said:
Among our numerous English rhymes
They say there's none to month;
I tried and failed a hundred times,
But succeeded the hundred and onth.

Teaser 'N' (page 124)
According to Professor Alan S.C. Ross, it is to be avoided because it is *non-U*. The U equivalent is **writing-paper**. A long list of words and phrases that reveal one's social class is to be found in this author's *Don't Say It*.

Teaser 'O' (page 136)
Nine — even though there are only about thirty *ough* words in English. The pronunciations are indicated by the following words: **bough, plough; though, dough; bought, fought; cough, trough; enough, rough; hough** (cut of beef = hock), **lough; through, brougham; borough, thorough; hiccough** (= hiccup).

Teaser 'P' (page 147)
A **Presbyterian** (anagrammatically) is **best in prayer**.

Teaser 'Q' (page 156)
In Australia. G.W. Turner, in *The English Language in Australia and New Zealand*, says that a *qar* is 'a car in Sydney's Q-patrol, a plainclothes traffic police with a name suggested by the Q-ships, mystery ships with surprise value, in the First World War'.

Teaser 'R' (page 159)
A **mushroom**.

Teaser 'S' (page 167)
It is the longest word in English — there is a *mile* between the first and last letter.

Teaser 'T' (page 187)
Its pronunciation — not just the silent *h*, but the fact that the *a* is pronounced as a short *e*. This pronunciation of *a* is very rare; the only English words where it is pronounced in a similar way are **any**, **many** and **ate** (though some people pronounce the latter to rhyme with *mate*). The silent *h* is much more common. Nearly all the consonants occur silently in one word or another. Example words, with silent consonants under-

lined, are: De_bt, indi_ct, han_dkerchief, hal_fpenny, gnaw, _honest, _knit, ta_lk, _mnemonic, autum_n, _pneumonia, i_ron, ai_sle, lis_ten, _who, bille̅t-dou_x.

Teaser 'U' (page 197)

The American writer Dmitri Borgmann pointed out in *Beyond Language* that this word is **autological** — it describes itself. Similar words are **English**, **adjectival**, **polysyllabic**, **short**. British word buff and Scrabble expert Darryl Francis brilliantly added to these what he called 'suggestive' words: HUMiLiTY, twogether, millionheire$$, erronious, Decembrrr.

Teaser 'V' (page 206)

Vair was borrowed from Old French in the 14th century to describe a white and grey squirrel fur, much used at the time for lining and trimming garments. The word is pronounced exactly the same in French as *verre* 'glass'. This seems to have caused confusion in the tale of Cinderella. The original version of the story says that she wears a *pantoufle en vair* 'fur slipper' to go to the ball. In the *Contes de Fées* of C. Perrault (1697) she is wearing the *pantoufle en verre* 'glass slipper' that is now firmly part of the legend. *Vair* has other homophones in French, including *ver* 'worm', *vers* 'towards', *vers* 'verse', *vert* 'green'.

Teaser 'W' (page 213)

It is an example of what has been called a **contronym**, a word which can be used in contradictory senses. In an article in *Word Ways* February, 1978, Richard Lederer drew attention to the sentences: 'I want a cloth that will wear' and 'I want a cloth that will not wear'. Both mean the same thing. Likewise, **cleave** can mean 'split away from' and 'remain attached to'.

Teaser 'X' (page 217)

The X is the Greek letter *chi* (χ), first letter of 'Christ' in its Greek form.

Teaser 'Y' (page 219)

Exactly the same as the. In this instance the letter that is now conventionally written as a y is really a *thorn*, pronounced th-, which was part of the Old English alphabet.

Teaser 'Z' (page 225)

Sample words with which one can make up the set are: **zigzagging**, **zoological**; **azeotropic**, **czarevitch**; **puzzlement**, **razorblade**; **brazenness**, **quizmaster**; **breeziness**, **horizontal**; **rendezvous**, **squeezebox**; **kibbutznik**, **stargazing**; **chimpanzee**, **deepfrozen**; **antifreeze**, **pocketsize**; **hakenkreuz**, **razzmatazz**. Hakenkreuz is another name for the 'swastika'. It is listed in *Chambers English Dictionary*.

INDEX

———————○———————

BUCKINGHAM:
My lord, whoever journeys to the Prince,
For God sake, let not us two stay at home;
For by the way I'll sort occasion,
As index to the story we late talk'd of,
To part the Queen's proud kindred from the Prince.

William Shakespeare *Richard III*

———————○———————

With the Envoi duly in place a writer's task would normally be complete, but this book ends as it began. Curiosity about the word **preface** was enough to set it on its way; similar thoughts about **index** now bring it to a close. Any word ending in -x is rather odd, and index has the additional interest of its two plural forms. This book has two **indexes**, but if mathematicians were discussing the exponents of a number they would talk of **indices**. The latter form more clearly reveals the word's ancestry and family connections, its links with other Latin-based words which have the underlying sense 'to show'. An index **indicates**, like an index finger or forefinger which is used to point something out. The same basic sense of 'showing' led to Latin *dicere* 'say' and *dicare* 'tell', then to words like **abdicate, condition, contradict, dedicate, dictate, diction, dictionary, ditto, edict, interdict, predicate, predict**.

———————○———————

The face is the index of the heart [mind].

Latin proverb

———————○———————

Indexes are now usually found at the end of a book, but it was not always so. Older reference books, such as Charlotte M. Yonge's *History of Christian Names*, frequently have them at the beginning. In H.B. Guppy's *The Homes of Family Names* there is an index at the beginning, a different one at the end. Shakespeare clearly expected an index to precede the book; in *Troilus and Cressida* he refers to 'indexes . . . to their subsequent volumes'. His more interesting use of the word comes in Othello:

IAGO:
Didst thou not see her paddle with the palm of his hand? Didst not mark that?
RODERIGO:
Yes, that I did; but that was but courtesy.
IAGO:
Lechery, by this hand; an index and obscure prologue to the history of lust and foul thoughts.

———————○———————

Index-learning turns no student pale
Yet holds the eel of science by the tail.

Alexander Pope *The Dunciad*

———————○———————

Pope speaks disparagingly of 'index-learning', but serious students as well as those who are lazy need their help. Few are blessed with the kind of memory which brings not only a comment, but its exact location, instantly to mind. Works of fiction do not have indexes, though Dr Johnson once suggested in a letter to Samuel Richardson that he should add one to *Pamela*, so that 'when the reader recollects any incident, he may easily find it'. This is not a very convincing argument, but indexes to the novels of Dickens, for example, would be justified on other grounds. Dickens's chapter headings often summarise the story incidents, but do not conveniently list his interesting remarks about a wide range of subjects.

'Index' is a thoroughly bookish word, of etymological interest, but can also

> ## INDEX
>
> Where the statue stood
> Of Newton with his prism and
> silent face.
> The marble index of a mind
> for ever
> Voyaging through strange seas
> of thought alone.
>
> **William Wordsworth** The Prelude

appeal to those word buffs who approach their subject from a more 'numerical' viewpoint. The mere fact that it is a word of five letters ending in -x will arouse thoughts in some minds, suggesting those 'useless knowledge' questions which torment and intrigue. How many words like it are there in English, for instance, not counting trade names such as **Rolex**, **Timex**, **Exlax**, **Xerox**, **Durex**? How many such words could be used in a fairly normal English sentence? Which English word of this type is most frequently used? More specifically — why were the words **bioux** and **hioux** quoted on page 151 of this book?

Try the 'number of five-letter -x words' question on a friend. He or she will do well to list seven of the following: **affix**, **annex**, **beaux**, **codex**, **desex**, **helix**, **index**, **latex**, **murex**, **phlox**, **relax**, **telex**, **unfix**. Be generous, perhaps, and allow **Sioux**. The sentence question is open-ended, depending on individual ingenuity. A sample sentence — one that ends with what must surely be the most frequently used word of this group — is: 'When a writer has completed a book, it is time to annex an index to it, telex the publisher, then relax.' The thought contained in those words is not elegantly expressed, but it is one on which this writer now proposes to act.

INDEX OF WORKS QUOTED AND CONSULTED

INDEX OF WORDS AND PHRASES